in search of satisfaction

d o u b l e d a y

n e w y o r k   l o n d o n

t o r o n t o

s y d n e y   a u c k l a n d

in search

of

satisfaction

j. california cooper

75617

PUBLISHED BY DOUBLEDAY
a division of Bantam Doubleday Dell Publishing Group, Inc.
1540 Broadway, New York, New York 10036

DOUBLEDAY and the portrayal of an anchor with a dolphin
are trademarks of Doubleday, a division of Bantam
Doubleday Dell Publishing Group, Inc.

All of the characters in this book are fictitious, and any
resemblance to actual persons, living or dead, is purely
coincidental.

Book Design by F. J. Levine

FRONTISPIECE COURTESY OF STATE HISTORICAL SOCIETY
OF WISCONSIN

Library of Congress Cataloging-in-Publication Data

Cooper, J. California.
    In search of satisfaction / J. California Cooper. — 1st ed.
       p.   cm.
    1. Fathers and daughters—United States—Fiction.
    2. Sisters—United States—Fiction. 3. Afro-American
women—Fiction. I. Title.
    PS3553.O5874I5   1994
    813'.54—dc20
                                       94-9555
                                          CIP

ISBN 0-385-46785-0

1 3 5 7 9 10 8 6 4 2

First Edition

Dedicated
With All My Love
to
My Beloved, Beloved
Only Brother
Joseph Carlton Cooper, Jr.
in
My Heart and Memory
Forever

Kay Cooper, his wife
Joseph Cooper III, his son

acknowledgments

I asked God so many times to help me with this book I have to acknowledge Him first. Thank You.

My daughter, Paris Williams, for her support. Always. The wonderful people of Doubleday. They are all so important to me. My editor, Casey Fuetsch, one of the nicest; smart and quick. Thank you for all your help, Casey. The assistant editor, Brandon Saltz, who makes it such a pleasure to work with him.

To the others, some of whom help me every day in some way and let me know they are concerned about my well-being. A special, special regard for Martha Levin. Other special people include Stephen Rubin, David Gernert, Evelyn Hubbard, Arabella Meyer, Janet Hill, Michael Coe, Charles Thompson, David Lappin, Jim Chandler, Ellen Archer, Byron Baker, Delia Kurland, Anne Bentley and Phyllis Mandel.

Then, the marvelous wonder-workers: Ellie Sims, Russell Thelen, Ellen Schoemer, Julia Neves, John McPartland, Karen Fink, Barbara Suter, Josephine Brooks, Bryan Petty, Steven Fruda, John Murray, Helen Ortiz, Dom Durante, Annette Trial, Marion Seith, Alan Trask, Beth Facter, Claudine Morales and all the other wonder-working people at Doubleday I have missed.

I miss Sallye Leventhal and that handsome devil of an excellent publicist, Russell Perreault.

I must say thank you to those at St. Martin's Press whose kindnesses are still so ready: Keith Kahla, Michelle Coleman, Yvonne Phidd, Betty Banks and John Clark.

A huge thank you for special things to Jessica Henderson Daniel, Ph.D., of Boston, Ms. Georgene Bess, Atlanta, Georgia, Susan Shorter of New York, Santelia Steven Johnson, California, and my Spirit Sister, DeDe Reagan, Encinitas, California.

Thank you all. I love you. God bless all of us. And everybody.

I cannot think of anyone—any age, any color, any sex—who is not in search of satisfaction. Everything living, in fact. From a king to someone sitting in the poorhouse or no home at all. From a murderer to a child playing jacks. TIME is to be used to build our minds, our tool to get to some satisfaction. We are building our minds, our values, as we find what will give us satisfaction, how to get it, how to keep it. Our minds decide the quality of our lives.

Take the story of the three little pigs. Say they built their houses as you build your mind. One built his house of straw. Was he in a hurry? Didn't have much time? Went out to play? Lazy? His house did not stand against any danger from the world outside. It went down at the first blow from the wolf, the world. The second pig built his house of sticks. Did he believe lies? Settle for whatever he could get easy? Did he not care? Was he lazy? It did not stand in the time of need. Was not safe from lies, the world, the wolf. Time.

The third pig built his house of solid, precious, heavy bricks: Truth. It took time, sweat and thinking. That house withstood blows from the wolf, the world. Lies. That home was a safe place of security where his life and happiness could live safely within.

Build your house, your mind, of truths. Bricks. Don't settle for straw-tinsel. Let the mortar be love and goodness, but, always remember everyone else may not be full of love and goodness; that is why you build your mind and house of bricks anyway.

Lastly, do not depend on anyone else for your happiness. Happiness is something a person acquires for themselves with their energy and the tools of their mind. Don't say to anyone, "Make me happy, please." Make your own happiness inside yourself and, when you have enough to share, find someone to share it with. We cannot blame anyone for our misery, aloneness and impotence. If we fail, we cannot say, "It is not my fault!" If we never have anything to give that another person might want, we cannot blame it on parents, wives, husbands, circumstances or lack of opportunity. We, alone, are to blame. I believe you can survive anything and move on . . . with the right tools. Move on to seek, to find what you need . . . in the search for satisfaction.

in search of satisfaction

Once upon any time, when a person is born, no matter what color of mankind you are, a body with a mind seeks for the truth of life. A way. A chest is opened for you, filled with many truths and things that pass as truths for you to find, pick, choose from, live your life with. Be the things you value.

Now, you may have a brain and still be a fool. Many people choose those things that pass as the truth but are false. Still others find real truths then twist, bend and misuse them, even bury them. Some, the lazy, don't search or dig deep for the truth but find a way and use it until they find it is not so good, then they pick up another way, often just as useless. They spend years and years, their lives, doing this. Very often to the detriment of themselves and others. Very often . . . just a nothing life.

It's a sad truth that many get all the way to the end of their lives then stop and look closely at their way, their imposter truths; then they cry out to life, "Cheat! Empty!"

The mind is a mighty, mighty tool. A body just has to think and reason.

I think one of the main ingredients to reason your way to the truth is, first, love. If love is missing from your soul, your mind, you won't be able to find what you need. You may not recognize it.

It's a wise, wise person who looks into the Ten Commandments. Christian or not, they are a universal, huge power. They are tools. They are good. They are the main wisdom, the main direction in the search for truth, peace, love and ultimately happiness here on earth. Don't just wait for heaven. What you believe has no effect on what is the truth. One thing is sure, you will bump your head hard on the truth if you don't recognize it when you need to.

Almost everyone on earth believes there is a God. Some god. Some wise people believe there is a Satan or evil power. This Satan laughs at God because he, the devil, the evil power, has so many people following him. It's a hollow laughter. Because who can really be pleased and proud of fools? But another fool?

God waits for His own time. Time is passing. His time is coming. He has a plan. He need not be concerned with the laughter of fools.

chapter

1

the past comes forward

Yoville was a small, legal township founded by the very rich for their own personal use. It had one lawyer, a two-room bank that belonged to the rich Befoe family, a doctor for immediate needs until they could go to larger, more efficient places. A mill, a gin, a blacksmith, a small hotel for uninvited guests or business associates unwanted in their homes, a small shop carrying all sorts of things. There was a dressmaking shop, often closed because the seamstress was nearly starving; everyone really shopped in New York or other places.

The gentlemen of the area had built and kept a house of quiet, ill reputation in which at all times there was at least one woman so the local gentry could go there to drink and talk and relieve themselves if they wished. But many were in Yoville only seasonally, and, as the original founders of this little house grew older and their young left Yoville for college and cities offering more to their greedy young lives, the old gentlemen stopped bringing in a new refined whore to replace the last one who had become inevitably bored and tired of Yoville. There were, finally, few customers. In the old times, however, it was a bright, gay place to spend a few hours with other friends who had nothing to do.

Yoville was close enough to the Northeast to call itself northern upon occasion, and it was south enough to have had some of the advantages of slavery. A river ran through Yoville, hastening away to some happier place and people. A railroad spur was built in Mythville, a larger town some ten miles away. A clean barge could be engaged to carry a person down the river if one did not feel like driving their carriage or riding a horse. Over the years since slavery ended, some of the rich had moved further east, still holding to their land in Yoville, returning seasonally. It seemed, now, to be a dying little town. But it was not dying. It just never grew.

Following slavery, there was a man named Josephus Josephus. He chose to take the name he hoped his mother had given him, twice, rather than take the name of the cruel owners he had lived under. He had never known his mother or father, a sister or brother. He did not think his father had been white because his own skin was of a deep brown-black color. Emancipation came when he was between fourteen and nineteen years of age. He had known no other home than the one he had in Yoville with the Krupts, who owned him.

After freedom came, all the other slaves at the Krupts fairly flew away, for all they could remember of their masters was the sadistic treatment of the slaves they had owned. Both the master and mistress had had very sexual proclivities, much indulged. Master Krupt had married his wife, Virginia Krupt, because of her love of pleasure and her youth. Her family having name but no money, she married him for his money. They'd been married about 25 years. During their later years together, their lives and land deteriorated. They had even grown to hate each other; they hated everything else already. In old age and sicknesses, their tired, abused bodies had dwindled away, his more than hers. They had no children to care for them now in their old age. She had never been pregnant for him, ever. At Emancipation time, no slave but one able to walk had remained behind to care for them. Those unable to walk were carried away by able-bodied ex-slaves to people who had heart and land enough to let them live out their short lives and die in peace. God bless them.

Josephus Josephus intended to go away someday. But he had absolutely nowhere to go. He had looked around the farm and its owners and knew he could work almost as he pleased, be his own overseer. He could have gone to work for the Befoes, the very rich family on the next plantation down the road, but he figured all white folks were alike anyway. And there, he would have an overseer. He stayed where he was. Years. Why change?

Among other things once produced on their huge farm, Master and Mistress Krupt had made their own wine and whiskey. This was one thing they continued, except now, they gave none away. They drank it all. They were not in any condition, most of the time, to watch anybody. Josephus could choose which cabin he would live in and worked just enough to keep food on the table, his and theirs, and to feed the livestock. He kept the place in a generally clean and livable condition. The Krupts depended heavily on him. Josephus thought of marrying one or two of the neighboring, courtable ladies, poor, without everything. But poor as they were, the ladies did not want to move and live with him at the Krupt plantation, such as it was. One, Bessel, liked him enough to let him make love to her once, even while she courted another and tried to decide between the two. But she did not want to live at the Krupts. She became pregnant, then promptly married the other whom she thought would be able to support her and the child decently. She bore a girl-child named Ruth Mae, around 1879. Josephus did not know whose child it really was, so he made no fuss. What could he do anyway? He just watched the child as she grew for signs that she might be his. He saw them and knew she was his child. But there was Bessel's husband now, so Josephus did nothing but watch the child, Ruth, and love her from a distance.

Ma Lal, with her little daughter, Mae, was the midwife. She knew all kinds of things about everybody. She knew the child belonged to Josephus even before she delivered it. The married father was so light, and the baby was brown like her father, even with tiny features like Josephus. Josephus watched the child, yearning for a family of his own. Anyway, time passed.

During the last years Josephus was at the Krupts', a fierce storm had blown the roof and parts of the poorly built slave cabins away, so he moved into the servants' quarters in the main house. There he saw money and valuables all over the house that it was his job to clean. That is when he finally began a real plan to move away. Then, his mistress really saw him one day when she was sober.

Mistress Krupt, in her late thirties, was not so old but was married to someone old she did not love, and her life of quiet debauchery had ruined whatever looks she once had. She was puffy and pasty looking, bruises smeared over her body where she had stumbled against something or fallen. Both she and her husband kept mostly to their rooms, coming down to the kitchen for meals when they could walk. Sometimes they ate what she threw together, sometimes what Josephus cooked. He cooked more often because he now had access to and ate the food they had delivered. Then, too, he was always sober enough to cook.

Josephus did not know why they did not hire someone to cook and care for them, they certainly had the golden money. But the once lovely mistress was ashamed to be seen lest the tale be carried along the roads to people who had known her when she first arrived in Yoville. Oh! So many years ago! Before she became—ugh!—a lovely young bride to old Mr. Krupt. When even the wealthy Mr. Befoe, Carlene's father, had loved her and given her gifts. She had been a lovely young guest at the wedding of Carlene Befoe when she met Mr. Krupt, a very rich old man. Her family had lost everything during the wars. She was in need. When she thought of Carlene Befoe, her friend then who hated her now, she would laugh to herself. And take another drink.

One morning as Josephus was bringing her food to her rooms again, she saw him through the fog in her brain and beckoned him, pulled him into her. Ever and even, the body does not want to be alone. In his fear of death, he resisted her. She laughed and said drunkenly, "Nigger, you are still my slave!" The slave did her bidding. "Fill me up!" she laughed. Her body was too sotten to have orgasms, she just wanted something done to her body, in memory. An emotional need.

Somehow, enough of these times and one of those times, she became pregnant. She had never been pregnant in her life. Never having had a child, she wanted this child. Not *his* child, but *this* child. Sometimes, the fact that it might be black faded from her mind. For her own reasons, she wanted the child, black or not. She had no one on earth except that ole bastard lost somewhere in his rooms, in his liquor. Mistress Krupt even took to taking better care of herself during her pregnancy, with Josephus' help.

When her time came, Mistress Krupt sent Josephus to the very rich Carlene Befoe to fetch a doctor or a midwife. Carlene did not even come down to speak with Josephus but told her maid to recommend someone. She looked at her husband, Mr. Befoe, whom she knew had admired Mistress Krupt briefly at the same time her father had "made a fool of himself!" about Virginia Krupt. Laughing maliciously, Carlene said, "At her age! Mother drunk, child probably drunk, too! How that ole sot Krupt made a baby at his age . . ." She laughed. But Richard Befoe's thoughts were, "She is, obviously, still a passionate woman. Living! While you are a dried up, beautifully attended prig who has hardly allowed me to touch you for years now." She had "given" Richard one child and then forbade him her body. She had hated him even then, when he had loved her. Now, you see, they hated each other. Sometimes he thought of how wonderful it could be, they had everything else, and he would love her for awhile. But she never cared and made it obvious, so he would begin to hate her again.

Ahhh, Satan was happy with these people. Hate is so helpful in things he likes to do.

With the white midwife finally come, bringing Ma Lal to aid her, Mistress Krupt gave birth to a girl-child with hazel eyes and curly, brown hair. "Ahhhh, now . . ." Mistress Krupt thought, "I have someone. The Negra Josephus and now, the child. Perhaps someone will be around to wait on me as I grow old." She laughed as she named the child, Yinyang. Then she called for a drink and slept. The child, Yinyang, was handed to Josephus by Ma Lal as she finished cleaning up and reached for her money. She smiled up at Josephus saying, "You sho works hard roun heah!" She laughed—wicked, gleeful laughter—and was gone. It was around 1885.

Some few people came to see the mother and child, but, espying the tinge of color in the skin of Yinyang, they left, some never to return. Carlene Befoe, the rich and haughty leader of Yoville society, came, lifting her immaculate and costly skirts far above her ankles, careful lest anything touch her. She left laughing. She would tell everybody, her father and husband especially, "This old love-bitch liked black meat! My, my."

Fortunately, Josephus took over the care of Yinyang. Unfortunately, Mistress went back to her bottle. She never sought Josephus' body again.

Josephus remained there another long thirteen years to see what would happen to the child. His child. Yinyang was his family. He cooked for her, bathed her, made toys for her, played with her, took her out to the fields to work with him. Everything he could do, he did for her. She grew up loving him. Somehow she believed he was her father. He told her, she believed him. She called him Pajo because she knew the white man upstairs was supposed to be her father. Children are like that sometimes. Josephus yearned to leave, get away, live somewhere clean, fresh, small and his own, where he could be with his daughter, away from the shit of this life. He saw no way. He had nothing. Lately, he had begun to pick up coins and bills lying around the house, even selling things "for the Master" and putting the coins by for "someday." Sometimes he even gave Bessel money for his first daughter, Ruth. She took it with a smile, holding his hand a little longer than necessary. Bessel liked money, but she did like Josephus, too.

Young as Yinyang was, her world was difficult. Yin knew who her mother was. She wanted to love her, but her mother was always asleep. She knew who her father was, because the old man Krupt, her white father, hated her, struck out at her often, called her "black bastard!" Sometimes Yin (as her black father called her) would crawl into bed with her mother, hold her as she slept. But there was often vomit and, lately, feces on her mother, which Yin would try to clean. She tried to comb her mother's hair, change her clothes. The old, old, once grand clothes were dusty, molding. They fell apart when Yin tried to put them on her mother or play grown-up lady in them. Yin cried, often, as she moved around her mother's rooms; the windows closed, the shades drawn, the rooms stank, so gray, so sad, so gloomy. So dead.

Once when the nightclothes were a bit ragged, Yin proposed to her mother to get some new ones made. Her mother smiled, said, "Yessssss, I think I will." After a bit of thinking, Mistress Krupt continued smiling and said, "Look in that drawer, look in all my drawers. And look in that closet, the small box, I think, way in the corner in back. Get the money there. And go order some clothing for me. And some sheets. Get me everything I need, my little light slave daughter." She laughed. "Get Madame Carlene Befoe, the rich bitch, to tell you who sews for her." Yin was about ten years old.

Yin took the money to Josephus. "We got to go to that lady, Miz Befoe, to find out who sews for her. Then we got to ride ole Sal and the buggy into town and get some material to make mama some new clothes. Why, Pajo, we got a heap of gold money here to get us some clothes, too! C'mon, let's go now!"

Josephus looked down at the box of gold coins in the hands of his daughter and he saw his dreams more clearly.

"Wher you git that, baby?"

"From mama. C'mon, let's go!"

"She tole you where to git that gold?"

"Yes, Pajo. Ain't it a lot?"

"Where she tole you to git it from?"

"Her drawers, her closet."

"Was . . . was it any mo? Thar?"

"I didn't look everywher, Pajo, cause this was enough, I'm sure on it."

"Giv it to me, so it don't spill everwhere. Let's wrap it up good and safe."

"Sho, Pajo. We goin now?"

"Let me go hitch Sal, you go get washed up, then we go." Yin ran off excited to be going somewhere.

Josephus took the box, took half the gold out and hid it. He hitched the wagon up and, when Yin came running back out, they drove away. Before they returned, he had bought shoes for Yin and even hired a teacher by "errand of the Mistress" for Yin to go to each morning to learn to read and write. He bought nothing for himself. His dreams were his satisfaction.

He took her to school faithfully. She taught him what she learned each day. They both grew. His plans grew huge. He stole more and sold more of the things he could. He had enough to go away, but he kept staying for more. Satan's philosophy is like that, enough is not enough.

Josephus began to keep the Krupts' liquor right on the kitchen table, with glasses ready. He kept liquor in their rooms; though they had been doing a good job of that, now they didn't have to think about it at all. It was always just there, like magic. He also began rummaging in their rooms when he knew they were dead drunk and Yin was asleep. In time, he found much. He also began to tell Yin to ask about her birth certificate. There was none, it seemed. So "the Mistress" sent money to the white midwife who sent Ma Lal to the notary with the papers for a birth certificate. Josephus carried all the money and messages. Ma Lal smiled as she handed him the papers. They named Master Krupt as father. His plan stepped up speed.

Josephus knew the master would not be living much longer, and the mistress didn't look like she was far behind. Would they have relatives who would take the child, ten years old, away with them? Away from him? Relatives did come from time to time, distant relatives from distant places, to see what they could salvage or take away with them. Her relatives who saw the sunshine tint in the skin of the child didn't think it was the Mistress'. "It must belong to the Master and one of his Negras he used to have, so it wasn't anything but a Negra." Wasn't nothin to worry bout in the inheritance, was there anything left. Still, some others, among his few relatives, thought she was white. This frightened Josephus. They could take his child away.

Josephus began stealing more, kept taking more things to sell in the name of the master. Rambled through the dark rooms at night looking for a hiding place where there might be gold or silver, sold all he could for his "master." Some things he found, he just put away, biding his time. With the white men riding and killing Negroes now freed, Josephus dug holes in places to bury his value. The plan stepped up speed again. Time was getting hard, scary and short.

Josephus knew that if the money was caught on him when he and Yin left, it would all be taken away; he might even be killed. And, he thought, heaven forbid, Yin could be taken and raped, beaten and whatever them men wanted to do if they didn't think she was white, and some, even if they thought she was white. Hadn't the Master in his diseased drunkenness tried to reach out and grab her with his long-fingered, scabby, dirty-fingernailed, gnarled hands? "I would'a kilt him!" Josephus snarled to himself as he tightened his fist.

One day when he picked up Yin from her teacher, she asked him, "Who is God?" Josephus had heard of God, but he didn't know anything about Him. He did not know what to tell her. "What yo teacher say he is?" Yin looked up at her father, "She say . . . said I need to go to church and learn about Him. She said I can go with her since my mama don't go." She held up a book to Josephus, "See? This here is His book. It tells us about Him."

That night they read in it together. Somehow they came to the verse about "Thou shalt not kill." Josephus held the book a long time.

"Turn the page, Pajo." Yin reached for the book.

"No, not right now. I got to try to read mo of it. Let me think, baby." He put a small rock in the place of the book and closed it. "But you can go wit that teacher to church. I will take you on Sundy." As he did. Soon they spoke again about God. Josephus asked Yin, "What you spose happen to a body if'n they was to do what God said not to do?"

Yin answered, looking up at him, "I blive whatever you do to somebody else, it will come right back on you. That's close as I can make out from what they say in the church."

However, later, when he spoke with God, on his knees, Josephus said, "So, this is who you is. Well, you know I don't know yo, don't know nothin bout yo. Much. An I done met yo awful late. I blive I could like yo, but I got to do what I got to do. Tha's my chile. Yo sposed to be done give her to me. Well . . . sir, I wants to keep her side me. So . . . sir, I gots to do what I gots to do it. Tha's all."

Time passed, slowly. Old Master Krupt was sick to death, but just didn't die. Josephus in his gardening had gathered poison mushrooms, put them in a jar of water. He did not want Master Krupt to die before he was prepared to run away with Yin. He wanted to know WHEN Master Krupt was gone for good. He fed Master Krupt a little of the water off the poison mushrooms in his food everyday. He sat things by. He gathered his gold and silver coins and the little paper money, sewing all he could into his clothes, clothes taken from the master, and bought a new-made coat for Yin.

Josephus did not want to wear worn, ragged clothes away, nor grand, brand-new ones either. He wanted it to look like someone who knew what they were doing had sent him out on the road. He did not want to go barefoot because he did not know how far they would have to walk. He managed to get some shoes. All the things he thought he needed were put by. Master Krupt was dying a little more each day. Alcohol poisoning and, now, mushroom poisoning. No doctor was called.

Josephus packed as much to take with him as he thought would be safe on him and Yin. But . . . the money remaining. He thought hard what to do with what they could not safely carry, had to leave behind!

Remembering when he had worked far out in the field, he thought of an old tool shack seldom gone into by anyone except a slave. Now he had been the only one in it for nigh on twenty years or so. He went there, dug a hole in the ground of the shack, putting half of the remaining gold, silver and jewels from Mistress Krupt into it, buried at the bottom of a tool box and covered with tools. He covered the hole and stomped the ground over it. Then he took a long look at the shack, sighed, said, "I see you again some day."

When the master didn't die from the water covering the mushrooms, which were now rotted, Josephus just mixed the whole jar of spoiled, smelly stuff into the next spicy meal and served it to both Master and Mistress. Then he called Yin.

"Yin, baby, Pajo is gettin ready to leave here."

She was surprised and alarmed. "Oh, Pajo, where you goin? When you leavin me? When you comin back?"

"I don know, baby. I do want to know, do you want to stay here? I don blive ole Master is long for this world . . . and yo ma ain't gettin on too well." He saw the fear and pain in Yin's eyes. He hurried on, "She be alright tho. If'n we don be here, people will come in and take care of her like she need to be. She sick." He hesitated. "She mayhap mighten die." Yin's eyes spilled slow, quiet tears. She looked at her father. She loved him. She loved her mother. But she knew him better than anyone in the whole world. He loved her better than anyone in the whole world. 'Cept God.

"Is . . . are you gonna take me with you, Pajo?" She sniffed. "Or are you gonna leave me here?" Her face was full of fear. Her heart was in her eyes, mouth, nose and ears, it seemed.

"I wants to take you."

"Will we come back sometime and see bout mama?"

"I . . . If'n you wants to. I know we will be back." He was thinking of the gold.

Yin sighed so deeply it hurt Josephus. "Then I want to go with you. Pajo."

"Good, baby, good." A weight lifted from his tired shoulders.

Finally, that night he removed a necklace from Mistress Krupt's neck as she slept fitfully, dying. A gold chain with a locket having one diamond and two rubies on it, clogged with the mushrooms she had vomited. He thought of the diamond ring he had already taken from her drawer that was now out in the shed with the other gold. He took a picture of the mistress from her bureau top. He took all the papers belonging to Yinyang. He packed all the things they needed that they could carry walking. Packed a little food. Hitched the tired horse, Sal, to the wagon. Then he changed his mind, unhitched her, thinking someone would bring Sal home and thereby find whatever might be wrong there. Then he changed his mind again, hitched her back up. Would drive all night while the child slept, then leave the wagon wherever he was when dawn came and walk till they was far, far away. If someone found the wagon, they would probably keep it, he thought, "wasn't nothin but a poor man gonna be out where they would leave it noway."

That night Josephus cleaned and placed the necklace around Yin's neck, saying, "From yo mama, a membrance." He laid her in the wagon, covered up warm, sat his shoes beside him in the wagon, looked around the old, run-down, empty and dead plantation and thought of the golden money that would be there when he came back for it. He heaved a heavy sigh . . . looked in the direction of where Ruth, his other daughter, was sleeping and, snapping the whip lightly over Sal's head, drove away.

The wagon slowly rolled down the drive to the main road. Master Krupt lay upstairs in the dark old weather-beaten house, dead. Mistress Krupt, in pain and anguish, heard the wagon wheels creaking and moved slowly to the window, sick to death. Face distorted with stomach cramps and confusion, she tried to understand the wagon leaving in the night. Was someone else sick? Are they going for a doctor? Was what she had really just a hangover from the liquor? Perspiration broke out over her body, already dripping wet from the labor of her movements. She bent over and vomited again. Brushing her hand at the vomit, she fell back into the bed, vomited again, then drowned in it, clutching the new sheet, never to awaken again. Her life gone, for riches and wine. Satan smiled. And though Josephus did not know it, he was never to see that plantation or his daughter, Ruth, again.

They traveled first by buggy, then, in the early dawn, Josephus left the buggy and the horse Sal and began to walk. At first Yin thought it was a fun adventure, walking through strange woods and sleeping on the earth at night, always in a new place. But in time she became tired and disgruntled, so Josephus stopped a while, worked for a month or so, helping a man build a barn. He received a mule; thereafter, Yin rode while he walked. There was no real destination, just away. Josephus thought of New Orleans he had heard a lot of, but he really didn't want to go further down south. They had to be already close to the North. They just traveled on and on, slowly.

Josephus and Yin grew even closer together during their travel. They talked of many things, new things they were seeing, old things Josephus thought about. He even told her about his daughter, Ruth, born before her, her half-sister. She was surprised and thrilled to have a sister, any kind. He taught her many things about animals, the woods, the night, the stars. They fished and he hunted for food. They had money to buy things with, but didn't want to show it. It took them nine months to even reach Southern Virginia.

In Virginia, Josephus found and worked for a seemingly gracious Negro lady of such years as his. Miz Nattie Lee ran a boarding house. Hers. He wanted a home for Yin, and he fell in love, too. He wanted to stay and marry. The lady liked his work. She had already had most her fun, she thought, as she looked down at her bulging, lack-a-shape body. When he told her about the gold, pouring most of it onto her bed where they had just made a little love, she married him. Josephus had a home at last! Yin had a home, and a mama!

But the new Miz Josephus turned out to be exceedingly greedy, a nag, a mean-jealous woman. She did not like Yin, though the young girl was sweet and obedient. She complained of Yin all the time, ridiculed her eyes and hair, tried to work her sweet, young body to death. Josephus began to frown all the time. He also began to look at the woman as though she were empty space, his mind off somewhere trying to understand how a Negro, a colored person, could be so cruel. He knew all people could be mean sometime, but cruel? Only the whites were this cruel! He decided to go back for the rest of his money. He had given just about all of it to Nattie Lee by now because she wouldn't let him rest or make love, such as it was, until he gave her "another one of them shiny pieces of gold." Plus, he would think, "I'm workin hard raisin all the food her boarders eat, raisin and killin chickens, milkin cows, all of it! Even helpin cook!" Josephus had seen the icing on the cake earlier and had given Yin a number of gold coins wrapped in one of her handkerchiefs. Josephus was mad at himself for giving up his gold and hurt because, of all the women he might have chosen, he chose the wrong one. He cried a hoarse, deep sobbing sometimes, off by himself, he thought, but Yin had seen him. Yin cried often herself as she went to sleep at night or would just cry softly over the sink, washing all those dishes, forever.

Josephus decided to go back for the gold hidden in the tool shack. He knew nobody had found it because it was "deep in the ground and mayhap no one was buyin and workin that Krupt land." He told his narrow-hearted wife about the remaining gold, thinking that would make her nice again. It did. But while he knew "he wasn't ever comin back this way again," so thought his wife! "He was gonna keep on headin out the other direction or just pass her right on by like a freight train passin up a hobo." Then he told her he was going to take Yin with him for the trip.

His wife looked at him with narrowed eyes and studied on him. She told herself that he was "just tryin to get away from her like her last husbands." Well, he was. She knew a few things about plants and herbs herself; she gathered some, cooked and fed them to Josephus. Sent fifteen-year-old Yin on an errand, then sat and watched him die, screaming "You ain't gonna fool me none, you ole fool! You ain't foolin me none! I knows what you mean to do! Ain't no man gonna leave me agin!" He died. She put him in a wheelbarrel and rolled him out quite a way into her fields, dumped him out, leaving him for others to find and think he had died of a heart attack. They did. At that time, almost at that minute, the gold he had left behind was being found in the old shack.

Miz Josephus cried hard, hard at the funeral, wearing a new black dress and the little diamond-ruby necklace she had taken from Yin. Flailing her arms about, handkerchief in each hand, screaming "My sweet husband! Lord, he gone and left me! I is alone agin! He gone! Gone!" To herself she smiled, "And I got the money and a servant for life." She reached over, patting Yinyang hard and heavy.

Yin sat on the church bench, lost, forlorn. She felt like she was dying of fear. She was alone. All by herself. She had prayed so hard to God for so long and everything only got worse. Harder. Sadder. Now Josephus was gone. Pajo. There could be no God and still let all these bad things happen. Where was God now? Her prayers dried up with her tears. She did not know enough to know that Josephus had made choices which he had just naturally paid for. That she would be making her own choices from now on, from which she would reap her own life.

Yinyang thought of what the future held in store for her, but she remembered what her father, Josephus, had told her about the gold hidden back home. She also had that little handkerchief full of gold coins given to her by Josephus, "just in case." She had never told anyone about these coins. Indeed, there was no one to trust or tell. She knew her stepmother though, and since Yin was outside doing some of the field work with the few laborers, she had hidden her gold coins in a crocker sack in a hole in a tree. Josephus had taught her about things. She hid it safely. It stayed there until one day just after her sixteenth birthday.

On that day, Yin stood at the kitchen sink, daydreaming out the window as the sun was coming up. Her hands were in soapy, greasy dishwater, washing dishes from the boarders' breakfast before she went to the fields to work. SLAM! The hand smashed against her nose and mouth. "You ain't got time to stand there restin!" Nattie Lee reached for a long, heavy, iron ladle and beat the girl on the head and shoulders until Yin sank to her knees on the floor, her arms trying to protect and cover her head. She cried as the blood streamed from her nose. She used to take such beatings for her father to have peace, but now, he already had the deepest peace in the world. Yin screamed from somewhere deep in her intimidated and frightened soul, a sound which encompassed her years of suffering from this woman and the death of her only friend, her father. She was used to taking the abuse as silently as possible, but the pain turned to anger and the anger lifted her body, ran down her arm and filled her hand, making it reach out and grab a large, heavy, black, greasy, frying pan which she swung, without looking to see what she did. With her own blood dripping down her face onto her breast, she turned to Miz Josephus and swung, hearing the impact of pan on flesh. The blood flowed from Miz Nattie Lee Josephus' head as her eyes rolled back, her body slowly crumbling to the floor.

Yin panicked, fearing Miz Josephus (she hated to call her that name) would wake any minute, get up and beat her again. But Miz Josephus was almost dead. Yin ran to her tiny closet-room ("We have to make money from these bigger rooms," Miz Nattie Lee had said), threw some of her things into an old carpetbag her father had picked for her when they left Yoville, the only thing Miz Josephus had not taken. She saw the blood on her own clothes, rushed to wash her face, removing the bloody apron. Grabbing her bag, she backed against the wall of the kitchen as she stepped gingerly around Miz Josephus. One of Miz Nattie Lee's eyes was open now, her mouth moving but making no sounds, her hand raised as though for help. Yin looked at her from the back door, her eyes caught the glint of the necklace. She went back, stooping to take it from the woman's neck; it held locked. In trying to loosen it, she noticed the handkerchief pinned to Miz Nattie Lee's undershirt. She raised her eyes to the one open eye in the face attached to the neck where her mama's necklace was held tight. Yin removed the pin from the handkerchief and put it in her pocket as she looked into Nattie Lee's eye. Reaching again to unloose the necklace catch, Yin tried not to look in that eye. Hate glowered there above the twisting, soundless mouth from which foamy saliva bubbled. The woman grabbed Yinyang's wrist as the necklace lock gave—at last!—and the necklace slipped loose. Yin gasped and, snatching her arm away, backed to the doorway . . . and out of it, to freedom.

Yin ran from the house far out to the fields, found her tree, found her handkerchief with the gold, stuffed it into her bag, ran through the woods to the road. Yin headed for New Orleans, the place her father always spoke of visiting because "everything" was there. She never looked back; there was nothing of value alive to her there. Her face hurt, the slap still stung. Her fear was great. As she made up her mind to move ahead into the future, she thought of Josephus, and her steps became firm, her resolve, strong.

Satan, the devil, happened to notice and smiled at both dead Josephus and dying Miz Nattie Lee. Then, as he moved on to bigger game, he glanced at Yinyang, saw her beauty and her tight clutch on the gold. He smiled again, saw fear and doubt in her heart, and left, thinking, "Beauty. And fear. Grand potential there. Particularly in large cities!" God saw in her, strangely, a respect for the truth and love of learning. He set in her future chances to learn; her choice as to what. The truth or the lies.

Just so you will know, if you like. Miz Josephus lay on the floor until a boarder found her. A doctor was called; she was helped. But she was unable to move with purpose again. Only one eye would open, her speech slurred. She had to pay dearly. Paid all that good money she had hoarded, cheated for and stolen as it were, for help the rest of her life. Since people knew her ways from the past, she was cheated, stolen from and lied to. Until she was broke, her home lost, and she was discarded to the back room of some old woman just like she had been, who forgot to feed her half the time and seldom changed her bed. The remainder of her life ran out with her tears onto the dirty sheet under her head.

c h a p t e r

2

In the meantime around the year 1894, when Josephus was being poisoned by his wife, and dying in Yoville, Josephus' other daughter, Ruth, was growing up. She was a good young lady, worked hard helping her mother, Bessel, after her husband had left. Ruth had called him her "first father." Her mother, thinking Josephus was still alive and could help her, told the child that Josephus was really her father. But when Bessel tried to find Josephus, he was gone. Everybody was gone! Wasn't nobody living on that ranch of the Krupts' since them two old people, Master Krupt and his wife, had been found dead. A bad batch of alcohol they said had caused it. But, just in case Josephus ever came back, now the story was told, she left Ruth with it. "You got you a half-white sister, Yinzang, or somethin."

Ruth had a favorite friend-boy, Joel Jones. She loved him, but he didn't know it. He loved her, but she didn't know it. She was only in her early teens, while he was going on twenty years. Her mother thought he was too old. Bessel also thought he was too poor. Owned no land, no nothing. "His family didn't even ever own nothin," she said as she scratched her head for dandruff.

Ruth used to say, "But, mama, we just only rentin and workin this here land. We don't own nothin either!" Bessel would answer, "That's why we got to make sure you marry somebody with somethin!" Bessel was one of two domestics working for Miz Befoe and tried to put on airs because of it. That's why she was always talking about "somebody with somethin."

Well, there wasn't anybody with "somethin" around. Hadn't been too long since everybody was slaves! Some Negroes had gotten a'holt of something, had a house, some farm animals, but not too many. A few rich families, mostly the Befoes, owned most everything in Yoville, and they didn't sell too easy, unless it was a little bit to a favorite Negro of theirs. And, who had the money to buy anyway?

Ruth and Joel would just see each other at church most of the time. Peek at each other, smile shyly. Joel was a good-looking young man, a teaser, liked to have fun and make people laugh. Girls liked him and didn't care whether he was poor or not. They expected poor anyway. Ruth was jealous and grieved her heart a lot because she thought she didn't have a chance with Joel on account of the fast, pretty girls round him all the time. Then, too, she thought Joel felt she was too young for him. So she just looked at him, blushed and passed on by. But Joel liked Ruth's shyness, loved her goodness. He respected her, so naturally love grew, because respect is what love grows on! This had been going on for about two years, since Ruth was thirteen.

Ruth had dreams of a wedding night with all the beauty she had heard her mama preach about. She was saving herself to be special for it. No matter how she thought she would never have Joel, he was always the person in her wedding-night dreams. Oh, how she loved that man.

Joel didn't like Bessel much, even though he knew Bessel was raising her child right and trying to guard her from life pains she had known. Joel would sit and brood. "Hell!" he would say to himself. "I'm gettin on to old. I got to be gettin married soon! Least she could let me court her! I ain't a slave no more! We ought to be free to pick who we wants!" But poverty, though he worked at the Befoes' as a gardener, gave him no control over their lives. He was too poor to take any steps on his own.

Joel was well-raised himself, so he waited, trying to find a way. He even worked over on Bessel's rented land at times, just to be near Ruth and to try to influence Bessel with how good he was and how hard he worked.

Bessel's land was next door to the old Krupt plantation. Her family had worked that land since slavery ended. Her closeness to the Krupt land was one of the reasons Josephus had gotten so close to her right under her daddy's nose. All her family was separated and gone, or dead and gone now. She just held on to the little house and land and worked even some Krupt land she didn't rent because there was no one there to stop her. The Krupts were dead, least them who had lived in that big ole house all closed down now. No one came to check around.

So, that's how things were going on—full of hopes, dreams, worries, frustrations and work. Life.

On one particular harvest time, the day had started out as clear and sparkling as ever you could see. A slight breeze stirred the trees and clothes hanging on lines, the corn stalks and all other vegetation. It seemed as though the sun would finish coming up any minute, but the sky in the east remained gray with only golden flashes now and then. Birds, all sorts, flew about the sky taking care of the business of feeding their young, building nests, all that birds do. All the field workers were out because this was the time to make money if you worked for someone other than yourself. If you worked for yourself, it was the time to make haste while the sun shone. Eyes and hands flashed as people met and passed, throwing words of greeting over their shoulders, or stopping to talk awhile or inspect what the other had to show. A good day!

Without notice, within a few hours, the day changed. The birds stopped their flying and their chirping sounds. The wind stilled. There is no evil sun, no evil sky, but the dark clouds that gathered slowly, silently, stealing across the horizon, hovering over the earth, were evil looking indeed. Darkness came where there had been light. First, scattered drops of water came down lightly then gathered in abundance and speed. The winds whipped up and around everything, gathering strength, hitting with force. You could hear it whirring through space. Sapling trees were bending to the ground easily. Bits of roof flew off, pots and buckets toppled over on porches. Ashes, sand, dirt swirled up and around in the fierce air. Fences leaned over, gates squeaked, hinges let loose, in time, broke. Soon the very air and land was being bruised with the great force of mighty nature. Before it would be over, all the houses and land would be changed. A storm had arrived without warning. Ahhh, but the harvest, the harvest! Shining, new, fresh vegetation, necessary food for the people and animals, tried to stand, rose and fell again and again, then lost the battle against the mighty storm. These things were the very LIFE to these people. They must be saved as much as could be.

No one could run for cover, be warm, be safe from the storm. Everyone must work to save the harvest so they could eat, cover themselves with clothes, continue to live even poorly. Everyone in the little houses and shacks must come out and work. Even some of the sick. So, the people jumped into action. Rushed into the fields to save what they could. Pulled, plucked, picked everything in sight, throwing it into bags, pots, sacks, aprons, anything. "God help us," they prayed as people do in a disaster, even those who don't believe in Him. At first, the elements don't scare you. Because you are man! Human beings who can do anything! Then it comes to you, you ain't got a hell-of-a'chance against nature. Man ain't nothing. You are fighting for your life. Yet, this time, they were fighting for themselves. To white folks, when they had been the slaves, they had seemed indifferent. But on land which these former slaves and their children knew they owned, they counted on for sustenance, independence and freedom, ahhh, this land was different. They were the kings. They were responsible to feed the hungry, themselves. To survive. And the days were already lean.

Those who had been committing adultery cried to God they would never do it again. Oh, how loud they cried. Those who had been lying, cried, "Lord, let me go this time, I will not lie again." Those who had stolen from others, cried, "Lord, let me go this time and I will take everything I have back to the one they belong to. I will, I will! I'm sorry, Lord, I'm sorry." None of them kept their word, of course. But, you see, He reads hearts, not words. And the storm wasn't the end of the world anyway!

during the storm Joel and Ruth were working the same field. Joel watched Ruth fight the rain and wind and keep coming back for more, always near where he was fighting to cut and stow the cane or corn. Bleeding hands, bruised arms, legs and bare feet kept at the fight for the food of life, the bare necessities.

After many hours of the grueling work, people already on their knees were falling to the side of their rows, prostrate in their tracks. Exhausted, breathless, worn out, drained. The fields were not completely clear, but more than expected had been done. Beside Joel and Ruth, others young and strong carried, dragged and helped those fallen to their damp but warm shacks. There was only cold food to give anyone because all had been called to help in the fields, none left behind to cook. Children had taken care of babies. But cold food was also good, good to the tired, grateful workers.

Joel and Ruth had been screaming admonitions to each other through the hours, always working close together. Now, Joel beckoned to Ruth and they fought their way against the pouring rain and wind to the side of the field where he had seen a shack just over the fence there. He used his cutting tool to wedge the door open then held the squealing door far enough open with his strong back as they went into the dilapidated shack once used for storing tools, cattle-birthing, slave-birthing or whatever necessary.

Ruth just fell stretched out on the dirt floor. Joel, ever the man, watched her. He liked what he saw. She was slim, not skinny, about five feet two inches or so, which put her at his shoulder; he was five foot eleven. They were both healthy. All these things he knew, just liked thinking of them again. Then his exhaustion made him fall to the ground right next to her, naturally. She turned her head to face him and just, naturally, looked right into his light brown eyes with her dark brown eyes. They didn't say anything and didn't look away this time. They just lay looking at each other, listening to the sound of the storm beating on the tin roof of the tool shack, trying to come in. Finally, he whispered to her, "You done good, girl." She almost smiled, but was too tired. She didn't worry about her mother, she felt safe with Joel. She closed her eyes and slept. Finally his exhaustion overcame him and he fell asleep, his crusty fingers holding one of her wet braids tightly.

Ruth awoke first, hungry. The storm sounded worse. She didn't wake Joel, just sat and watched him. She liked his strong, muscled arms, the curve of his round face, strong chin, pretty, wide, short nose and the short, thick lips so well defined as though drawn. She was getting ready to sight-travel down his body when he opened his eyes and looked at her. She smiled through the dried mud and bits of weed or grass on her face, and the sun came out for Joel. She did not look like a young girl anymore; she looked like a young, lush woman.

The rain was coming down hard, hard. The roof was holding up, but water was coming in under the loose floor boards. Ruth got up as quickly as her tired body allowed and shook out her wet dress. As Joel became more aware he moved quickly to push loose dirt to the wall with his hands, trying to stop the water. Ruth hastily searched and found the broken end of a shovel and handed it to him. They smiled together. He looked around for loose boards laying on the ground of the shack. Finding them, he dug a trench around the edge of the walls and set the boards in, shoring them with dirt. It worked. They rested, sitting close for warmth. As a place in the wall would weaken and let water through, Joel would dig dirt from the uphill side of the shack to strengthen the shoring. Ruth was happy being there with him even in all that mud and cold, but she was now very hungry. The only thing that kept her from being ugly-evil about it was being there with Joel. She had liked him before, mightily. Now, she loved him more. He knew how to do things! He was a man. And . . . best of all, he looked at her with such sweetness in his eyes. She didn't know whether to thank God for the storm or not.

Between bouts with the water and dirt, they talked. She, shyly, which made Joel more bold. A potato-bug could tell they liked each other, a lot. When their stomachs growled, they laughed. Nothing was too hard to stand while they were together. A few hours passed, the storm hardly seemed to be letting up.

Time passed. There was now a deep hole where Joel had been digging for dirt. The storm seemed to slacken, but any light from the sun behind the dark clouds was really gone now, and it was dark, truly dark. As the time to go came closer, the hearts above the empty stomachs wanted to linger. They were holding hands for moments at a time now. They were sitting closer now, for warmth, yes, but mostly for the thrill of it. Joel didn't want this time with Ruth to end, nor did she, so they decided to shore the wall one more time before they made a run for home. As he moved on his knees over to the dry-dirt hole, he smiled over his shoulder at her. He spoke, "You sure no fella have spoken for your heart in marriage? Your mama ain't promised you to nobody?" His foot hit the bug's new mudpile and the bug rushed out.

Ruth laughed softly, blushed, shook her head no. The bug, seeing no immediate harm coming, rushed back in to its toppled mudpile and began repair on it.

Joel laughed happily and bent deeper in the hole to break the dirt with the piece of shovel. Suddenly the shovel flew out of his hand as he hit something hard in the dirt. Ruth screamed, because you know there are all kinds of snakes and animals in the country. Joel started up, then, quick as a minute, he grabbed his piece'a shovel and began digging in the ground again. "Help me," is all he said. Then there was silence except for the sound of heavy breaths and grunts, and they were covered again, with dirt clinging to their sweat. They pulled a long, narrow toolbox out of the ground. The water was rushing in again at the floor, but they did not see it now. Nor did they care. What wonder was this? was in both their minds. The bug's new home was flooded. It fell on its back, legs scrambling wildly to right herself. She could not understand what was happening. She righted herself and began burrowing, seeking her place. She felt the birthing near.

Joel and Ruth looked at each other over the box, reading each other's thoughts. Their future could be in that box! Or nothin! Why would anybody want to hide an old toolbox if wasn't nothin in it?! Everythin or plain ole, useless, Confederate money!

Ruth started crying from nervous hope and a built-in, lifelong expectation of nothing but some man she hoped she would be able to love, who might someday get a piece of land of their own or . . . be a share-cropper forever. She had never known anyone who got ahead or got over. They got away. But then you didn't know what happened to them, mail and transportation being what it was. Some of her mama's sisters and brothers had "gotten away," but were very seldom heard of and almost never from. Just there, there where she was born, lived and grew, was all she knew. But her mama worked for the Befoes, and Ruth knew there was "better" than what she had ever known or would ever live, don't care how long she lived or how old she got! But . . . maybe? She looked at the box. Maybe . . . her own house, Lord? Please?

Joel stared at the box. His thoughts were like Ruth's except in a man's way, because their experience with life had been the same. He wanted a wife and children he could take care of. Would this box change his life? Could it be possible God had . . . No, God wouldn't. For him? Why? He didn't always live right. Joel, dreaming and praying, looked into space beyond the walls of the shack. He looked back at the box. Maybe wasn't nothin in the damn ole thing noway. Then hope and need beat out despair. Money? Gold? His own house and land and . . . Marry his woman he wanted? Or just plain ole Nothin? The bug, feeling secure within her scarcely finished mudhole, began to give birth.

Joel and Ruth looked at each other for several moments, not eager to lose a dream to just discover more of nothing in their lives. Then, without saying a word, Ruth grabbed the shovel and beat on the lock. Joel took the shovel away and hacked at the lock. It loosened . . . and fell off. He threw the lid back.

There were tools, old rusty tools: an old, old hammer, a chisel, some measuring sticks, nails, nails, nails. Joel turned the box over, dumped every thing out. Ruth put her hands on her face and burst into tears. It had all happened so quick! The nothing, the hope, the fear, the dream, the hope, then . . . nothing. Joel pushed the tools around, searching, even though he could see there was nothing. He looked at Ruth, sniffling now. He tried to smile. Said in a cracked, strained voice, "Nothin." He shook his head sadly. The bug, burrowed in now, breathing hard, still patting the earth down to make a place safe to leave her young.

"Well," he sat back on the now muddy floor. "Well, the shack kep us dry. And we kep warm . . ." He looked down at the box, "This ought to be good for somethin. I'll clean up the tools can use em to work, make money maybe." He slowly stood and reached for the box, but Ruth kicked it over and grabbed her hurt foot the same time the bottom fell out of the toolbox and the heavy black bag lay at their feet. They both reached for it, then Ruth said, "Go head" and held her hurt foot again. Joel cut the strings of the black bag and gold and silver coins fell to the ground along with a small jewelry box.

Ruth could count quicker than Joel. She did not know the value of the gold coins, but there were fifty-eight of them and about forty silver coins. She opened the jewelry box and the large one-and-a-half carat diamond ring flashed its brilliance for her. She pressed the ring to her breast and asked Joel, "Whose things is these?"

Serious, Joel answered, "I don't know they name, but I know it was a white man."

Ruth thought a moment. "Didn't have to be."

Joel smiled. "A Negro would'a done come back and got his gold already!"

Ruth thought some more. "Well, if'n we ask anybody, they gonna claim it!"

Joel started putting the coins back into the bag. "I knows it."

Ruth held the ring tighter to her breast. "What ought we to do? Is it yours or mine?"

Joel smiled. "It's ours. Somebody else gonna lie and take it, so we might as well lie and keep it."

Ruth leaned forward. "How it gonna be ours?"

Now, Joel, back on his knees, was thoughtful, but he knew his answer already. "Well . . ." He leaned back, rubbed his chin like he remembered seeing his daddy do long ago. "Well . . . I don't know if you blive me or no, but I was gonna ask you to marry up wit me, be my wife. I loves you. I knew that already."

Ruth's smile grew until her nose was at her hairline and her mouth covered her face and seemed like you could look in that smile and see her heart. "You was?!"

Joel smiled big, too! "I is askin you now!" He reached for her hand. "Well? C'n you see yourself a'marryin up wit me?" Ruth looked at him as if he was losing his mind and like he was her heart, all at the same time. He went on, "We c'n get our own land, our own farm. Our childrun c'n go to school. I c'n build you a big, good, nice house. I c'n buy a mule, naw, a horse! Two of em! A plow . . . tools. I'll work hard for you! For my fam'ly!"

Ruth, still smiling, "I'll make a good home for you, too, and give you beautiful babies what look just like you." She blushed. "Joel, you so beautiful." They reached for each other's hands and held them.

Ruth spoke first, "Who must we tell?"

"Don't tell nobody!"

"We can't spend that gold like that!"

Joel nodded. "Let's think bout it. Don't tell nobody, even your mama. I'm a man now. I'm your man now. This is 'tween us'uns."

Ruth nodded her head, yes, slowly. She looked down to the hole in the ground. Joel followed her gaze, and said, "Let's fill it back, much as we c'n and set the toolbox back in it. Ain't nobody looked out here in a whole lotta years, I bet."

"Must'a didn't."

So they worked until the floor was uneven, but filled. They stamped the earth as they laughed and planned. Joel put the bag of money inside his damp shirt; Ruth held the ring in its box in her hand. They were happy! Isn't money something sometime? Then they held hands and, running lightly, laughing and bumping into each other, found their way back to the field and to home as they made plans for the marriage and how to change the gold into money they could spend without worrying who could notice them and think on it. They, now, had a life!

The mother bug had now cleared a circle of space she did not really like. Her other, first home she had prepared for the birth had been done slowly with care for her babies. Now this would have to do. Her little eyes blinked sadly. Finally all the babies were born. The rain was gone, the water stopped. The mother bug spread her arms and legs around her brood under her stomach and, blinking her eyes in the dark hole, she settled down softly to being a mother.

and that is how Josephus Josephus' other daughter, Ruth, got her inheritance from him. Yinyang got hers from the tree, Ruth got hers from the ground. The dead ex-slave had helped both his daughters.

chapter

3

having finally reached New Orleans by train, Yinyang walked the
streets of the beautiful, dirty, fun-filled, sin-swollen, rich-poor, parading,
busy city filled with all kinds of smells of good food. Hungry, but afraid
to take her money out, fearful of everything and everybody, she walked
until she came upon a school building. She walked around it a few times.
Finally she went in, asking to speak "to a KIND woman."

"Is . . . is there a nice person here who likes . . . people? A kind
woman?"

The lady behind the counter sniffed down at the dirty, little street
urchin. "What do you want? Is this some sort of joke?" She stepped
back from Yin.

"No mam. But . . . I need . . . to talk to a . . . nice person.
Someone kind."

"Are you registered here? Who are you? Who are your . . . parents?"

"They are . . . dead." The face before her looking down at her
with such disdain made her panic. "I . . . never mind. I'll go."

"Well, I should hope so, young . . . woman. We are busy here!"

A rather tall lady dressed neatly in black with a white lace collar, stepped into the office, rushing, carrying papers, and heard the last remark. "What is the matter, Miss Wench? Who is this?"

"Nobody and nothing, if you ask me, Miss Able. I was . . ."

The woman turned to Yin. "Nobody and nothing?" She smiled, "What is the matter dear?"

Yin turned to go, almost whispered, "Nothin, I just wanted to . . . Nothin, mam, please."

The woman reached for Yin's arm, gently. "I have no business to attend to right this minute, why not come in and have a cup of coffee with me?"

Yin looked at the clerk behind the counter with fear. The woman, Miss Able, understood. "Come now, there is nothing to fear. We might even be able to help you. My name is Miss Able." Yin slowly stopped pulling away, dropped the muddy carpetbag and started crying. "Oh, my." Miss Able soothed. "Oh, my, I hope there is no need for tears. Come with me, dear. Let us talk." In about ten minutes, Miss Able excused herself from school business that day and took Yin home with her. Yin still pouring out her story to the kind woman.

The next day, bathed, dressed neatly in things Miss Able had gathered, Yin was found lodging, registered in school, bought clothes with contributions garnered by Miss Able. (Yin did not tell her about the gold.) Yin's new life began. Thinking of becoming a young lady, she hugged herself with joy. She would be in school and learning; she laughed out loud with pleasure.

Yinyang had not been to school since she had studied with the teacher back home. Students her own age were now beyond her capacity. She stayed with the younger students because she was learning, but she was so embarrassed with the older students teasing her. They say children can be cruel; many children grow to be adults and stay that way.

Yin stuck with school about two years, mostly because of the caring Miss Able. Then, she stopped going a few days a week. Gradually, she quit going all together. Miss Able urged her to continue, because an education would be so important to a young lady. But Yin's thoughts were already beyond the school.

Yin had taken to stopping at a small, genteel coffee shop each day as she walked home from school. She had noticed the young ladies, only a bit older than she was, talking so excitedly, looking so fresh and lovely in such becoming clothes. Beautiful clothes, grand hats, superb, laced shoes. With heels! Because she was so well mannered, she had made friends with the serving help and she asked about a job. Wonder of wonders! They hired her to walk around the shop with the silver coffee pot, filling the cups, keeping the coffee warm. Mostly ladies came to the coffee shop. They talked of love, lovers, clothes and things that sound so glamorous. Very few men came.

Yin had continued going to see Miss Able for tutoring, including manners, dress and such. She admired and respected, even loved Miss Able. But Miss Able could not get her to come back to school full-time. Yin had decided she was going to find a man to take care of her so school would not be necessary. A man to settle down with. A man of means, so she could be like the ladies she admired so much.

When Yin thought of it, she was ashamed she had never told Miss Able about the gold and had let the good woman beg for her, but her shame didn't make her any more honest. She thought of God and His suggestions hardly at all. So she cashed in most of her gold without Miss Able's help. With honest help like Miss Able's, she would have found out she had enough money to buy a house, a home and all she needed in it. She was cheated, of course. With the money, she bought a wardrobe she thought was equal to the ladies she had envied, to find and attract a man who could give her a home.

During her search for the man of substance, she was used by more than a few. She kept running into men in her same circumstances looking for a woman of substance. If they took her home to an apartment with rich, rented furniture and appointments, she "just knew" this was it! Well, it wasn't. She gave her virginity, her lovely fresh self, to a liar. A thief. When he left, she had just what they leave you with: a puff of sweetly scented air, dirty sheets, and nothing. Some don't even leave sweetly scented air. She behaved slavishly toward men in her eagerness to please. Now, you know, most human beings seem to value you less when you make them more important than you are. She was left often and always. She was pretty . . . but, she was not rich, not even wealthy. And pretty won't buy anything . . . unless . . .

The gentlemen she yearned for, she was not well-bred enough for. Those who might have wanted her sincerely, were not well-bred enough for her and had no means. In seeking places to meet gentlemen (ladies could not go everywhere) she ran into her share of pimps and gamblers.

One pimp of high personal standards for himself (he had none for his women) did indeed steal her heart for awhile. She forgot her plans for a man of means and the "good" life. She was in such need of love by that time, she accepted a substitute, as people will. One she had to work for. He also had other women. Women he treated better. White women. He was white and he was one of those who knew she was not. In time she began to feel insecure, inferior, as, of course, he made her feel. Yinyang found herself in the arms of other men more than she was in the arms of the man she thought she loved. It was for money. Money for him, the man she thought she loved. At his request.

When she thought of God, she frowned and liked Him even less because of what her life was. Yin blamed God even though these were her own choices. To pray was now stupid to her. To pray made her more lonely. Her life went on this way for a couple of long, barren, sad years.

One morning Yin woke up used, hung over from liquor, smelling of smoke and Lord knows who. Her fine dress spotted with the waste of a stranger's seed. The stale liquor fumes made her think of her mother. Her soiled dress made her think of her losing dreams. She thought of the lovely, tastefully dressed ladies with the lively eyes in the coffee shop. Surely they did not live like this. She thought of Miss Able, the only KIND person she had met. She started to cry when she thought of Josephus Josephus, Pajo.

Suddenly the man came from another room, frowning, "Here, here! What's this now? Crying!? Are you trying to say I cheated you? Get out of here! Go, now, go! I must have all this mess cleaned out of here anyway! Take your money and go! Tears!? What are you trying to pull? Not another cent are you getting!" He pulled her roughly up. "I've been around some. You can't pull that one on me!" He pushed her toward the door. "Where's your wrap? Ahh! Here!" He almost threw it to her. "You're mighty young to have learned so much, so soon! Bad, all bad!" Then she was out the door. As it slammed she heard him muttering, "Trash. All trash. Not near worth my $20 gold piece!"

Yin, still crying, snot trailing down her reddened nose, eyes bleary as she reached frantically into her pockets for the gold piece. Twenty dollars!? She was used to handling smaller money, paper, different metals. Her gold coins had been cashed in and, at that time, she had been given the bundles of cash without division of value per coin. Her youth and inexperience had made her gullible, trusting. Just right to be used in the devious, bustling city. But she knew it now. And she was supposed to hand this over to her Man since he took care of the rent for her tiny room with cooking privileges in a very questionable area of town. Yin cried even harder.

Stumbling down the hall, down the stairs, through the lobby, oblivious to stares and whispers, she reached the streets. Walking aimlessly as she cried her child-woman heart out, she was thinking of all she had been through since her birth. She did not think of it as violence, but it was. Her life felt like shit and she smelled much the same. Of low life. "What have I done wrong?" she wondered. "Why does my life keep turning out wrong? God?"

The noise of children running down the steps of a church caught her attention. She stopped and stared at the church, feeling a quick sense of the need of God. Was there a home in there? She lifted her spotted frock and, going up the steps, went in.

There was instant quiet inside. Peace. She did not know what to do so she knelt, waiting for God to do something to show her He was real, that He cared. When her knees were tired, she sat, thinking about her life. Thinking of God. But Satan had a friend here in this beautiful church. Yinyang felt a light touch on her shoulder. A soft voice spoke, "My child, do you need help?" The priest had noticed her rumpled condition . . . and her beauty.

"Oh, sir! Oh!" She burst into tears afresh. The soft voice bespoke kindness. She felt herself lifted gently as the voice continued. "My child, let us go where we may talk without disturbing others. You can cleanse your soul." She was being led down an aisle, tears held in her eyes by her relief that someone cared, God cared.

"Now, now," he urged, "tell me what I can do to help rid you of those tears on the face of such a lovely child. Tears do not belong on your face. Such a pretty face. How old are you?"

Between sniffles, Yinyang looked into the soft blue eyes and poured out her whole story, holding back only those things that caused her too much shame. The priest patted and consoled.

He sighed, "You must get away from this man who takes you into such degradation. He does not know what he is doing. God is frowning on the both of you. Do you wish to continue this life?"

"Oh, no! No, I do not! I am ashamed."

"Then you must get a job, find some means of support that will be cleaner, with a possibility for happiness. Do you agree?"

"But where, sir? How?"

The priest was writing with a tiny pencil on a small sheet of paper.

"You must take this, if you wish to change your life, to a friend of mine. She has a dress shop in an excellent area for a woman such as you will be. She will help you . . . give you a job." He handed her the paper. "Er . . . is that all the money, . . . gold you have?" Yin nodded yes. He sighed, "Then you must take the gold coin you have. With her help you will find another place. Then pack your things and move where this man will never find you again. Leave nothing behind."

Yin's eyes shone with love and gratitude. Her young tears wet his hands as she kissed them. "Oh, thank you, thank you, bless you. When I am settled, I will come back and learn about God. I want to learn how to live a good life. I never meant my life to turn out this way."

The priest patted her hands which held his so tightly. "Yes, yes. We will see." He led her to the door, pointing her in the right direction. He had never once mentioned God to her except to say He was frowning.

Yin walked briskly, her spirits lifted, her resolve firm. She thought of Miss Able; perhaps she should tell her everything, regain her friendship, return to school to learn better ways to make her living. Yin almost decided to do it right then that minute, she was so filled with happiness. But, then, Satan pointed to her clothes, her hair, her condition. She looked down at herself, raised her hand to her hair. Shame filled her again and she resolved to see Miss Able as soon as she was settled. Then Satan pushed her age into her mind with the memories of when she was younger and tried to go to school with younger students. Besides, who knew if Miss Able would help her again? Or even where Miss Able was? It had been several years since she had even seen Miss Able. Satan knows how people think and how to help them think. His way, you see.

Finally Yin stood outside the grand, little dress salon. It was more than she had expected. She had spent some of her own money in a few stores like this, but had quickly come to where she could not afford such beautiful creations. She looked down at herself again, almost turning to go away and return another time. Satan nudged her at the same time an extremely well-dressed, short, plump woman opened the door and spoke to her. "Well, now, dear. Do you see something you might like?"

Yin stammered, "Oh, no! Well, yes! You see . . ."

The woman smiled, "Come in, come in. You can see much better and much more inside." She reached out a friendly, white hand. "Come in, come in."

In a moment, Yin was inside, hardly knowing how it all happened. She was embarrassed in the midst of such finery. The few well-dressed salesladies were looking at her. The kind, plump lady waved the bejeweled, soft, white hand to dismiss them. "Would the beautiful, little one like a cup of fine coffee? Come along now, I have just had some made. Miss Will is my name, and what are you called, dear?"

"My name is Yinyang . . . Krupt," she added suddenly. Yin winced at this little seeming betrayal of Josephus.

"What a strange, but lovely, name for a lovely, young woman. And how old are you, Yinyang?"

"I am twenty-three now. And people call me Yin."

Sitting in a soft, luxurious armchair, a saucer balanced on her knees, Yin poured out her story for the second time that day, leaving more out, crying anew. Plump, comforting hands patted. The soft voice soothed. Finally, Yin finished her part of the intimate little talk.

"Well, you dry your lovely eyes right now! That part of your life is over! We shall start all new! First we shall choose a few things for you to wear. Never mind going to . . . where you live to retrieve anything. You shall come with me. We will get you settled and then see what is to come! You should never have to go back to that life again! You shall stay with me until we know what to do with you. Your decision, of course!"

Yin thought of her papers, her birth certificate. She stood, "Oh, but I have to get some . . . papers and things that are, may be, important to me." She saw the frown appear on Miss Will's face and added hastily, "Oh, but it will only take a moment. I promise."

Soon, Miss Will was filling Yin's arms with so many lovely things Yin could scarcely believe this was happening to her. Her dreams! Her eyes and soul all aglow with happiness, she thanked Miss Will, even taking the liberty to kiss the plump cheek in gratitude. She even thanked God, but what He had sent—thoughts of school, returning to the good woman, Miss Able, finding a good and clean comfortable way to live her life, to learn life—she had not taken. Yinyang rushed into the future again, leaving behind all thoughts of returning to Miss Able and school . . . and seeking God.

Later that night, full of champagne and a sumptuous dinner, sunk in the fresh, clean, soft, downy bed, body covered with a plump-sized, lacy nightgown, Yin could hardly believe her luck. She was just about to thank God, when her door opened and someone came through the darkness to the bed. She could not see anyone, but she could hear their quick, panting breath. Her cover was pulled back by an unseen hand, and a soft, plump voice with a gentle roughness said, "I felt lonely. You are such a nice, lovely, kind, young woman, I want to sleep here, with you." Miss Will moved easily into the bed. "Sometimes I feel so lonely. I have no one, like you have me, now. Here, put your arms around me . . . and I will not feel alone anymore." Yin closed her eyes tight, hoping this was not what she knew it was. She forgot to be thankful for her luck.

"Yes, dear. That's right. Yes, come closer. Ahhh, you're a pet. A sweet pet." Moments passed, Yin's heart beating fast, her mind disgusted, again. The voice spoke again, softly, "Oh, such warm feet, such warm, smooth legs." A soft lamp flicked on. "Here, raise your legs so I can see these beautiful things." Yin raised her legs toward her chest obediently. "Lovely, lovely," Miss Will continued, as she stroked Yin's legs. "Yes, dear, you are lovely. Such terrible things have happened to you because of this beauty, you know. Now, we will care for it right, and those horrible things will never happen to you again. MMMMMMmmmmmm. Don't put them down yet, dear. Here, let's turn this awful, old light out. There. Now, let me feel that lovely, smooth skin. Up a little, up a little, dear. Now . . . there." Yin felt her legs caressed, spread open, then the head that greedily sank to its prey. Miss Will knew what she was about. Soon Yin forgot to feel anything but the pleasure spreading through her. She had decided to stay.

Satan happened to notice as he was passing on his way to his business; he smiled. Well, he didn't have to worry about her for awhile, she was in good hands. He moved on, after all, he is always very busy.

Yinyang met the old priest again many times, he was a friend and frequent visitor of Miss Will. But, he never, ever, spoke of God. Yin was living by her own wit, alone.

c h a p t e r
4

In Yoville, Joel and Ruth were trying to plan their future. Being Negroes with restricted education and very small experience with money, they did not know exactly what to do to further their dreams. After weeks of courting and counting, Joel and Ruth decided they HAD to tell somebody because they didn't know what else to do. Joel sweated over that bag of money ALL the time, didn't trust hiding it. He was scared to keep it on him all the time, which he tried to do, but it jangled and was so big. Ruth wore her ring when she went to the toilet-out-house. She kept it on a string tied around her waist other times. She was scared the string would break and it would fall into the hole in the outhouse. She didn't know what to do either. They wanted a house of their own where they could hide the money and she could wear the ring without anyone being able to see anything. But they had to spend some money to get the house in the first place.

They decided to trust Bessel, Ruth's mother, who worked for the Befoes and would know about money. Bessel wanted to take the money from them for safekeeping since they were just "children." They weren't just children so they didn't let her do that. "A little at a time," they said.

The mother said, "I know Miz Befoe is a good enough woman. She ain't like these other southern crackers. She'll help. If I take too much to her, she might get greedy, so I will take one and tell her I found it."

Joel spoke, "Found it where?"

Bessel immediately understood, she wasn't dumb. "I'll tell her I found it . . . over by my church! She can look there forever and never will find nothin!" This is what Bessel did.

Asking permission to speak to Miz Befoe "bout somethin portent," she got it. Mrs. Befoe turned the coin round and round in her slender, well-cared-for hands. "Where you say you found this, Bessel?"

"Over there round by my church, mam."

"I haven't heard . . . anyone say they lost a gold coin . . . lately."

"I just wants to know how much money is it worth, mam. Lord, I can't do nothin with such a money as that! I needs to know what kinda real money can I get wit it, mam. I is so sorely broke, mam, I needs everything, an I got a growin daughter what is askin bout marryin, I sure could use whatever that thing is worth! What you say it's worth, mam?"

"I'll have to check into it, ahhh . . . what's your name again?"

"Bessel, mam, I works in the cleanin end of this house for twelve years now."

"Yes, Bessel, now I remember." She looked hard at Bessel. "Why didn't you go to my husband? He's at the bank today."

"Cause I don't know him, mam. You my fren who I work fo an knows."

"I am?"

"Yes, mam."

"Well Bessel, I will let you know in a few days. You have to leave it here so I can show it to . . . somebody. I will let you know in a few days. If it is not too much, I will save you some time and trouble and let you have it myself."

"Yes'm." Bessel looked lingeringly at the coin as she turned to leave the room.

"That will be all now. You may return to your work. I'll send for you, Bessie."

"Bessel, mam."

"What difference does it make? I'll send for you. In the meantime, look around that place where you found this and see if there is any more."

"Yes'm."

"Good day, Bessel."

When Mrs. Befoe called Bessel to her, she spoke shortly about the low value of such coins now, and grudgingly (because what did Negras know what to do with money?) gave Bessel twenty dollars for each fifty dollar coin. Bessel was elated. Before she left Mrs. Befoe, she asked, "Miz Befoe, mam, what you spose you would ask for that little piece of land I lives on? I mean could I, maybe, buy that for my younguns to live and marry on?"

The land was worth about twenty dollars on the market then. Mrs. Befoe had so much land in her family that no one but the Negra might need, that she agreed to sell the land to Bessel for seventy five dollars. The deal was made that day, and Bessel left for home to tell the good news to Joel and Ruth. On the way home Bessel pocketed the remaining money in her homemade brassiere and only gave the waiting Joel and Ruth a note of purchase for the land her own house was on, thinking that would keep them from ever moving her out.

Joel and Ruth spent their wedding night in the room Ruth was born in. She had hung new curtains, had a new spread, sheets and a brass bed. The new dresser drawers were full of new underclothes, some she had made, for Joel and her. Her mother had given her a nightgown, pale and gossamer so you could see through, and Ruth was ashamed to wear it. But when all the guests were gone, she placed the diamond ring above her wedding ring, put the lovely gown on, slipped between the new sheets and pulled them up to her chin . . . and smiled.

Joel came in as happy as he could be. This was his bride! His woman! He had been squeezing his toes in his shoes all day, knocking his knees together all day, touching her whenever she passed close to him. He smiled so much it began to hurt him. He was happy!

He pulled the covers back, turned up the lamp Ruth had turned down and got in his bed with his wife.

He spoke softly. "That's a mighty pretty nightie, baby, but take it off."

Ruth whispered back. "What chu talkin bout, Joel."

They were both whispering. "Talkin bout you takin that gown off. I wants to see my bride, my wife!"

"Why? Ain't nothin to see."

"Oh baby, it's plenty to see. You is my body now."

"Joel, I ain't takin this gown off nothin."

"You my wife and I wants to see you. Girl, you know how long I been waitin to be like this wit you? Well, it's my turn."

"Joel, I'm shamed to take everythin off!" Still whispering.

"Baby, I loves yo body. It's the only one I ever wants beside me anywhere." He put his hands on her waist and began to move his hand down across her lower stomach, reaching for the hem of the gown. She grabbed his hand.

"Stop Joel, don't make me do that."

"Here," Joel stepped out of bed and started pulling his nightclothes off. "Here, I let you see me!" Still whispering.

Ruth let go holding on to her gown and covered her eyes. "Naw, Joel, don't you do that! I don't want to see it! . . . No!" But it was too late, she had.

He reached for the gown, now free, pulled it to her waist, before she stopped him again. "Joel!" She forgot to whisper, "Please baby, don't, pleeeeeeeasse." Joel answered, whispering, "Please, baby, do, pleeease." They laughed. He hugged her. She held him close to her body so she could hide it from the light. That was all he wanted anyway. He held her, kissed her tenderly, gently but hungrily. Her legs opened of their own accord. He laughed softly. She covered her face. He moved over on her, holding his weight off her. He was gentle like a cat's pad on your cheek or a butterfly on your hand. He loved this woman. She opened herself up to him, gave him her virginity she had saved for him. She loved this man. It was a beautiful honeymoon no further than a minute from where she had been all her life. They woke up smiling and whispering and kissing. It was nighttime again before he said he was hungry and needed to eat. That's how they became husband and wife.

With them all working together over the gold, Bessel felt very competent and smart because they depended on her. She felt like the ruler of the house. But Joel said he was not going to live in a house where he had two rulers. He spoke up. "Well, Miz Bessel, mam, this here is goin to be my house and my wife's house. If you wants to you c'n still live with us. I is goin to build on to the front of this shack a place for my own wife and childrun. You c'n stay on here if you wants to."

Bessel glared at him. But then he handed her ten more gold coins and a silver one, saying, "Tell her you done found these more monies. See what c'n you git for em. I needs to get mater'al to build wit. This here weekend, if we c'n."

When Bessel took the new coins, found at the same place, to Mrs. Befoe, Mrs. Befoe noted, "I need to start attending your church, Bessel." The price had gone down some. Bessel got fifteen dollars for each gold coin and five dollars for the silver one.

One hundred fifty five dollars!!! Free and clear! Bessel took $50 for herself again, and gave Joel $105 which could handle his building and the wedding debt. She didn't take too much because that was "her daughter he was doin for!" 'Sides, she had more money now than she had ever had at one time in her life!

When she went yet again to Mrs. Befoe, Mr. Richard Befoe was there this time. He asked, "Where do you . . . say . . . you find these coins, Bessie?"

"At the church, suh."

"These are the fifteenth or so gold coins, at least, and the third silver coin, Bessie."

"Yes, suh. I don't knows suh, I just be walkin home from my prayers, still prayin, an then, all in a sudden, I looks down an there be a piece of money!"

Mr. Befoe smiled what he thought was a warm smile at Bessel. "If this keeps up, I shall have to buy your church and go pray there myself."

Bessel tried to laugh, but she was scared. "Yes, suh."

"Ahem," Mr. Befoe cleared his throat. "There is so much work involved in doing this . . . thing for you, I am only able to give you one hundred dollars for the gold coins and ten dollars for all the silver ones. I have it here for you." He opened a desk drawer. "Bring me any others you may . . . find . . . and I will see what I can do."

"Yes, suh."

When Bessel got home that day, they all sat down, the newlyweds and mama, and decided they had to find a different way to change the coins. It was finally decided Bessel would have to go north to one of her sisters or brothers and change it where it was really possible to find out the truth about the worth of them and maybe get more money for them.

In no time at all, Bessel got sick and took leave from her job, which put Mr. and Mrs. Befoe on alert. They argued about running her off while they were still making profit. This, when they already had millions. Bessel went east, found her brother who was worrying about her living off of him and "he a poor preacher," he said. All he had was a broke-down church, some rental shanties, a home and wife with one child, two women on the side. Satan "loved" him, he was a good worker. Yes, her brother cheated Bessel, but he was cheated by his friend, the banker. Still, he gave her a bit more than the Befoes had. She took the money home to her daughter. Less a bit for herself, of course.

Bessel quit her job, "too sick," she said, and the Befoes sat up straight. They bought, or rather took, the grounds the church was on, tore it down, dug up the grounds and found nothing, then sold the site back to the bewildered preacher who began to poke around in the dirt himself. Joel watched all this and sold no more gold in Yoville.

c h a p t e r
5

Time had passed quickly for Yin the last few years. Miss Will was very good to her. Yin had asked for only one thing she really wanted: it was to learn something special. Miss Will allowed that to be harmless to any plan of her own, it might even prove to be a help because she had not decided what she would finally do with Yin when the end of her passion came. Miss Will wanted to speak better French, did not like to cook, and if Yin could sew she might be useful at the salon. So Yin had teachers in French, cooking and sewing. She could already read and write, but her studies much improved these things, too.

God gradually faded from Yin's mind, He won't live just anywhere. Lacking any self-motivation, Yin remained with Miss Will. It seemed to take bad luck, or tragedy, to make Yin think enough to remove herself from unhappiness or degradation. She seemed easily led. Closer to the truth was that she took the line of least resistance. If she wanted something, she made decisions without thought of the consequences. She didn't really care, or not care, about others but would treat them nice and try to make them happy as long as they did something she wanted. She seldom took thought; instead, she took things. Even false love.

But, she was learning. French, cooking and sewing. And she was learning about envy; she wanted everything material. She had pride in abundance, too. Of what, she couldn't have told you. Just "myself," she might say.

Around this time, the old priest who had sent Yin to Miss Will had a young priest he wished to corrupt or control, so he began to invite the young man to accompany him on his visits to Miss Will. He thought the proximity to such a lovely woman as Yin who was submissive to Miss Will might seduce the faithful young priest, Paul. He needed Paul to owe him his loyalty or a favor for secrets kept. Paul did indeed like Yin and, after they were set up to have a tryst, Yin liked Paul. But for quite different reasons.

Paul, fully dressed, lay across the bed and spoke to Yin of God. The things he said went over and around her head, making her mind whirl in confusion.

She clasped her hands to her cheeks in exasperation. "But why does He leave me here if He thinks this is all wrong, all sin?!"

Paul smiled gently. "Does He leave you here, Yin, or do you stay? What is stopping you from leaving here? Did He send you here? Or did you decide to come here?"

Yin shook her head. "I didn't decide to come, I just . . . oh, I don't know what happened! I had no place to go! That awful man . . ."

"What awful man?"

But Yin didn't want to tell that part of her life. "Just . . . someone who caused me grief, did me wrong. Taught me things I didn't . . . need never . . . Oh, never mind. You are a priest, you would never understand."

Paul shook his head. "Yin, I study the word of the creator of life. He knows it better than anyone. He tells us how to live it, what to avoid. I may not 'understand,' as you may think of it, but I would know if it were a wise choice or a good person." He smiled. "And I knew enough not to take that path myself."

Yin threw herself back on the bed. "But I didn't choose any way, it just came to me. What could I do?"

"You could have refused it."

"But why should I?"

"Are you happy? If you are, you chose right for yourself."

"Well, I'm not exactly 'happy,' but who is?"

"Those who own themselves. Those who respect themselves."

"I do respect myself! I have furs, clothes, a carriage for my use. I have . . ."

"Nothing. Nothing that cannot be taken from you in an instant!"

Yin thought seriously a moment. Looking into his eyes, she knew he spoke the truth. "But I have no money, no way. Nowhere to go, even now."

Paul smiled again, gently. "No, Yin, I will not accept that, and neither will God. There is always somewhere to go. And I'll wager you have some money somewhere. You are not a stupid woman. You are not a child. Do you like what you do? Do you want to stay with Willie (that is what he called Miss Will) forever? You can't, you know. She will not want you that long, I don't think. Has she ever asked you to make love with anyone else before?"

"Nooooo, not like this. Not a man. Once or twice her friends from her social club or whatever she calls it. I refused, though."

Paul's smile disappeared. "Ahhh, you will not be able to say no much longer. She is now offering you to men."

"No, a man. Only you."

"Yin, you are old enough and smart enough to know when a thing is beginning and where it might lead. In any event, do you like what you do with her? Is this how you want to live your life?"

Yin fingered her gown, rubbed her hands down the silky pillows. Paul caught her thoughts. "Yin, Satan always makes his dirtiest deeds look good and feel good, until you are beyond help, then things will change."

"Might change."

"Will change. Read your history, watch people. Everyone at the bottom, in the gutters, diseased, sick, misused, abused and bereft, poor and friendless, did not start there. Many of them started where you did, as you do, or even better. Satan gives no reward beyond your time of use to him. He does not love you, or even think of you beyond what you may do for him."

"What does God give you?"

"The greatest things on earth."

"You mean the sun, the moon, stars, maybe the ocean or the rain? The air?" She looked at him with derision. "He never gave me nothing!"

"I should think breath is the most important thing to all of us. Life. But, no, there is much more."

"What?"

"Love." Yin stopped smiling. Paul went on. "He gives us love. Satan never, never does. Satan deals in lust and infatuation. God gives us Love, that which goes out from us and which comes in to us. Living His way gives us respect. And without respect, respect . . . there will never be true love, any love. Think. Think and tell me who you have loved whom you did not first respect? He gives us kindness, kindness that does not depend on a return favor. He gives us . . ."

Yin interrupted him. "I have really respected and loved only one person. My father." She thought a moment. "Maybe my mother. But I never thought of going home."

Paul sat up. "Then you have someplace to go! Leave here!"

"And God made me lose him. Josephus. He died. He told me my mother died."

Paul flung his arm up. "I am so tired of people blaming God for death! God did not bring death to man, Satan did. Satan told the first lie! 'You shall not surely die.' He fooled Eve and death came to be! Do you ever hear Satan offer life everlasting?! No! Only God!"

"I never thought of it in that way. I never knew all of that."

"Then go! Go where you will have time to learn, to think! Time to live, to seek your own soul, to find your peace."

"Willie says I am too young to speak of peace."

"What else would Satan tell you?"

Yin thought of her life as she looked into the eyes of the young priest. She knew he was right about Miss Will. More and more lately, she had asked Yin to be kind to one of her friends. Implicit in the request was the reminder that all Yin had was put there by Miss Will, at her will. Yin always complied because she held her mind in abeyance. She didn't want to think about her life, she just wanted to live it as softly and gently as possible. Just wear things, go places. Not to have to worry. She sighed. "One last question, Paul."

"Anything."

"Isn't your life boring? I mean, doing everything right? You don't have any fun!"

Paul laughed as if Yin was a child. "The 'fun,' the joy I get from life, is in not being caught up in all that nasty, sticky, stinky doo-doo that people like you get caught up in. You see, this is not the end if you don't leave and find something to do with yourself. You can stay right here and go down, down, down. You are already well on your way. Looks don't last forever."

He shook his head, sadly. "Are you bored when someone is kind to you? When someone does not lie to you. Loves you truly? Are you bored by me?" Yin shook her head slowly. He continued, "How can you be bored when your head is filled with beauty, love and truth? When all the arrows of life that try to pierce your hungry, hungry heart cannot reach you because of your knowledge of what makes these arrows? And what makes your heart hungry? Ahhhh, my little friend, wake up before someone decides it's time to let you slide further down. Don't wait for the end to come first."

Yin was not naturally dumb, probably more lazy. She looked at Paul and said thoughtfully, perhaps testing him, "I don't know if I can trust God again. He has never been as good to me as the devil, if what you say is true and the devil led me here."

Paul shook his head sadly again. "You play. I will not play with God, nor you."

"Well, what shall we do for the next few hours we are left alone here?"

Paul smiled and sat up. Looking at the lovely woman before him all dressed for bed and love, he thought, "Get behind me, Satan, you are far too lovely to be in front of me right now." To Yin he said, "Get a Bible, let's reason together for this little while." Yin hesitated. Paul laughed, "C'mon, let's do something Willie and the old priest won't like!"

That did it, Yin jumped up to get a Bible. It took Yin quite a time to find a Bible among all the unread books on Miss Will's shelves. Finally, way at the bottom in a corner, dusty and unused, the gold lettering flickered through the grit—HOLY BIBLE. She laughed, grabbed the book and, thinking of Miss Will, danced all the way back to her room. Handing the book to Paul, she fell back on the bed, ran her hand down her voluptuous length, threw her head back and laughed, laughed, laughed.

.   .   .

When Miss Will and the old priest returned, Paul and Yin were sitting in the parlor. Each held a glass of wine, each looked pleased and satisfied. This was much to the old priest's delight, while Miss Will did not know whether to be pleased or not. She decided she would be pleased for her old useful friend's sake; she would not be pleased with Yinyang though. She would soon replace this woman who could be so pleased with a man.

On their way home, the old priest put his arm affectionately around Paul's shoulders and said, "Well, now. I suppose you have had a very good and . . . fulfilling afternoon?"

Paul moved away slightly. "It was a good afternoon, after all."

The old priest patted him on the back. "Well, that was what I planned for you to have!" He laughed and rolled his eyes gaily.

"I have never had a bad time yet, doing the will of my God."

"The will of your God?! My Lord, boy, that was not . . ."

Paul interrupted, "Yes, the will of my God. I was able to speak to her about Him and what He means to us."

The old priest was annoyed, his voice lowered, "At such a time, you felt that was necessary?"

"It is what I live to do. Am committed to do. Teach."

The old priest turned to Paul, "It is not what I intended you to do. I did not tell you to convert her! It . . . it . . . wasn't . . . the right time!"

Paul turned to him. "I do not take my instruction in these matters from you. I take them from the Bible."

The old priest turned red with chagrin. "You presume to know more about these matters than I? I have been a priest for forty years! You do not know, can never know, as much as I about the ways of God!"

Paul smiled slightly. "It is not the number of years a man knows of God that gives him wisdom and understanding. It is his brain. His soul and his heart. Sincerity. Love for God. Faith."

"Careful, young man, careful. You do not know what you are doing."

Before he walked away, Paul nodded and said, "I am afraid I do. Yes, I am afraid so. But I believe my care need only be that I do the will of God. Then I need not worry about man. At all." Of course Satan heard all this and began to think of troubles to lay upon the young man to take his mind away from God. Satan also cast a glance at Yinyang. "Hell," he thought, "There is so much to do in this world!"

Yinyang was a bit more quiet and thoughtful through the next few months. She watched Miss Will for signs of fading affection but instead she was more abrupt and demanding. So Yin began to think about and try to plan, as had her father, as have millions of people, for a way out, for a better life for herself. She believed her mother was dead and did not want to go back to Yoville. But as time passed, Yoville began to look better to her in her mind. "After all, Yoville is my home. I must have some property there. Anyway, where else is there for me? I am a woman, alone." Her plans took firmer shape.

In Yoville, Joel and Ruth were trying to raise their family and working hard to improve their life and home. The gold was a huge help but posed problems in trusting others to help them fairly. They had to trust Bessel. Bessel chose to trust her brother in the East.

After a year or so with a few trips east to change money for Joel and Ruth, Bessel had a powerful, new wardrobe and had rented her own apartment in Philadelphia. She'd met a man and was trying to get him to marry her, which he really planned to do since Bessel kept coming up with gold money from somewhere. I mean, times were hard, very hard. And money was money. These were some of Satan's favorite times. People could be made to do things so easily. (People needed a place to live, needed liquor, needed drugs, needed food, needed everything.) It was a very good time for him. And Bessel.

Joel and Ruth had had two babies. Ma Lal and, now, Ma Mae had attended Ruth. One child had died, they didn't know of what. Ruth was a good mother and Joel a loving father. They had gotten most of what they wanted. The house was built. It was lovely and dear to Ruth, and Joel was proud of his family and what he had been able to do for them. Still, even with the money, there was work, babies and death. They loved each other though, oh, how they loved each other. The gold coins were being changed and spent too fast, however. They now only had about fifteen left and several silver ones. Bessel had been cheated and in turn had cheated Joel and Ruth out of so much.

Joel gave Ruth five gold coins and told her to hide them for herself if the need should ever come. He kept five for himself and sent five to Bessel in a box of pecans for her to cash in. She seldom came home to Yoville now. She didn't send any money. They waited and waited. Another child had come. They had a boy, Luke, and a girl, Lettie. Joel wanted to build another bedroom, so when the new babies came, he could have a room for the boys and a room for the girls. They waited and waited for what seemed like forever. No money came.

When, finally, Bessel came back, she brought no money with her. She was broke. And broken. Her man hadn't married her. Hadn't worked to help her. Had left when the money was gone. Ole good, slick Bessel. Not really slick though, just hadn't ever had anything before in her life and didn't know what to do with it when she did have it. And didn't know much about love either. Now she took to just sitting on the porch all day in the spring and summer and sitting at her window in her old room in the cold, wet, snowy winters. She didn't smile much and often found much to complain about to Ruth about Joel. To Joel about Ruth.

In a house in the country, things are always needing to be fixed, repaired, replaced. Animals continue to eat and need all they need. Money just goes and goes and goes. It does not always come in. Ruth had buried her gold coins in the dirt in the chicken house. Joel spent his last doing things that needed to be done on his farm. He finally turned to a white man he had worked for and with, whom he thought could be trusted, Mr. Kindle. The Kindle family was once quite well-off and had fallen on hard times gradually since Emancipation. Mr. and Mrs. Kindle's children were grown; one had left, the other had married but stayed in the area. Kindle was not a greedy man. He sold the gold coins and even almost refused to accept any pay for doing it. He gave the right money to Joel. Mr. Creed, Joel's Negro friend, helped Joel build the new room at almost no cost because he had gone through the same thing while raising his own family. He had money hidden away, but he would not bring it out and give it away. He kept in his mind the thought, "That money gonna send my son Lincoln to school, to college!" But he worked hard helping Joel at whatever he could.

When Ruth became pregnant again, Joel was full of joy. He had a good crop planted, the animals were well, and nothing bothered him except Bessel. Bessel was always in bed now and Ruth had to wait on her. Bessel said she had no life and she just didn't want to get up. She complained all day and called Ruth sometimes during the night for anything that would break her loneliness. She resented Ruth having a man, while she, the smartest one, the real woman, didn't. Plus, Joel was a good man. Not like the ones who had left her. She loved Ruth, but she was just what some humans call human.

Bessel was a country woman. At that time, what constituted a good life was having your man or your woman. Love. You had children and hardships, but you loved, fought and loved some more. Some cheated, but it was all still in the name of some love breaking the monotony of nothing else to do. Bessel knew she had had a chance at SOMETHING. But, what was it in the end? At least she was on her own land, in a way. Had done a bit of travelin. Had had a city man! Her own little apartment. Had paid for one of them cars for him. But here she was sittin, dryin up, dyin in her daughter's house, pract'ly stolen from her, Bessel! What was it she had done? She had always been smart to look out for herself. What happened?

She hadn't made it. She had stolen the money. The days, the hours. They faded away like smoke. She hadn't meant to cheat her daughter. She hadn't meant to steal. Didn't call it that. But if that's not what it was, why did she hide what she had done? Satan liked her because she fooled herself so easily. But she wasn't much use except for creating little problems for Ruth and Joel, so she could live or die, Satan didn't care. The world was full of bigger fish to fry, so to speak. His agents had more than enough to do! He had to keep busy, busy. With the important things.

Ruth was kind so she did all she could for her mother and, of course, for Joel. This pregnancy was a bit more difficult, for some reason, and Ruth had to go to the white doctor for care, there being no Negro ones almost anywhere. This took up a lot more of their money. Mrs. Befoe's slightly retarded daughter, Richlene, was sick at that time and she was seeing the same doctor. On learning Ruth was seeing the doctor,

Mrs. Befoe told him, "Those niggers have money. They have solid gold coins they steal from somewhere!" The doctor charged accordingly. Ruth even sold two of her coins to help pay him. That left three of all the gold coins.

Now Joel and Ruth talked long into many nights about the money and the hard times. Joel said, "We shouldn't not never had no mo hard times wit all that money we found! Now, don't you go a'spendin no mo of yo money! You save it! Times is hard and don't look like no let up! Everbody is doin poorly!"

So even with the gold coins out in the chicken house, times got hard for the little family. Bessel was no help, she needed medicine for her imaginary ills. Now she said she couldn't get around well when she did get up. Joel had to carry her from one chair to another or to her bed. She liked that. Her grandchildren didn't always make her happy, they meant age. Ruth held the sides of her growing belly and made those deep, heavy, low-down tired sighs.

The two small children had to help now in the fields, kitchen and Ruth's small garden near the house. Ruth had to help in the fields, also, even as she grew larger. Then Mama, Bessel, just up and died. She had gotten up, quietly. Already had a paperbag ready full of her clothes and was going to walk back to Philadelphia and find "that man." She had stolen coins from Ruth earlier and, now, put them in her mouth as she reached for her bag so they wouldn't jangle as she sneaked away. On her way slipping out of the house, she tripped on one of the broken front steps and fell. The fall caused her to swallow the coins, and she choked to death even as she tried to struggle up and keep running, her feet digging in the earth trying to get a foothold to move on. Away.

Ruth and Joel had to bury her and it cost their few last dollars. The undertaker didn't give them back any of the coins he must have found during the embalming. They were broke! Ruth still grieved for her mother. That was her mother that had died. Joel patted her, held her when she lay crying in her sleep as he looked into the darkness and wondered what had happened. What had gone wrong? What was going to happen to them? They were back where they had started. He refused to touch the coins Ruth had buried in the chicken house. He determined he would find a way. Least they had the land.

Joel and Ruth's family were considered poor, again. It made them argue, though half-heartedly. Joel felt Bessel had cost them their good future with her ways with their money. But he knew that was not Ruth's fault. They always ended up hugging and making up. They still loved each other deeply, even so. But little, teeny scars remained.

Ruth had dreamed of having Joel's babies. Loved having their children, their blood mixed. But her last months of this pregnancy were long, tired, sad. Washing, trying to cook or teaching her children to cook, ironing, cleaning, working in the field sometimes, working her garden. A needed late autumn harvest. Tired, tired, tired and sick. Wondering how they were even going to pay the midwife, much less the doctor. He wasn't coming out there anyway, and she didn't want him to.

Joel had planted pumpkins, late winter greens, to make up for the slack in his regular crops. When he didn't get fair money for them, he tried to wait the buyers out until he could find one who would be even a little bit fair. Then when some of the pumpkins spoiled, he fairly cried without a sound. He ended up selling what was left for even less money. The jack-o'-lanterns in November glared at him through blank fiery eyes and crooked teeth set in wicked smiles and grimaces, and Joel truly believed life was laughing at him. Satan sometimes gives poverty to people who cannot do him much good. He works, of course, through his human agents on earth. In this world where gold, money and power are gods to most people, poverty is, they say, the cruelest way to have to live on this earth. Satan also knows poverty will make some people attempt things, do things they would never do otherwise. He misses no opportunity.

Yoville was still a small town when Hosanna was born. On the darkest, wettest, freezing cold winter night, Ruth's water broke and the baby decided to come. Oh, it was so cold. Pipes froze, water froze, windows creaked and cracked, people froze. Luke and Lettie, six years and four years old, sat around the kitchen stove wrapped in blankets, trying to keep warm. Joel returned from fetching the midwife, Ma Lal said she was getting old, so her daughter Ma Mae came. She said she wasn't going to stay any longer than necessary for the baby to come, because she was not going to get paid this night. She didn't mean to be mean, but she was poor, too, and had to get back to her own children huddled around her wood stove. Joel was to take her back to her poor home right after the baby was born.

The hot water was boiling on the wood stove. Joel kept running outside trying to find wood and twigs to put in the stove to keep Ruth warm. He had put some by earlier, but it was so cold and the birth took so long he had used it all up. So now, he kept putting on that threadbare coat of his over his raggedy, long underwear and pants, whose patches had even been patched (in order to have enough clothes for his children and the one to come), and going back out in the black night to gather that cold, icy wood and kindling. He would rush back into the house, ice on his mustache from his nose running. Ice around his nose and eyes. Lips cracked, frozen. Hands cold to numbness, scratched and bleeding from pulling on wood that was frozen stuck or nailed onto something. Like that fence he was so proud to build around his little home. Getting that wood because it might mean life. Filling the stove while he cried silently. Hurt, mad and hating himself because he couldn't do any better. Blaming everybody who was holding him down with their smiles and a shake of their heads. Blaming those who wouldn't be fair, pay him what was rightfully his. Wouldn't treat him like a man! But, instead, like a fool! Like he didn't know how hard he worked in those fields or what he should earn by the labor and sweat of his back. Like he didn't want his family to have what they wanted their own smiling families to have. And not even ALL they had. Just some! Some! There are things love wants to do for the people it loves. Keep them warm, keep them safe, keep them full! Well, that's just the way times were then. Hard. It's the way a lot of people are always. Hard.

Joel was holding Ruth close and hard, crying, when the baby finally came. Ruth was crying, also. That is a mighty terrible way to be born. The people who made the baby, hate to see the baby come, even though they love it once it does. That's the way some things are, sometimes, for some people. Does not matter what color you are!

the baby was born right on top of midnight, December 31, 1899, and January 1, 1900. They didn't know what year to call her birth. "She can take her own choice," Ruth said, smiling weakly down at her new baby.

Now, through the years, Ruth had gone to work at the Befoes with her grandmother and mother. Once or twice, Ruth had listened to Richlene Befoe's lessons, heard and remembered the magical stories. The stories of Cinderella and Snow White had remained in her dreams. She fantasized about the wonderful, magical things that happened to them. She wanted the magic to happen to her new daughter: love. She wanted to name her Snowella.

Joel was cold and wet and on his knees praying, thanking God the child was altogether in one healthy piece. When Ruth said "Snowella," Joel said, "We betta name her Hosanna, by the Bible, cause she gon need some REAL help that she won't get from no story tale." Together, they agreed upon Hosanna Snowella Jones. It was the only new thing Hosanna got when she was born.

There was no nourishment from the milk of Ruth. She was hungry, too, always giving others what she should have taken for herself in her condition. But little Hosanna had a strong will. She intended to stay alive. She lived.

By the time Hosanna was five years old, Ruth had had three more births. One she miscarried in the fields, one died right after its birth, one lingered awhile trying to breathe, then died also. Now, Ruth and Joel were not dumb. They were just desperate! How in hell, in this world, could they find some pleasure, some reason to keep struggling everyday, getting up every morning, facing work for so little profit and sustenance? How in hell could they find some reason for living, except in each other's arms? They still loved each other. Didn't know anything about any birth control! If they had they would have used it. This is just another place poverty takes you. Believe it! Even to death!

The next baby was going to be a winter baby again. It turned out to be twins though—a boy and a girl. The boy seemed to be physically all right. He didn't cry at all at first. The girl baby, her little legs were twisted a bit, but she showed signs of being a beautiful baby. She wailed a little, frail sound. Hungry. Inside his soul, Joel was in pain; he hurt for Ruth. Outside on his face, Joel was proud; he smiled and laughed to express his joy, but the laugh froze and cracked hoarsely. He held Ruth's calloused, thin hand tightly as they looked into each other's eyes and tried to smile.

All the other children were wrapped in blankets in bed, close together for warmth. Joel kept going out in the freezing weather again, trying to gather more wood, more anything to keep Ruth and the new babies warm. He had no coat. Ruth had tried to make him let the white man, Kindle, trade at least one coin of the last three, but Joel would not do it. He said, "That ere is all we got, all I got, to have fo my fam'ly. If we sells that then we won't have nothin behine us. I'm a man, I can make it! Things got to change round. Trouble don las always. If I could jes make this wood burn a little longer." He watched as the wood burned down, flickering weakly in the cold room.

He left, pulling that threadbare shirt and jacket round his thin body. An old hat, no gloves, no socks. He was weak from going without food, full of cold from going without clothes so others could have them. Somewhere out there in the frozen night, he found the remainder of a broken fence. He bent over to pull the pieces apart so he could carry them. The cold, icy wood was frozen together, stuck. He pulled with all his meager might and strong will, tears freezing even while they ran down his face. Old clothes tearing from his efforts. First, his knees gave, then his bent back would not pull. The frozen wood pulled him down and he couldn't get up. He had been already half frozen when he went out this time. Now . . . he froze too much to get up. He lay there . . . and he died there. Frozen to death.

Some said he could have got up, that he just gave in and lay there crying until he died. They were thinking about those two lines of tears frozen on his face. But, they were not tears of weakness, no, because he was a strong character man, wasn't used to giving up trying. They were tears of frustration and desperation. Poverty! Believe that!

This had been a good, manly man. He didn't really do too much wrong, so Satan had no use for him. They say the angels in heaven cry for the plight of some mankind on earth. But what can they do? So many choices by so few people have been made for so many other people so long ago.

After an hour or so, the oldest son, Luke, thirteen years old now, went out to find his daddy, couldn't. But he brought in some wood, taking his daddy's place already. He wore a warm jacket his daddy had sacrificed for.

All the children stood at the windows for the rest of that night, looking to see their daddy's form coming through the dark. They were certainly not poor in love. He was all they knew to look up to, to count on, to believe in—their daddy. They knew he was more than just poor. He was a man, their daddy.

They turned toward their mother whenever the new babies sounded those thin wails, trailing off as Ruth tried to put her nipples in the little ones' mouths. The boy would spit the nipple out, as if the milk did not taste good. The little girl tried to hold on and suck.

In the first good light, Joel's older children wrapped themselves in their blankets and ran out into the snow and wind to find him. Even Hosanna did. Only five or six years old, but she was counted! They searched until, at last, they found him. Imagine looking for something, thinking something you don't really want to find. He was dead. In death, his body looked so much thinner and worn. He was bent over, bowed, trying to hold any warmth to himself. They knew he had prayed for help.

Ruth's milk didn't come up at all anymore after that. There was only cow's milk from their lean cow. The babies could not keep it down, threw it up. So . . . the boy baby finally took a tiny, gasping breath and died, too. I guess Ruth's body and mind couldn't take anymore. She kept saying, "My chilren, my chilren. My husband, my husband." Then she would say in a sort of delirium, "The chicken house, get that chicken house!" She meant the gold, but they didn't understand what she meant. One morning, all of a sudden she sat straight up, grabbed Hosanna and screamed, "That chicken house, git it! I love my fam'ly more!" Hosanna held her mother around her waist, crying, "Mama, mama, don' cry lak dat!" They all gathered around their mother, but they never found out what she meant. Because then Ruth fell back, and, screaming with rage at life, she died. Her last thoughts were, "We were supposed to make it! We had everything! God! Where are you?!"

All was gone. All but the new little girl-child with the strange, little twisted legs.

Later, the older children tried to share the remaining milk. None could keep it down. No one could keep it down except Hosanna and the little girl-child they had named Lovey. Hosanna did not know the story of the milk then. When she was grown, she would feel that milk in her throat. She hated that she drank it. In some way, she believed she had deprived Lovey or the little boy who died. But there was enough to keep little Lovey alive after all.

The children, young as they were and hard as the thought might have been, built a coffin for their papa. There was not much wood, so the coffin had big spaces between the boards. They put him in it, bent over with his head down like he was praying. They had to keep him until a thaw came and the ground softened. They tore down more of the wood-shed and built another coffin with no spaces in it because they wanted Mama and the baby to be as warm as possible. The coffins stayed in their room behind a curtain, because some of the children still had to use that room to sleep in. There were no radios or TV's to make a lot of noise, and, at that time, the children did not laugh and talk a whole lot; they could hear a sound for miles around. One day their daddy thawed a little enough to straighten out, and he slid down into place. They heard the lid close with a tiny little thud. They heard the sound of the lid closing and no one, not one of them, said a word, or moved. O death, where is thy sting? In the heart.

for the funerals, there was a man from their church who wanted to be revered. He called himself Reverend, though everybody ought to know you don't revere anybody but God in Heaven. When the ground was soft enough to be dug for graves, Joel's friends Mr. Kindle and Mr. Creed came to help with the work. They gave a little money, very little, and food, very little, along the children's way. The men could not let them starve.

The reverend came by, said a few words over the knotty, crooked coffins, asked the children, did they have any money, any food? They said, "A little food Luke had caught, fish and rabbit his Indian hunting friends had helped him with. And a little money, about $1.10 our mama kept in her saving can." Looking around at the children, even the little baby, it took the reverend a long time to say, "Well, keep it then. You don't have to give me nothing for coming all the way over here in this cold weather. Just keep it and the Lord be with you." He had about fifty dollars in his pockets. His church women were good to him. He left after eating the last piece of fish left in a pan and patting everybody on the head. He lingered on the oldest girl's, Lettie's head until she moved it out of his way.

The three children, one of them holding the baby Lovey who had a rag on for a diaper (clean rag, though), watched the reverend ride away on his horse. He had prayed the Lord would be with them. The boy, Luke, was thirteen years old going on fourteen, Lettie Mae was going on twelve, Hosanna was going on six, Lovey was new. All the numbers missing in between were dead.

They had seen love in their mother and father all their lives. They loved each other very much. But they were children. They thought they needed someone older they could trust, someone who cared. Love was too much to hope for. They didn't know that, exactly, at that time, but they learned.

Two of Bessel's sisters, Esther and Jessie Bea, came to Yoville after the funerals. Esther lived in Washington, D.C. Her husband was a deacon, among other things. Jessie Bea was a live-in domestic in some other large city. It was not known how they got that far away from Yoville, but they had. Just left, that's all. Bessel's brother, Dick, the preacher came also. After much discussion about what could be done with their sister's children, Esther said she would take Hosanna because her husband, the deacon, would like that name. "I can't take any one more 'cause I can't expect my husband to take in somebody else's kids," she said. "We's already havin a hard time. Amen."

Jessie Bea said she couldn't take nobody, really, 'cause she lived on the job. Everybody just looked at her and frowned. She finally said she could take the oldest girl, Lettie, cause "might be she could help her find a job. Twelve years is old enough to do some kind of work! Bessel should'a told that daughter of hers not to lay round havin all these babies for no shiftless man! I ain't got no husband no more and may never get another one with all these kids!"

Jessie Bea sniffed and kept on talking, "I told Bessel she ought'a try to leave here and come where she could live decent! Have somethin sides babies and granbabies she ain't here to take care of!"

No one paid any attention to the children sitting and listening. Lettie didn't like the way they were speaking about her mother and father. She spoke up saying, "I might not be old nough to say nothin, but it don't look like YOU got nothin and is livin so big and decent neither. Your husband gone! You ain't even got no babies to love!"

Jessie Bea looked at Lettie, then at Esther. "I ain't takin that one aft all. You all do what you want to!" She looked at the baby with twisted legs in Lettie's arms. "I can't take that one neither, I work." She sighed. "I guess I can take the boy. Dammit. People ain't got no right to leave their own problems on nobody else!"

The brother preacher, Dick, spoke up and said he would take the boy. Said he had two good women . . . ahem . . . friends, and they would help him, a bachelor, raise the child. Teach him how to live and all. (I guess he was going to show him how to be a preacher and have two women.) Then Dick said, looking round the house (he had already looked over the land), "We can sell this little piece of land that blonged to my sister and give the boy, the kids, some kinda start. Cause I can't take nobody to nobody empty-handed."

The young boy Luke spoke up for the first time. He took his baby sister in his fourteen-year-old arms and looked at his aunts and uncle. Said, "I don't want nobody takin me. And this is our land. My daddy said so. He payed Gramma for it. We gon work it and take care our'sef." Lettie looked at him with such pride. Hosanna looked at him, her little eyes just beaming.

But the uncle preacher puffed out his chest, took his handkerchief out, wiped his forehead, waved Luke aside and said, "You ain't old enough to decide for yoself. We'll decide for you. We gonna sell this place. I done already talked to a few people bout the worth of it. I know what I can do. So that's settled!" He smiled at his sisters cause he was a business man.

Luke said, "No sir, ain't settled. My daddy said age don't make you able to do things, sense do. We got sense enough to know we don't want to sell what blonged to our daddy and mama. Ain't gonna sell it . . . sir. We was mostly workin the land anyway, helpin papa. We can keep doin that right on. We done settled that between us." He indicated Lettie.

Lettie spoke up. "And I'm gonna stay and help him, cause it's my daddy's land, too. I can cook and wash and work in the fields with em. The little chilren can go for a little while, cause we ain't gonna have a lot to eat for awhile, but I'm gonna stay here and work it out with my brother."

Aunt Jessie Bea looked down at her lap and didn't say anything at all. Aunt Esther took Hosanna's hand and smiled a respectful smile at Luke. But still, no one wanted Lovey, the baby, because she was crippled.

So that's the way it was and that is what they did. The uncle preacher left angry, but you could tell he respected the boy-man, Luke. Aunt Jessie Bea left empty-armed and glad. She did say, as she looked back over her shoulder with a sad little look on her face that had a little love in it for these children she did not really know, "I will try . . . I will send you a little money from time to time, to help you along." She sighed. "Cause I know it's hard out here on this land. Course, it's hard everywhere IN this land if you po." She sniffed. "It won't be no whole lot, but I will send something." She came back and kissed everyone good-bye. Then she was gone.

Aunt Esther left with her lips pressed tight, holding on to Hosanna's hand as Hosanna pulled back. Hosanna looked over her shoulder as she was pulled away. Tears were in her eyes, but she did not cry out loud. Even as young as she was, she was trying to think of some way she could get back to her own home, her own family. It was around 1906 or 1907.

A neighbor with a wagon took all the relatives to the train and bus stations in Mythville. Helped them get off all right and on time. Well, thank God for Himself, because the man who called himself the reverend wasn't going to do anything. Don't you know?

The reverend didn't come by before Hosanna left. Didn't send any food or money. Just sent word by somebody in his church. Said, "Tell em I ain't seen em over to the church. Tell em they gotta come to God's house if they want His blessin! Tell em God bless em all, He will take care of you."

It is not certain if anyone sent them any money or not, but the children kept that land. At fourteen and twelve years old, Luke and Lettie were grown. All the children would be far, far older than most others their age by the time they turned twenty-one, twenty and seven. But proud and independent! They kept that land, believe that!

God gave us a plan long, long ago on how we can make it in the world. It was good for that time and it is good for this time. For all times. He told us it would be hard, that sometimes the more you did right, the harder it could be, but not to stop doing the right things because they will pay off in the end. Not just in going to heaven, but you CAN have a good life on this earth. You just watch those Ten Commandments and watch out for people who do not respect and try to do them.

.   .   .

hosanna stared out the window and watched the land through little blurry eyes filled with tears. Thinking of her home getting further and further away. Hosanna's little heart kept repeating "My mama gone . . . ain't comin back no mo. My daddy dead. Who gon care bout me?" She would turn her head to look at her aunt who looked worried, then turn back to the window. "Who gon care bout me? I want my mama!" She didn't cry out loud, but such painful little sounds her heart made in that tiny breast. She wished she could have done something, anything, to save her daddy and mother.

As Hosanna grew up she heard about the "Goddess woman," but she told herself, "Only Goddess I know here is Mother Earth. People make gods and goddesses of too many things that die, can't help their own self. That's why they confused. What they blive in dies. Or if it's money, you can't always count on it for what you need. As I see it, we too confused and doing wrong to be gods and goddesses. We are people! Just people. And that is more than plenty to be!"

chapter
9

hosanna's new home was in Washington, D.C. A small, crowded, tenement house. Aunty lived with her husband in a tiny, apartment crowded full of things gathered over the years from the people she had worked for, and thrift shops. Most of the landlords of the area were white. Ninety-nine and nine-tenths. Aunty's landlord was one of the preachers at their church, but all the tenants, (except a few nice-looking ladies the preachers looked after), suffered with things that needed fixing or replacing. All they ever got was promises and a "waiting for the Lord to provide." They not only paid him rent but put money in his collection plate at church as well! Several nights a week and Sunday, too!

There was no place to play except in the streets and most of the youngsters around there wanted to boss or fight you like their folks did them. All colors! Everybody lived together. Church-goers, domestic workers, prostitutes, pimps, old folks, a few dope dealers, a few dope users, winos and plain alcoholics, wife beaters and wife lovers (somebody else's), thieves and con men and women, no-church preachers, kids with no parents and no homes except an empty house if they could find one, yes, even back then. Someone said the poor are with us always and I believe "poor" makes all these types of people, that and what is already in their hearts. Satan loves these type of places and poverty. Babies and babies are born. Some make new problems for people and many make new followers of his.

Even some grown people who wanted to work had no home except a park bench or doorway. Hosanna had to watch everything she had all the time, because somebody needed it and wouldn't back-up from taking it! She wouldn't even close her eyes at nap-time in school. Her aunty told her not to. "Sleep at home where you safe!" she had said. She didn't know about how Uncle Deacon was at home. Home wasn't safe for Hosanna either.

As she grew older, Hosanna found that all these things were hidden behind the things you had to stay busy doing to make a living. In the country where there is some space you can see these things clearer. You even see where there is something you might do to help. But the city is too big, too many, too busy and too fast to stop to see sometime . . . until it's your turn.

She also looked up many times at the white house the president lived in that she was learning about in school. She would see the flag waving that they told her to love, while she was learning to hate some of her fellow men because they had something and she hadn't. But she had sense enough to say to herself, "It ain't the flag's fault. Flag ain't done nothin! Man what waves that flag to keep your eye off him sometime. Them's the one makin people hate each other."

Hosanna knew somebody was lying. Too many people were using and stealing from each other. Love was for sale and for free. It just depended on what side of rent day or how full a belly was when love came up. She heard of some of the poor women with children to raise, exchanging love-sex for food, insurance and favors, whatever they needed most. Pretending it might be love . . . someday.

As Hosanna lived and learned she found that everybody wanted everybody ELSE to do right and be truthful and honest, while they did whatever they wanted. She learned that while learning the rules of being "grown and responsible."

She watched her friends. Some parents made their children go to school. Some dreamed of their children going on to college. Aunty made her go to school. Thank God! Hosanna studied hard because she wanted to get out of there and back to her "Home" home. Aunty worked hard all day, stayed in church with the deacons and other women just like her most nights until she fell, dead on her feet, into bed.

Aunty tried hard to keep up a thing like she was a normal, happily married woman. But her life was not normal. She had to worry about everything. Don't even talk about smiling when your husband comes home. Her husband didn't even work, just went to church, though not as much as Aunty. He was a deacon and liked to be called that. Aunty liked him being a deacon so that's what he gave her. When she got home, he was not only not smiling he wasn't waiting for her either.

When Aunty first brought Hosanna home, Uncle Deacon did welcome her. Hugged her a lot, until Aunty looked at him sidewise and said, "You gonna spoil that chile, stop huggin her so much." He stopped, for awhile. The first five or so years, he wasn't home much, but when Hosanna got to be around eleven years old, he started staying home a lot more. Maybe because he was getting older, maybe because Hosanna was getting older, her little body filling out a bit, tiny budding breasts and all.

Uncle Deacon liked to play games. He had a lot of children's games to draw the children in the building to his house. He would meet them at the door, smile (as he seldom smiled at Aunty) and have them come on in. He never had any money for Aunty, but he always had money to buy ice cream or cookies for the children. Boys and girls. They were all welcome.

He was a toucher. A digger with his fingers. These were poor kids who did not get much chance to play indoor games, checkers and such. Or eat ice cream, cake or cookies. Hosanna had fun with the kids and the games. She knew to stay away from Uncle Deacon because she saw him, now and again, touching the other children.

It was a rainy day the day he decided to put his hands on Hosanna. The few children who had come to play this day had gone on home. Aunty wasn't home yet. Uncle Deacon reached for Hosanna and sat her on his lap. Hosanna had been watching out for this day because she did have good sense. She straightened her body and fell out all over the floor, against the wall, rolled her eyes back in her head and hollered, "Jesus! Jesus!" loud as she could, like she was in the middle of a fit! She tried to throw up on him and acted like she was retching when he would try to reach for her. He would snatch his arms back. Then, "Jesus! Help me!" again. Loud, loud. She hadn't really planned it that way, but she knew it was coming one day the way some people just know things. When she found out this scared him, she did it everytime he got his nerve up again. When Aunty was home, too! It got to where he went as far around Hosanna as he could in that small apartment. He didn't even want to touch her even accidentally! He kept his hands off her. Well, for a long time anyway. Then she had to map out another plan. Being wise was an everyday job.

In the meantime, to pay him back she said, when Uncle lay a little change down Hosanna would pick it up and save it until it was a dollar. She would exchange it for a paper bill and fold it into the letter going home she got a stamp for once a month. Hosanna thought this would let them know she was the family, too, and her home was where they were. And that she loved them.

chapter
10

The hotter New Orleans became that summer, the more Yinyang and Miss Will seemed to get on each other's nerves. Each seemed to have thoughts about changes in their lives. Yinyang had now determined to leave and go home to Yoville to see if she could be at home at last somewhere.

While Miss Will was thinking of ways to get rid of Yin, Yin was thinking of ways she could leave and take all the things she so loved with her—clothes, jewelry, just things you get used to. One day Miss Will spoke to Yin, "Do you never think of going back to your home to see whatever became of that property that belonged to your family?" She smiled wryly as she placed a particularly juicy piece of candy on her tongue. She was sure Yin had come from sharecroppers or some poor white trash. She never for a moment believed that story Yin told about rich parents. She had seen that birth certificate among Yin's things when she had gone through them secretly, but even some poor people had birth certificates now.

Yin opened her eyes wide as the words struck her. She covered her shapely legs with the soft, silk dressing gown, unnecessarily, and said honestly, "Why, I would love to go see about those things!" She smiled brightly at Miss Will, then lied. "But I have hated to think of leaving you! I do not know how long I would have to stay, but whatever I am able to retrieve, I would bring back to you for all the wonderful things you have done for me." She looked Miss Will directly in the eye as she lied however it was sweetly, "I never want to leave you. I want to give you what is mine. As you have done me." Yin looked thoughtful. "I remember the house as being huge. . . . And . . . I do . . . believe there is still some . . . gold there my father told me about."

Miss Will popped another piece of candy onto her tongue, thinking what a little liar the cur was. "Oh, poot! You don't have to give me anything. Keep it, my lovely. I have enough. I love being with you just for yourself! You will want your own home someday, here in New Orleans, I hope. Near me. Use it for that."

Thoughtful again, Yin said, "Perhaps I should go soon. Anything could have happened. You are right! I shall pack and prepare to leave. Let me see, I will pack up most of my things so they will not be in the way . . . And I will store them until I know when I shall return! Oh! You are so smart to think of everything!" She ran to embrace Miss Will.

Miss Will smiled and hugged Yin back as she thought, "Yes, go. Go! I will always remember your face when you were with that silly, stupid man. You liked it! You are a silly, stupid woman! Yes, go!"

It was not long before all was packed and done. Miss Will wanted to take back the fur coats to hold until Yin "returned."

"You won't need these dear, you will be back before winter." Yin looked at her coats longingly. Instinctively, she reached out for one of her favorites, held it to her so that Miss Will understood that she would not give it up. "Oh, my dear, I will just take this one. One can never tell about the weather, and we must be prepared like you always tell me!"

Miss Will spoke softly, "I have another one, more suited to the country, with a fur collar. You should take that one, I think."

Yin also spoke softly, "Oh, no, my dear, this is the one I shall take. It pleases me so." Yin had spent almost three years with Miss Will. In her mind, some of that time was for that coat. When Yin left, she took the coat.

She went to see the young priest. He was having trouble with several other priests because of his honesty and faithfulness. He was sad for

God. He and Yin promised to write, to keep in touch somehow. She left him the name of her home, Yoville.

But listen, Yin had taken everything Paul had said as it was meant that first day they talked, but as time passed, the devil had changed her thoughts into her own interests in another way: she would look out for herself, she would get out of this with something. She could be rich on her own with the gold her father had left behind. Her thoughts did not dwell on God, her thoughts dwelt on material things. Ole Satan held on.

She liked the honesty the priest Paul had given her, she just failed to know such honesty would be so hard to find, would be the only thing that would carry her on, that she would have to hold such honesty to life.

Looking from the back of the train as it pulled away from New Orleans, Yinyang thought of her last years. "Well, New Orleans, you have given me one friend, Paul, and I am leaving him behind. I don't know what I am going to, but I will never forget you New Orleans, you big, fun-filled bastard!" She laughed. "And I swear, I swear, I will end up with far more than all those lovely, fresh-faced ladies in their finery I saw here! I will, I will!" Oh, Satan was pleased. He loves wild ambition! It so often turns into greed and envy, hate and even murder in some search for satisfaction.

Then. She thought of God in the midst of her laughter and became serious. She thought, "Is He real? I can only lose if I follow that Bible." Yet? God always hopes, it is written. Yin remembered Paul's words, "It is your choice and your life. You will be able to blame no one or no thing for your life but yourself." Yin shook her head to clear it and the thought flew away.

Yinyang settled back in her private room on the train. Everyone thought she was white. There was a young, handsome, jet-black porter that attended to her needs. Yin had never in all her sexual life had a black man that she knew of, though she had heard much about them and been told to avoid them. She smiled to herself, thinking, "White men would rather see a white woman dead than in a black man's arms." Yin reached for a magazine, still thinking about sex and love. In fact she had not had a man in these several years. She watched the young porter as he moved gracefully through his duties, she liked his movements, quick and sure. She watched him when he came to make down her bed. She thought, "What have I to lose?"

She asked, "What goes on in these trains on these long traveling nights?"

The porter smiled. "Sleep."

Yin smiled. "That's all?"

The porter made a few more deft moves, smoothing the sheets. "Well, I guess it's just like bein at home for some. You do whatever you feels like."

Yin opened her expensive suit jacket. "Do you have liquor to sell?"

The porter looked more closely at her. "A person can most always find some liquor."

Yin stretched her arms and legs as much as possible in the small cabin. "Well . . . why don't you see can you find some?" The porter said nothing, wondering just who and what she was.

Yin pursued. "What do you do when you finish helpin everybody to sleep?"

The porter reached her door to leave. "Well, play cards, read, think, whatever is okay to do."

"Well . . . why don't you get the liquor . . . and come back and have a drink with me?"

The porter just turned and looked at her, this pretty woman who was invitin him to come back . . . in the night. "Well . . . I don't know, Miss."

"Well, don't think about it so much. Just do it. I . . . need to talk to someone . . . I can relax with." She smiled up at him, moving her body just so. He stood there a moment, looking at her. She gestured for him to leave. "Go on now, and hurry back." He left with a frown.

He did come back. She was undressed and in the narrow bed. He did bring the liquor. She paid for it because he asked for the money. They had the drinks. Then he had her. They were tired then, almost falling asleep. But the porter knew his business. He got up and left, wondering about what had just happened to him and why. A new porter was there to help her the next morning. Yin didn't care, she was glad. She treated the new man as a servant, barely giving him a glance.

Anyway, she was on her way to Yoville. She had saved a nice piece of money. Had a marvelous wardrobe. Her mind was on the nice cache of gold Josephus had left behind, waiting for her at home. The diamond ring hidden there would be worth a lot of money, or she just might keep it. And the girl, her half-sister, Josephus had told her about. And the

land, her land. In Yoville. "Hell!" she thought. "At least I'm not pregnant with Willie's baby!" She laughed as she looked out of her window
at life.

No, it wasn't going to be Willie's baby. But, she would be pregnant.
She never would know the father's name. It hadn't been important
enough to ask.

Yin was a young woman on her way home. A few people thought she
was Negro, a few people thought she was white. Very few had ever cared
what she was inside, except for what was useful to them. What can you
know about people? You don't know enough of time to judge, do you?

c h a p t e r
11

Washington, D.C. was sweltering hot when Aunty lost her job and came home disgusted, tired and mean. Hosanna was around fourteen years old, and Aunty looked at her as if Hosanna was a grown woman, as though Hosanna was the cause of her losing her job. Aunty went right back out the next morning to seek another job but was unable to find one right away. She was out of work for several weeks. Finally they had to move because Uncle Deacon "couldn't find any work," he said. The preacher landlord said, "Sometimes God tests us to see if we are worthy." He had them evicted. "For your good," he said.

Put out of even that low place that needed everything, Aunty got way down in her heart, feeling guilty. She did a lot of crying over the sink and into her pillow. Hosanna's heart needed to love someone and Aunty was her blood. She loved her, when she could, and she felt sorry for her and angry at her, too. She knew that woman, her aunt, knew right from wrong and should not be fool enough to believe her preacher or her husband was doing her right! If grown-ups knew so much about life, why didn't they do it better!? Hosanna's young mind was reaching to understand things no one ever talked about. She was building her mind so she'd know how to make decisions. She made up her mind never to get married . . . for a long time, that is. She started finding excuses to keep from going to church with Aunty.

They didn't move far. Couldn't. Black folk could only live so many places. They moved around the corner. Same apartment, different address, less room. Hosanna's space was especially cramped. Her bedroom was rolled out at night in what they referred to as the living room. When Hosanna made the mistake of complaining sometimes, Aunty sniffed and said, "I reckon there is more room back there where you come from." She wiped her nose with a gray, wrinkled handkerchief. "Chile, I'm the only one bringin any money in this house. I ain't got no help round here. This the bes I can do for you." Hosanna would bow her head and Aunty would continue fussing at her because she couldn't fuss at Uncle Deacon. "You young. You eat and sleep and go to school while you here livin under my roof. I bring the clothes off my job so you will have somethin on your back! You cries bout that, too! Either they too small or too large. Or somethin's wrong wit em!"

With tears in her eyes, Hosanna rushed to explain. "No, Aunty, no. I preciate what you do for me. I'm glad to get em! Just tired of some of them kids laughin at me sometimes."

Aunty slammed a piece of cold meat brought from her job on the table. "Some kids ain't got nothin! And you ain't such a kid no mo! You gettin mighty grown-up. Look at you! Mos a woman! Too old for me to take care for by myself!"

Walking to and from school, Hosanna would think of ways she could make money. Some girls even younger than she was stole, begged or prostituted themselves. She shook her head, "I am NOT going to do any of that. My mama and daddy done left me a home and some land and I got a brother and sisters I can go to before I do that! I don't give a damn what nobody say or what they do, I know what I want my mind to think and what I want my body to do." Hosanna didn't think much of the church she went to less and less with her Aunty and Uncle Deacon, but she did hesitate in giving up believing there must be a God. He had taken the place of her mother and father. She talked to Him. He had to be there!

"You ain't my chile! I'm just helpin my dead sister out! You jus my niece." Aunty didn't mean to be mean again. She was just poor and could see no way out ever. Nothing in her life was really good. Not her home, not her job, not her man. Just her church, she thought. It got the little change she could not really spare. Took it with a smile and a hurried, whispered blessing.

Then, sometimes, Aunty would sit on Hosanna's cot and talk about the "old days" when she was back home with her family. Nights around the "woodstove eatin hot sweettaters out the ashes, Papa tellin stories, everybody kinda cold from the drafty old farmer's shack but laughin and happy and lovin each other." She would speak of her sister, Hosanna's grandmother, Bessel. Seemed she was the sweetest one when they were young. And "Oh! how we all hated that field work! We all lef, but just Bessel stayed." Aunty would laugh, and tell more stories of back home. So, Hosanna had some good evenings with her Aunty. But . . . they were too few.

c h a p t e r
1 2

a way for Hosanna to help herself came up in an unusual way. Aunty found another job, of course. She worked on Saturdays, naturally. Saturday mornings, while Hosanna was still asleep Uncle Deacon would come in and she would wake up with him feeling on her, digging his nasty, dirty fingers in her fresh, clean flesh. She hated him too much to act out a scene with him sometimes, so she just slapped the fatal shit out of him and tried to scratch his face so he would have to explain it to Aunty. Then one time, he slapped her back. Hard. She ran out of the apartment in her gown that time, screaming in the hall where others could hear. Uncle did not know who was home and who was not, and they might call the police, so he did not follow her to make her come back inside the apartment. When anyone would pass her in her nightgown, she would look down at the floor until they passed. She did not return inside until he said he would go out. When he tried to come in later, she would go out and stand in the hall. Uncle Deacon called her "stupid." But that evening, she asked Aunty if she could go to work with her on Saturdays.

Aunty's back straightened as she looked at Hosanna. Her brow wrinkled, her eyes softened as, tilting her head, she looked at her niece with gratitude. Hosanna went to work.

Hosanna did not like the work Aunty did, but she learned and did it. Then Aunty got Hosanna her own job for weekends. Cleaning and serving. And, see, Aunty said you could miss church if you were working. This way Hosanna could go to school during the week and still bring some money in.

This arrangement went on for several months. There began to be days when Hosanna had to miss school to take some extra job. Aunty would say, "You a smart girl, you'll make it up, chile." Hosanna got most of her food from her own jobs now, and there were a few more smiles in the apartment. Hosanna let her schooling slip. She almost forgot that schooling was her real way out of her situation.

One Sunday morning when Aunty had left early for church, Hosanna woke up having to struggle with Uncle Deacon. She rolled her eyes back in her head and fell all over everywhere and hollered, "God, help me!" But this time, somehow, it was different. She just quit trying to fight and started crying silently. That didn't stop Uncle though, he just put his arm around her, whispering, "Now, come on now, Uncle make you feel better. You don't know what you fightin, girl. Let me show you, let me make you a happy girl."

Hosanna's anger made her come to herself. "You ain't made nobody else happy, you ole bastard! Lying to the Lord, lying to Aunty, and now you gonna keep tryin to lie to me!" She clamped her teeth down on his nose and bit with all her young might. Now, that worked. As soon as he could get loose, he was gone, saying, "You gonna get your little ass outta my house! You ain't got sense to preciate what I do for you, lettin you live here all these years! You owe me!"

Hosanna screamed through her tears of anger. "I ain't gonna let you, NEVER let you, do nothin to me!" Then she fell back panting, and lay there with her face turned to the wall, staring into space.

When Uncle Deacon had finally gone to church to pray and the house was quiet, Hosanna turned her mind to looking at her life. She was the one who would have to change things. She thought of all the ladies she had been working for. Some, a few, were kind of nice, and they were rich, too. "I can talk to em, I'm a good worker. I can see can I live in. Then I can save my money and take my self home. Home."

When Hosanna decided which ladies she would ask, she left church behind that Sunday. She took the change she could find (she knew where all the money was hidden in that apartment but didn't want to take Aunty's blood-and-sweat money) and started out across town to speak with them. "I'll ask can I move in for just a while to help them more at the same money. Then I'll see can I add a little more from extra work on my own." Mrs. Doll, the very first lady Hosanna spoke to, needed a live-in kitchen helper and laundress. She said yes.

Hosanna asked for a small advance so she could move in that day. The lady looked at Hosanna sidewise and said, "Now if you take my money and don't plan to return, I will call the police." Hosanna said to herself, "Oh shit, this kind." But she assured the woman of her good intentions and took the money. She didn't have much, so moving in one day was no problem. Just leaving Aunty like that presented a small one.

Now . . . listen. Aunty was not a mean woman. Just stuck in a hole in life with poverty and a husband who escaped into little feelings on young children. He evidently could not think any larger, and being poor and hungry for any pleasure out of life kept his mind in some dark, tiny, dirty place. Kept him from growing. Or maybe his brain wasn't the kind that grew.

Aunty had been glad she had come on out of the country and bare feet and what she called hard work in the fields to better times. To Hosanna's mind, Aunty had just changed one hard time for another hard time. Plus a burden, a liability on her in the shape of a man who wasn't poot! It was Aunty's life though, she had mapped out her own plan.

Hosanna had grown to love Aunty, felt sorry for her. But, as that same time went by, Aunty was getting evil from her life. She was hard to be around. Resented Hosanna making her own decisions without her say-so. Hosanna knew she did not have time to be a fool, not for a fool. "My mama and daddy wasn't no fools, they got their own house and land!" So, even though Hosanna appreciated and even loved Aunty because she was of her mother's blood, she didn't respect her or her life.

Still in her early teens, almost all Hosanna's experience had been hard learning experiences. She had never lived as a child. The love that comes from parents had long been denied her in life. As anyone would know, that in itself is enough hardness to start life with. Her aunt's love was there, but it was a taking love as well as a giving one—hard-edged, lukewarm, from a tired, unfed heart. Day by day, Hosanna never knew what was to come next. There was always some struggle to be made, a fight to be fought.

Now, she was leaving even this small family of such, to be on her own. By herself. To survive. In some kind of peace, if possible. All she had was her brain, her mind, her hands and feet.

Some would have had their god to lean upon. Hosanna believed in God, but not the god of the little church she had attended with her aunt. She knew people to speak with their open mouths, seemingly full of God, but the devil was there, hiding behind holy words. She knew that the god her aunt and others like her served, gave no peace, no joy, except maybe when they opened their mouths to sing out. With heads thrown back, eyes closed and voices raised, they declared more pain than joy and the reverends' and preachers' hands were held out and open, beseeching even as they sang. So Hosanna put God away somewhere in her mind and went on to take care of her own problems herself.

She waved all thoughts of boys, men and love away with a "tsk!" or "humpth! I ain't never seen love done good!" She remembered only slightly her own mother and father and their love.

But work now. Hosanna had been hearing that to work in service was a low job. For her, it was not. There was always heat, food, even learning and some little money at the end of the job. She knew there were mean people who hired you, tried to work you to death, did not want to give you much for your sweating labor, but she guessed there were mean people in every walk of life. She thought, "That man up there in the white house sure wasn't too nice to everybody either and people voted on him to be nice to them. We in a war now! Somebody's dying right now!"

Besides, Hosanna had seen servants who ruled the house! Servants who were secure and even protected from the outside world. Some people were very lucky that other people were rich and lazy. When they came to depend on you real good, some of those people would ask for advice. Some even let a servant tell them what to do. Hosanna had even seen some servants who frightened their employers! She had also seen lazy servants who did as little as possible and did it poorly, and they were still paid and fed. Be full and have a little money, too! So service was not low to her. She decided she would use it to do what she had to do. Free herself. From Uncle and this life that was going nowhere. Take care of herself.

The alternative for her, right now, was to steal, be a whore, lie, cheat. In her little wisdom from her study of God and the streets, she knew the alternative would be giving her life away to some jailer, some prison. What's lower than that!? She wanted freedom, not prison. She would work for it!

She thought of school, sadly. She would love an education. To go to college! But it was 1914 and education was not given away. And you couldn't get it in thirty minutes which was when she needed it.

Hosanna sat on her little sofa bunky bed in her aunt's house, her few packed things waiting at her feet. She was not so afraid. But she was so, so lonely. Her young little heart was a graveyard begun with the tombstones of her Papa and Mother dear. In her time at her aunt's, life seemed to be chiseling her name on a stone to sit forever in her mind. She did not think this, but it is true: What she did now would decide so much of the quality of her life. But her feet kept moving and her mind, sometimes leading, sometimes following, reached out to get away, to live. Oh, the pillows that have been soaked with tears by those in this world, trying to find a way.

Hosanna picked up her little sad belongings and walked slowly out the door, leaving her key behind on the table. She had written a note but did not say where she was going.

hosanna worked hard on her new, steady job. She watched the cook, the maid, the gardener, everyone with a job to do. She learned to care for fine lingerie and to iron anything to the rich woman's joy. She learned to cook special foods and to serve them. She learned to clean and polish things to the rich woman's satisfaction. The other help said she was a fool, a slave, to work so hard. But Hosanna was thinking of what she would someday do for herself. She learned all the skills called drudgery because each is a skill, valuable knowledge. Be without it and see how things feel, look and taste.

Mrs. Doll was very particular about all things, but she especially loved rich, good foods she had discovered on her travels with her husband all over the world. When she discovered Hosanna worked hard and learned quickly, Mrs. Doll removed her from all other tasks except washing and caring for her very best underwear which she had taken much time to teach her, and had her concentrate on the cooking of special dishes. She taught her what she knew and liked, gave her books on the culinary arts and was delighted with the results.

Of course, this made Mrs. Doll call upon Hosanna at any hour of the day or night for something special for herself or her guests. A job, after all, is a job. Mrs. Doll even loaned Hosanna to friends. Hosanna didn't mind. It meant more money to save or send home to her brother and sisters.

Mr. Doll was a politician and had many kinds of friends. A very rich, old and gay gentleman, Mr. Went, often entertained all sorts of people and, on occasion, used Hosanna to help. Finding her more than efficient, he began to use only Hosanna at his smaller parties.

The first time Hosanna went to Mr. Went's house, the door was opened by a gentleman of color whose name was Mr. Butler, though he was not the butler. He was of medium height, color of a polished walnut, smooth, clean, soft-spoken. A lean body stood in good posture. Hair graying at the temples, neatly trimmed. He was in a casual morning suit, impeccable. He smiled and welcomed her in. The house was dimly lighted and expensively furnished. Soft music was playing—Mozart, Rachmaninov. Later, Hosanna also heard Billie Holiday or Bessie Smith softly singing the blues. Mr. Butler led her to the kitchen, spread his arms wide, saying, "All yours." Then he left her until she was through. He paid her more than she was due, smiled, said, "Very well done, little madame. We shall see you again, I hope." Hosanna went down the steps feeling like a real person. In the times following, whenever Hosanna saw Mr. Butler, he was the same; he always made her feel as though she mattered.

One morning, she arrived to clean up a dinner party from the previous night. Mr. Butler was still in his robe. He seemed weary, tired and sad.

"Are you all right, Mr. Butler? Can I do something for you?"

"I'm . . . fine. I'm fine. I . . . just don't feel well today."

"You need anything? I can go to the store."

Mr. Butler smiled a sad, grateful smile. "Well, it is not my body. My body is fine. It's my mind . . . my heart. They are murdering Jews and so many unfortunate Chinese who have come here to work. The Irish suffer, also. Small children—nearly babies—work! And God help the Negroes and the American Indians. Politicians speak about it in private, as though they are getting rid of or handling junk. I've been listening to them for nearly twenty years now. And not only do they not know how I feel, they do not care. Yet they call themselves my 'friends'."

Hosanna turned to him with surprise. "They been killin niggas for years and years. You a Negroe man! Why you feelin sorry for Jews and Chinese and somebody white like them Irish?!"

Mr. Butler held up his hand as though to stop her voice. "Because . . . they are human. Because I am human. We are all human." He wiped his hand across his brow. "I can't understand this hatred of others."

Hosanna stood looking at him for a few minutes, thinking. Finally she said, "Somebody ain't human. A whole lot of em. They holler God but they don't love nobody. They work hate and hate sposed to blong to the devil!" She waved her hand back at him as she went on to the kitchen, "Aw, I don't know! Who the hell knows?!" He heard her mumble to herself, "They been doin it for a million years! They killed Jesus Christ! He sure didn't hurt nobody! And if they killed him, they'll kill anybody! Human beings! Huh!"

Hosanna wondered about Mr. Butler. What was his job? He lived there, ran the house. She seldom, if ever, saw Mr. Went, but she knew he lived there, too. At least once a week, she prepared food or cleaned for them and left. The dinner parties they had were mostly small. They drank a lot. She thought they all must be men because she never had to wash lipstick off of glasses or silverware. She wished she could work there all the time, full-time. It was so quiet, so peaceful. Mrs. Doll and her children sometimes ran her ragged.

One day, Mr. Butler sent her upstairs to fetch something for him. The rooms startled her. There were two of them, and they were large and as beautifully furnished as any other in the house. Even better. It seemed hundreds of books lined the shelves on one full wall—floor to ceiling. The colors of the room were muted, soft. The carpet tones so soft and delicately colored. Small pieces of sculpture stood here and there about the room. The paintings were real ones of forests, storms and trees. There were no people in any of them. There was a fireplace with two great and comfortable easy chairs sitting in front of it. A beautiful, gleaming table holding a brandy decanter with gold-rimmed glasses beside it. All sparkling clean. The room looked content. Hosanna touched the books lightly with reverence as she read the titles. She pulled one out and opened it.

That was how Mr. Butler found her when he finally came to see if she was having difficulty finding what he had sent her for.

He smiled his soft smile. "You are a lover of books? Or do you just like to browse?"

"I love to read. I'm sorry I took so long . . . I . . ."

He came into the room. "No problem there. Do you see something you would like to read?"

Hosanna gave a little laugh of embarrassed pleasure. "There are just so many!"

Mr. Butler touched her shoulder and smiled. "Yet, not enough. They are where I live most of the time." He waved his hand to include the books. "You can see, I live many places."

"You read all these books?!"

Mr. Butler laughed, "And sometimes I go back and live in one again." He moved to the chair and sat down, reaching for a cigarette. "They are the best company in the world, except," he blew the smoke out, "when I have a question about one of them. They cannot answer me."

Hosanna sighed, holding the book to her breast.

"But," Mr. Butler continued, "if they could answer, like people, perhaps we would argue and one of us might get angry and I might lose a friend. And I need a friend, now and again."

Hosanna stepped closer to him. "Mr. Butler, you must have lots of friends. You are such a nice man."

He smiled sadly. "Nice does not always get friends, sometimes it gets leeches. You are a very nice person, also. Like a little mother. You should be careful of strangers. They watch for people like you." He laughed. "Doesn't your mother tell you about friends?"

Hosanna shook her head sadly. "My mother is dead. My daddy, too."

Mr. Butler's voice was somber. "I'm so sorry. I didn't mean . . ."

Hosanna's voice was sad. "I came from . . . somewhere else. Seem like a thousand miles away." She sighed heavily. "I lived with my Aunty and her husband here. They was gonna be my friends. She was, most times. He never was. They said Jesus was their friend, their true friend. But Jesus don't seem so friendly to me. I don't have no friend."

Mr. Butler stubbed his cigarette out. "Many people say Jesus is their friend. And God, too. But," he smiled, "we haven't heard Jesus' side of it. I have read that Jesus was a sad man around most people."

Hosanna sat down in the other chair. "I use to . . . I use to love Him. But in the churches my Aunty go to, He didn't seem so nice."

Mr. Butler leaned back in his chair. "Ahhhhhh, I see. You know, not many churches or people, very few, stand or speak for Jesus or God. You have to let them speak for themselves. That is why He created the Bible, so he could speak for Himself and you don't have to listen to what any man says."

"But they reads it all the time."

Mr. Butler laughed. "So, probably, does the devil. People see what they need to see, or want to see. Something that original benefits them. They will even change a thing if they need it to be understood a different way. Like Satan did in the beginning."

"You believe that?!"

"I believe there was a creator. The earth and mankind are too perfect even now for it all to have been an accident! Women have human babies, apes have apes. And if one original person was an accident, how could there now be millions of accidents as there are people now? All looking alike for the most part."

"Do you live by the Bible, Mr. Butler?"

He thought a few minutes; Hosanna waited in the silence. Finally, he spoke, "I believe the Bible. But I do not always do God's will. I do my own will and I do not like myself for it. I cannot seem to . . . stop . . . myself. I . . . I do pretty good on most of his commandments though —I choose not to lie, not to steal, not to kill, not to . . . covet. Not to envy . . . But . . ." He hesitated.

Hosanna spoke softly, "I don't do none of them things either. Cept maybe envy a little. I want money. I want to go home. I want . . ."

Butler spoke as though to himself, "Money. That's it! We all have something we want, I think. And it's that thing we have to choose . . . or fight. Ahhhhh, to fight and win . . . must be a marvelous thing."

He remembered Hosanna. "If money is everything to someone, then, money is everything. But let me tell you, Hosanna, the real truth is money is not everything."

"What is, Mr. Butler?"

"In truth, love is everything. You can live without money. You cannot live without love . . . of someone or something. Everyone is forever trying to find love in some way. Everyone is trying to win something. Wanting some satisfaction."

"Do you win, Mr. Butler?"

"No." He spoke so softly she could hardly hear him. "No . . . I do not fight . . . and win. I have fought, but I did not win." He was quiet a moment, then looked up at her. "But, here, how would you like to read some of these books? Are you in school ever?"

"No," she sighed. "I have to work. I need money."

He leaned back. "Oh, Hosanna, you cannot stop your education. You may have a long life to live. You have to be prepared for whatever comes . . . if you can."

"I like school, I just got to work!"

He smiled his soft smile. "We'll fix that, if you would like. Everytime you come here we will spend an extra hour or two and play school. You'll get paid anyway. You can read and do homework. I'll be the teacher. Would you like that?" His voice held excitement and hope.

"I would like that, but you might be . . ."

"Hosanna, I would be so pleased to have something else to do. Something I love to do. Your English could stand some work! And we'll just talk about life . . . to learn to speak better. The way you speak can make a huge difference in your life. Knowledge can be a sign pointing down all the roads of life."

"Oh, Mr. Butler, I sure would like that . . . and . . . and you don't have to pay me for the time I don't work."

"I insist. Now you go finish your chores and I will select a few books for your first homework . . . and pleasure." He was smiling.

Hosanna turned to leave then looked back at him. "Mr. Butler, this mean you my friend? You my friend?"

"Hosanna, we are friends."

For the next few months Hosanna read, learned and thought. His questions made her think so hard sometimes her head began to hurt. But she loved it. She learned so much. And . . . she had a friend. She believed if she needed him, he would answer.

c h a p t e r
1 3

Yinyang's train arrived in Mythville, the closest stop to Yoville, and she had to go the rest of the way by wagon or pay an exorbitant fee for a coach. Even very few rich people had the new motor cars and she didn't have any idea about the river barge. Yinyang thought of her choices and smiled, "Hell, I rode away from here in a wagon, so I can ride back in on one!"

She asked the station clerk, "Is there a stop between here and close to Yoville where I might change and rent a carriage?" The clerk looked back at the pretty, well-dressed lady, understanding her, pursed his lips and said, "No. There ain't! This here is where everthin is done!"

"Well, then I'll take the wagon." Yinyang watched to see if there was ever any thought given to her race, her color. She could see none in the white station clerk or the white wagon driver. She smiled her dimpled smile and carried on.

On the ride to Yoville, Yin contemplated the countryside—plenty of tall trees everywhere, occasionally little lakes and creeks could be seen from the road. A few houses, mostly farms. A few people. She saw Negroes working in the fields, theirs and others. This brought to her mind the decision she had to make about what color she would be. There was no doubt that being white held all the advantages, she thought. She sighed deeply, thinking, "I do want to find my half-sister, Ruth." Her father Josephus had told her the name. "I have no family. Nor even seen anyone with my blood in years. I will find her and see how she is doing after I see about my property and where I am going to live . . . if I stay." That decided, she sat back and enjoyed the scenery, every once in a while asking the driver a question.

"How large a town is Yoville . . . now?"

"Oh, it's a purty good size un."

"Do they have stores, a department store with clothes? A lawyer or a hotel?"

The driver rubbed his bristly chin. "Welllll, yeah, I reckon. I hear they got a lawyer fella workin in them Befoes' office, over by the Befoe bank. But they ain't no good hotel no more, like I spect you mean. It's a Miz Whitman runs a clean enough roomin and eatin house in what used to be th' hotel."

They rode awhile in silence.

Then the driver spoke, "You gonna need you a room? Who your famly down here?"

Yin didn't like questions. "I am going to surprise them. I simply want to freshen up and change before I see them." She interrupted his next question with one of her own. "Do we have much further to go?"

"No'm."

"How long?"

"Bout anotha half hour or so."

She leaned back as well as she could on the board set in the wagon for that purpose and said, "Well, I'll just be quiet and rest then." And they just jiggled along until they came to Yoville.

The driver took her directly to Mrs. Whitman's. Though the hotel was a bit dilapidated, it still stood. It was set back from the street, neat and clean looking, painted white. The yard had trees with casually attended flowers scattered about. Mrs. Whitman opened the door, called to her colored woman, Mazel, to get the colored yardman, Tillis, to come help with the baggage.

As Yinyang stepped into the vestibule she gave a quick glance at the furniture which deserved no more, although they had been chosen with an eye to looking somewhat rich anyway. There was a heavy wooden settee and thick coarse drapes. Shelves filled with bric-a-brac and a large round table covered with a theatrical, long-fringed cloth on which sat a tarnished silver tea service.

Mrs. Whitman came into the room, brushing and smoothing her collar and bodice. She was a very thin woman with a more than ample bust unusual for one of her size. They were her pride, her breasts. Mrs. Whitman was a whiner. She seemed to sing her words as she spoke, as though she was moaning. Although she spoke softly, it was a high, plaintive sound. "Mmmhmmm, I haven't been feeling so well, so please, do not grade the look of this room. I'm tellin you, it's so hard to get my help to do what I neeeeed. They are sooooo laaazy. They knooow I am not well and can not watch them alllll the time." She sniffled.

Yin turned to her, smiling. "I was thinking more of what I would need. I would like a room or small apartment."

"How long you plan to need the room?"

"It's uncertain, but I shall know soon."

Mrs. Whitman's sharp eyes took in Yin's clothes and all the luggage. "Yesss, mam." She recognized rich fabric and tasteful design. Mrs. Whitman stepped backward and forward and every which way, thinking out loud, moaning words Yin could not understand clearly. She finally decided on the second best room, next to the very best room in the upstairs front—second best, just in case someone else came who was better. It was not likely anyone would, but Mrs. Whitman was a business woman.

She turned toward the rear of the house and her voice became hard and harsh as she hollered, "Tillis! Send Tillis in here, Mazel! Right now!" Turning back to Yin she spoke in a soft whine again, "He's so slow, but I'll show you your room, if you like. He'll bring them things of yourn up." She began to lead the way upstairs slowly. "You in our little town to visit somebody? Kinfolk? You must be kin to Miz Befoe." She turned her head to smile down on Yin. "Or else you done come to marry our barrister, Mr. Syntoll. He ain't been here long and he is a single, bachelor man, but I been sayin he sure needs a wife. Lease I think so. Mmmmmhmm."

Yin smiled and said, "I must see the barrister, then I shall know everything I need to know to determine my stay. Until then I have no answers." Mrs. Whitman's little eyes became alert. "A pretty woman needin a lawyer! Ahh huh!" she thought to herself.

Mrs. Whitman finally reached the landing and stopped to lean against the wall to catch her breath, smoothing her bodice, which seemed to be a nervous habit. Then she moved on, whining again, "Mmmmmhmm, well he just hangs out his shingle in old Mr. Befoe's office. Mmmmm, musta knew you was coming." She laughed and it sounded like a little cry.

"Well, here we are," she said as she opened the bedroom door wide. The room was of a good size, clean, with a high-poster bed, flowered wallpaper, flowered bedspread, flowered dresser doily and curtains, imitation flowers in a flowered vase. "This is my best room. I planned it for a lady. Mmmmmhmm."

Yin looked at the room so full of flowers, smiling inwardly at the pretentiousness. "How far is the bath and the . . . toilet?"

Mrs. Whitman seldom took a bath now, nor did she even when she was married, before her husbands had died, each one. She said to herself, "This one is either a whore or a lady." She said to Yin, "Well, mmmmhmm, you hav'ta work that out with Mazel, she have to bring the water up, mmmmmhmmm, or you come down there. And we all use a chamber pot. Only a few people round here like Miz Befoe and such has any inside baths and toilets." She thought of her water. "If I was you, I wouldn't bathe too much cause I know for a fac' that it only puts the skin open to germs and diseases. Mmmmmhmm." She sniffled. "Now, if you think this ain't gonna be good nough for you, then I don't know where you gonna go, cause the onliest thing left is a rooming house a colored woman keeps over there near the colored part of town. I won't live with coloreds myself, never have."

Yin thought of the two coloreds downstairs that she was pretty sure lived in. "How much will it be costing?"

The room went up two dollars. "Oh, mmmmmhmmm, $3.50 a week for you. Five dollars if you plan to grace our table. Mazel is a mighty fine cook!"

Yin moved into the room, taking off her gloves. "May I be served in my room?"

"Mmmmhmm, well it ain't . . . aren't our regular practice, but for a little extra, fifty cents or so, I can have one of em bring your meals up.

Mmmmhmm, you will have to eat at the time we eat though, cause I have to get everythin cleaned and locked up. Once I put everythin away, well, mmm, I don't let em out no more." She crossed her hands upon her breast and looked humble. "Mmmmhmm, I'm a widder woman, you know, nobody here to see for me, but me. People's all time takin advantage of women all alone in the world. Why, my help'd just steal me blind. Mmmmhmm . . ."

Yin broke in hastily to stop the barrage of words, "Yes, yes, that will be fine. Now that is settled."

Mrs. Whitman didn't seem to want to leave, so Yin moved to the door. Mrs. Whitman stepped further into the room. "Mmmmmhmmm, we pays in advance here in Yoville."

Yin moved aside to let the man Tillis bring some of her baggage in. She then reached for her purse, *"Certainiment.* I will pay you now for one week."

Mrs. Whitman, hand to her lips, eyes opened wide, asked, "What is that there you said? Was that a forei'n tongue you spoken?"

"Yes, French."

Thoughtfully, Mrs. Whitman said, "Lovely, I'm sure." So that accounted for her color and looks! She was a white woman, just a forei'ner.

Tillis went downstairs to get the remaining bags, taking his time so that Mrs. Whitman would be gone from the rented room when he got back. Whenever he got a tip, Mrs. Whitman deducted it from his dollar a week pay. He did not want her to see whatever the lady might give him. When he heard her coming down, he started up. They met and dodged back and forth as Mrs. Whitman fussed, whining, "Tillis, you should'a waited 'til I was all the way down! You know two people, 'specially one weak and one with bags can't pass on these here stairs!" "Yes'm" came the words from the bowed head. Tillis was laughing quietly at Mrs. Whitman. He laughed at her airs and liked to see her uncomfortable as she so often made others.

Yin was placing her things around the room, clearing a way to hang dresses in the closet. Tillis came in with the last two bags. "You wants me to hep you open up all them bags, mam?"

"No, thank you. I'll wait until I know how long I am to stay here." She looked at Tillis wondering if he could perhaps be one of Josephus' relatives and therefore one of hers. She frowned. "Where is the lawyer's office. Is it far from here?" She reached in her purse, deciding how much to give him by determining how much use he would be to her.

"No mam, ain't far." He pocketed the change and smiled, looking down, away from the white woman. "I'll show you soons you come down ready."

Yinyang found the Befoe legal office easily, it was right next door to the Befoe Bank. There were few people about so she did not have to wait long for the lawyer. The only jail, a converted barn, was for coloreds who didn't always remember how to act. The occasional white man who had to go there belonged there, they said—done gone bad anyway or he wouldn't be there, was the prevailing opinion. The small courthouse attached to the jail was locked until a visiting judge appeared in town, usually by request. Sometimes a year would pass between judicial visits. So there was not a lot for a lawyer to do except settle small business problems and agreements or complete business papers—land, wills and things like that. He was really there to keep up with Mr. Befoe's business. Even so, Mr. Befoe kept his main files at his house. Most people with the real money had attorneys in huge corporations in large cities. And the lawyer Syntoll was very glad things were that way. He liked to pose and even strut in his pride at being a lawyer, but he was deathly afraid of being discovered in court as a fool or failure. He was smart, he knew he was smart. But suppose he lost a case?! He could never show his face to his friends or family again! The only answer was to practice where his friends would never see him and where court rarely convened.

The rich and powerful Mr. Richard Befoe was a very important client of one of the most important firms in Philadelphia, which is where Mr. Syntoll grew up. Mr. Syntoll admired, nay, practically worshiped, Mr. Befoe and the firm which would never invite him to join it. Consequently, Mr. Syntoll chose to move to Yoville when Mr. Befoe suggested it, having heard it was small and court seldom convened over anything very demanding. Mr. Syntoll's family had a little money and, knowing his weakness, were very glad he had passed the bar exam and spared them any embarrassment, so they helped him from time to time and he was able to take his time moving along, posing as a lawyer or how he thought a lawyer should act.

Mr. Syntoll seemed not to look hard at his new female client, but he did and saw all things that pleased him.

"My name is Yinyang Krupt, and I am in need of legal advice."

"Shall I refer to you as Miss or Mrs.?"

"Miss or *Mademoiselle* shall be fine."

He smiled, she smiled.

"Please, have a seat, please, and tell me how I may help you."

Seated, Yin spoke in a soft, southernly voice, "My parents, the Krupts, lived, had property and died here. I was sent to school in New Orleans and stayed on after my education for there was nothing and no one to come home to." She took a handkerchief from her sleeve and wiped at her eyes. To her surprise, there really were tears there. "I have come home to ascertain what the situation is with the property and all our other belongings." She took her birth certificate from her dainty little bag. "Here is my birth certificate, and you must tell me what else I need so to regain my papa's proper estate."

The lawyer Syntoll took a deep breath and looked over the certificate. "I have not been here very long, but I have looked for a home to buy so I am familiar with this area."

Yin smiled through her tears. "That is very good."

"I do believe," he continued, "I remember the Krupt land to be deeply in disrepair and overgrown with thistles and thickets, trees gone wild, yet . . . a beautiful piece of property it could be. Do you plan to live here on the land or do you wish to sell it and return to . . ."

Yin moved forward in her seat, "It all depends on the costs. Is there . . . any money in the estate? I mean, I did not inquire ever . . . if I had inherited anything. I was too heartbroken for so many years to speak of money . . . after losing my parents, you see." She dabbed at her eyes daintily.

Mr. Syntoll laid a paper pad in front of her. "Give me your address. I do not have a phone yet. They are very hard to get here unless you have a million dollars." He smiled at her. "I hope to have one soon, but I dare say you don't have one either. Only one or two local families do. Give me the address and I will find out all I can this afternoon and call on you this evening with any news I have."

They talked a few moments more, then, all things done for the time being, Yin rose to leave. She did not ask him about his fee but sauntered rather primly but sexily out of his office. Mr. Syntoll steadily followed, reaching around her to open doors and make her way convenient. No, Yin did not intend to seduce him for the fee. She just knew that if he admired her a good bit, the charge should not be too high.

Returning to the rooming house, Yin was met by Mrs. Whitman who had been through Yin's things and had a million questions to ask about Yin's business, but Mrs. Whitman was asking a champion evader and she didn't learn much. Yin plead a headache and fled to her room, closing the door, thinking, "That nosy, ole bitch!" and looked to see if anything was missing, although she had no way of knowing if Mrs. Whitman had been in there. "I will make friends with Mazel and ask her anything I need to know."

Later, when Mazel came to her room to bring water and admired a pretty scarf laying on the table, Yin gave the scarf to her. It was one of the most beautiful things Mazel had ever owned. She was grateful, but whenever she could, she looked over other things Yin had, too.

When the lawyer Syntoll called on Yin that evening, he told her, "Mrs. Befoe has been tying up the property for years, you see. So no one else has tried to buy it. The only thing to your advantage is they have not paid any taxes on the land. They may be waiting for it to just fall in the hands of the judgeship of the town, which they own, you might say, and thereby they would get it for a little of nothing or less." He smiled at his attempt at a joke. "There does not seem to be any names on the estate as relatives waited ten years for closer relatives to show up, none did, and those who had waited were then awarded all cash found in the Befoe bank. There might possibly be a trust . . . ?" The question hung in the air.

Yin brushed that aside knowing there was none. "What do I have to do to acquire my property?"

Mr. Syntoll was glad all these questions were easy. "I would say pay the taxes and establish yourself as rightful heir. I can do that with your certificate. But the estate is in awful condition."

Yin placed her hand over her breast. "How much are the taxes?"

Mr. Syntoll looked at her hand. "So much land, so much time, perhaps two hundred dollars now."

Yin shook her head slowly. "So much money."

Mr. Syntoll, who did not have very much money himself, nodded. "Well, yes . . ."

Yin made two quick decisions. Looking into Mr. Syntoll's eyes, she said, "I will, naturally, pay the taxes. But it will not leave me much to pay you."

Glad she did not ask him for a loan, Mr. Syntoll made two quick decisions. "Well, certainly we can work that out, in time. But there is another thing. The Befoes have spent some money keeping the land clear near the road going through town. You will have to reimburse them, I'm sure, and, after all, I do work for him as well as myself."

Yin rubbed her hand slowly across her breast, taking a deep breath. "How much is that?"

Mr. Syntoll picked up his hat and stood. "Well, we should wait and see how much I will have to do for you." He smiled down at her, trying to make it a warm, handsome smile. "We don't have to worry about the costs now. However, I do not think I should do any more at this time. I understand Mr. Befoe has been ill. I believe you will have to speak with Mrs. Befoe yourself."

Mr. Syntoll hesitated a moment, thinking. Perhaps he might have liked to speak with them himself; he was a social climber. But his final thought was, "If she cannot or may not pay for what I have already done, I will not do too much more until I can see what is going to happen." He smiled at Yin again. "If she has problems," he thought, "I'll see what I can do." His smile was now wicked. "She is a pretty piece of baggage and," his eyes shone brightly, "if it turns out she has money . . ." Finally, Mr. Syntoll went back to his empty office to wait, to think, maybe even to dream of never having to go into any court or even work for anyone else again. "After all, she must be a single woman. And if she has business with the Befoes, she could very well be a very rich woman." So far in Yoville, the people Yin had met were thinking of her money. Not of her.

chapter
14

Yin decided to pass by the Befoe mansion before going back to the hotel to plan her next move. It was huge, stately and beautifully kept. She saw the gardener trimming the large, old hedges in the late heat of the sun. She did not know he was her nephew, Luke, son of her half-sister, Ruth. She looked back over her shoulder at the mansion as she walked back to the hotel, thinking, "I shall be visiting you very soon, I think, Mrs. Befoe. Tomorrow."

The next morning Yin awoke with reservations about her hopes and plans. She had had a restless night. The bed had been even more strange to her body than the train bed had been—both transient, but the bed in this house seemed to hold unclean secrets from what had gone before whereas the train seemed swept clean of the past. All night, Yin's mind had revolved around the past. Fear had brought misty tears to her eyes. "I have always been alone since Pajo died. Josephus. Life has dealt me the lowest of blows. I have not had anyone, not anyone to truly be with me since my father died. And I am lonely . . . and scared. Why must I be alone among all these people? No one cares whether I eat, where I sleep, whether I have a home or not. How did I get out here in this world all by myself? I am not ugly, what's the matter with me?" She was frightened. "If I don't think about it, I'll be all right." She turned on her side, trying to sleep, to forget her thoughts. "But, how can I not think about it?" The thoughts continued.

Yin was a young woman at thirty. Old for some in those times, but if you could afford to take care of yourself, pamper your skin and body as Yin had, a woman could still look good at thirty. "I am tired before I have even begun." Her thoughts made her turn again. "On my own. I must do all my own thinking. Not with, but against everyone else. Oh, God, why am I alone? I'm not ugly. I'm not mean . . . and evil like some." She sighed. "Why should I ask you? You may not even be there. And if you are there, you surely don't even know me." She opened her eyes. "I wish that priest Paul was here. He would know what I'm supposed to do. I want my house. My home. My own. My own everything!" With these sad thoughts in her mind, she finally drifted off into restless sleep.

Now she was awake early and her natural exuberance tried to overcome her sadness. She rose, bathed as best she could. Then she looked over her wonderful, fabulous wardrobe. She did not want these small town folks to think she had too much money, "They will charge me out of it!" A wave of emotion swept through her. "I'm alone, dammit! Alone, alone, alone, alone. I'm thinking against people I don't even know. Where is somebody for me? Is he here? Is he here, or did I leave him behind in New Orleans without even knowing him yet?" Sitting down slowly, she felt sad and sorry for herself. Tears formed in her eyes and slowly rolled down the fresh, pretty cheeks. "I am not loved. By anybody." Yin laughed a sad, little laugh. "Well, at least I do not love anyone. I don't have that kind of pain. And I almost have a house." The tears dried. She stood up again. "I am going to get my house! Now," she began sorting her clothes again. "What shall I wear? Something soft and feminine, yet businesslike. Something muted or dark to imply I am serious. And very rich in feel and looks and value." She clapped her hands together like a child, once. "I have just the thing . . . I think." She opened a different trunk and found what she wanted. "And a hat! Yes, that little pert 'you can't beat me!' hat! Dark, with a bit of no-nonsense veil." She was breathing heavily when she finished finding gloves, stockings and all the things she wanted to go with the chosen outfit, but she was smiling. "I got as much right as anybody to get out here and get what I want. I have to be satisfied, too!" She dressed and was gone with hardly a word to anyone but Mazel, who handed her a hot cup of coffee. "I don't want it. I may spill it, and I don't want to have to change."

It was still early, looking like the beginning of a beautiful day. She walked, enjoying it. She remembered the way to the old Krupt house. With every step she said to herself, "I will do it. No matter what I have to do, I will get my house! I will do it, I will do it!"

The landscape around the Krupt house was in deplorable condition. Yin could have cried. Everywhere she looked she saw weeds, uncut bushes taking over the yard and lawns, a board hanging, a door off its hinge, steps broken, even some wood torn away, taken away. Dollar signs floated before her eyes at the thought of the costs. Hers!

The door to the house was locked, and she broke the lock with a rock. She went through the house touching and remembering. It had been a very rich house. Had been very well built to last. It needed work, but . . . She almost cried again as each room reminded her of times past. Josephus, her mother. "Oh, what has kept me away so long? Why didn't I come back sooner to see what really happened? Oh, my mother, my poor mother." Yin thought of the happy few days when other people looked after her. She went to her mother's room, studying it a long time, remembering her childhood. Then to her own bedroom. Everything all over the house was covered with cloth and dust. Food left in containers, long dried up or mouse-tracked, ridden with dead bugs. It was a huge amount of work . . . and another huge amount of money. She did cry, but she stopped herself soon. "Even with the house like this, I feel a little bit secure. This is my home." She knew she would have to do most of the cleaning work herself. "You bet I will!" she declared to the empty house. Then pulling the door to the yard closed, she left, walking down the same long road she had left there on with Josephus. "Well, I'm back."

Thinking it being perhaps too early to try to see Mrs. Befoe, Yin decided to find the shack where the gold was. It was, in fact, uppermost in her mind. She took off in the direction she remembered Josephus telling her about.

. . .

On the same early morning, Mrs. Befoe lay in her bed thinking. She was feeling old and wondering where her life had gone. She didn't ring for Minna, her maid, to bring her morning coffee right away. She just lay still. Her body felt like crying, but she hated people who were criers. Her mind kept repeating to itself, "I am alone." Her mind began to go back over the past—all her life and what it had been.

But now as she reminisced, a visitor was on the way.

The foliage surrounding the old Befoe mansion was lush and deep with years of closely attended care. Moss and ivy were yet everywhere, hanging from trees, sheds, even from parts of the house. There were many communities of insects beneath all the green beauty at this time of year—living, birthing, dying of old age. Some can live a long time if left alone, not sprayed or, if lucky, not caught by some predator.

In foliage very near the house was a young black widow spider— newly courted, newly loved and impregnated. She had just had a huge meal, her lover, and was sitting quietly on the earth. Before her ran a river of water from the drain spouts attached to the main house. Ahhh, she was so full. She was pregnant now, she knew. She should have been happy, but she already missed the closeness and attention of her lover. He had even brought her food while they courted. Well, he was gone now, and she must carry on alone, give birth to their brood alone.

The spider looked beneath the brush around her, watching carefully lest something catch her and end the cycle that was started. She looked at the wet end of the drain pipe and, for no reason at all, she decided to climb into the dark, damp inside. She must find a place to birth her young. She liked the dark, damp dirt, but she was sleepy and wanted to be away from harm, so she climbed.

She began the ascent, slowly, carefully, looking for natural enemies along her way. She could handle most, but a small spider a half-inch long had to be wary. She climbed straight up, zigzagged a bit, then straight up again. Past the first story of the house, she felt as though she had put in a full day's work, and here it was all slimy, still dark and no nest to sit in and wait for the birth. Then, too, the babies must be fed. I have chosen badly, she thought to herself. She looked straight up, thinking, how far does this hole go? Ah, but there, up ahead, was a shaft of light shining into the darkness of the pipe. With renewed energy, she continued her almost content but still hesitant ascent up inside the drain pipe. Her concern was that what might be up there could destroy her and her young.

When she reached the hole where the light shone, she crawled out, still cautious, through a rusty hole to the outdoors. She looked around carefully, thinking. Tall tree branches were there, no brush and just a ledge. Deciding to go on, she continued across the siding and up to the window ledge. The spider climbed to the glass. It was warm, ahhhhh. There were small chinks in the wood around the window and the paint was chipped. She darted anxiously into and out of the chinks, but the short tunnels ended before crossing over to the other side of the glass. In her excitement, she crossed over to the next window close by. Ahhh, this one was open, showing a huge tunnel. The plump black spider scurried in. Ah, oh! There was movement inside this space. A huge movement for something she had no name for, but she knew it could kill her. She froze. She did not realize she was black and easily seen in this white room with white curtains which moved softly in the breeze. Instinct moved her to a side corner of the wide ledge. She pressed herself into the darkness of the corner and, tired now, decided to wait, to watch awhile. To wait and to sleep. She was, she remembered, going to have babies. She must be quiet now.

As the spider sat staring at her, Mrs. Carlene Befoe began her day.

Old Mrs. Richard Befoe, Carlene, heard the sound of her maid quietly opening the bedroom door. The strong smell of her morning coffee filled the large bedroom in this huge, old house. As she had planned, there was no other sound to be heard. She had arranged that her daughter and grandchildren were in other, far parts of the house. Her son-in-law, Arthur, had long been gone. She did not like to think of her family until she was ready. Not to hear them was not to think of them.

She watched as her maid set the tray down with the usual "mornin, mam" and opened wide the curtains and drapes at the windows. Rising slowly because of hip pains, she moved her plump legs and feet over the side of the bed and held her hand out for her morning robe, which was at the foot of her bed within her reach. The maid stopped what she was doing and, going to the bed, handed Mrs. Befoe her robe. There was no "good morning," but the maid was used to that. Mrs. Befoe pointed to her desk by the windows overlooking the land surrounding her home. She wanted to have her coffee there. She liked to look at her possessions. She didn't really see the true landscape; she just knew it was there.

A sunrise or sunset was wasted on Mrs. Befoe. There were beautiful mountains, as mountains are always beautiful, off in the distance—purplish-gray with the sunlight catching glints of the green trees growing richly on the smooth, graceful shapes. She didn't see them either. Of course, she didn't own them, all of them, but a little, a little. She did like to look at the river flowing about a mile in the distance. She was always glad she had not allowed her father or her husband to let the railroads come through here. It might be inconvenient for her, but this way she did not have to deal with all those dreadful people who would have come, too.

This morning the river was sparkling with the fire of the sun-filled morning. She did not see that either. She just knew it was there.

Without looking at her maid, she spoke in a low, steely voice, "Where is my cane? That damned thing is always disappearing." The maid found the cane for her. Mrs. Befoe did not say "thank you." She continued in her crochety voice. "You did not check with me to see if I would want anything different."

The maid blinked with surprise and her eyes opened wide. "You never, in all the years I been here, want anything different, mam."

"I know that. But I want you to check with me."

The maid took a deep breath. "Does you want anything else this mornin, mam?"

"No. But I want you to check. Do your job. I shall wash my face first, you dumb woman. My coffee will be cold. I should have let my husband bring the railroad through here, then I would have more help to choose from and would not have to put up with such as I have." She stood balancing on the cane looking at the tray. Mornings were the hardest on her hips. She would not use the cane outside of her rooms and not even there if anyone but Minna was around. She detested the age the cane indicated. "Here now, go back and heat the coffee again. I detest cold coffee."

"But this coffee is scalding, mam. I saw to it myself."

"Did you hear me?"

"Yes, mam."
"Then, do it!"

mrs. Befoe looked in her mirror a moment. She frowned, then sighed. Turning, she went to the bathroom built especially for her. Inside water. Even long ago. Her father, Carl Befoe, could get anything done anywhere. All it takes is money, he used to say. Someone, the maid usually, had to light the mechanism down in the basement for the water to be hot and turn it off after a certain time, but hot water right in your bedroom was a luxury in the little town of Yoville. A few of the other rich families had had the mechanism installed soon after the Befoes, using the engineer while he was there. "But we were first!" the Befoes said loudly.

Finishing her morning toilette, she returned to her room, yanked the bellpull for her maid to hurry and went to sit at her all-purpose desk-table. "Ahhhh, what I must endure!"

She seemed to be looking out of the window. Musing. But she was not looking out of the window. She was still looking into her life and those lives around her. The past. When the maid returned with her morning tray, Mrs. Befoe asked, "Is my . . . Mr. Befoe up yet?"

"Yes, mam."

"Has he taken his medicine? Is he almost out of it? Is it time for more?"

"I don't know, mam. I didn't talk to Baily yet."

"I suppose he is going to want to sit out in the garden and drink his . . . coffee."

"Yes, mam." The maid was through and wanted to leave.

Mrs. Befoe turned to her, "Yes mam what? You silly woman! See if he has taken his medicine, let me know, then leave me alone until I call you again! And see if he needs his prescription filled again."

"Yes, mam." The maid fairly flew from the room. She had been working for Mrs. Befoe several years now. They were not the slightest of friends. Mrs. Befoe wanted a French maid, but none would stay. "Putting up with that ole bitch and the isolation of Yoville. No men! It is too much for me!" were their parting thoughts.

. . .

alone, Mrs. Befoe sipped her coffee and looked at her room. She had sent for or brought back all this splendor from her travels to Europe and other far places. Her rooms were quite elegant and luxurious. Crystal lamps, Aubusson and Brussels rugs and carpets. Huge white furniture, glowing, gleaming from daily polishing over the years. Lace and satin coverlets and quilts, satin settees and deep, soft chairs. A white, marble fireplace, yellowed from polishing with poor wax, held a fire burning small but bright, for winter was just leaving and the morning chill still clung to the air.

In these rich rooms, in this rich house, a profound melancholy had long settled on everything. And almost everybody. Especially Mrs. Befoe.

the maid returned with the newspapers that Mrs. Befoe saw first every morning. "Mr. Befoe has took his medicine and I blive he is going out to the garden. Baily wasn't sure if he needed more pills, mam." Mrs. Befoe took the papers, looked at the maid and smiled, not at the woman, but at her own thoughts. Then she waved her hand and said, "Send for more of his pills anyway. Bring them directly to me. I'll call you when I am finished."

As she hurried away, Minna spoke to herself out loud but softly, "I don't know why you wanna know," she mimicked, "if he took his medicine anyway. You know ain't nothin in it when you gets through with it! You all white folks is crazy! Chile!" Minna was the daughter of the midwife, Ma Mae. As the granddaughter of Ma Lal, she knew almost everything about the goings-on in Yoville, and she was a direct line to Ma Mae and Ma Lal of all that went on in the Befoe house. Ma Lal loved gossip, it was almost all she had to spice up her life in her old age.

mrs. Befoe usually read the financial sheets of the papers, but this morning she lay them aside, turning back to the window. She looked out at the sun-filled morning, the trees and land still wet with dew, that dew sparkling on the grass, nature glittering in the sun. She sighed, leaning her arms on the desk. All the pictures from her family and friends throughout her years were before her. She looked at the loveliest picture of herself, then sighed again. She looked down at her own body and shivered with distaste.

Her body felt suddenly cold. Empty. Of all good things. Withered and aged from lack of everything but greed and need for the symbols of plenty. The unadmitted loneliness she had felt for many years. Her mind, her life, was empty of everything but herself. Oh, yes, it was full of money . . . and hate.

There was no one to come to her or for her to go to in friendship. No one spoke soft, gentle words to her nor put their arms around her with true concern. No evidence of affection. She thought, "There are those who come to me because of my power. If I do not give them something they want, they do not come back." She forgot these things were evidence of affection she had almost never given to anyone except her father. And yes, her uncle Richard, her father-in-law. But not to her daughter, Richlene. Even the lovers later, much later, when she knew her true love was never coming to her again. These later lovers through the years had been more useful for her self-adoration than they were for feelings of lovers. Their lovemaking was proof that she was desired; she lied to herself if she thought it was proof that she was loved. It was necessary in the sophisticated world she had moved in for others to know she was desired. She spent enough on clothes and jewels, furs, perfumes and potions to have someone desire her. She had pretended and they had pretended. Perhaps not all of them, but most. In truth, only her husband had ever really loved her. And she hated her husband Richard because she believed he stood between her and who was right-fully hers. She chose to deceive herself.

She turned her head to the side, looking at herself in the mirror for a long moment. Then she looked again at the pictures in front of her, thinking, "What is it? When does it all happen . . . the change in life? It comes so slowly . . . yet so surely. One day you are young, full of life, surrounded by love"—she had never been, but lies were so easy—"and there is a future! A brilliant future. There is surely love somewhere in your future. A love you can . . . keep. It belongs to you. Everyone tells you that." She leaned back in her satin-covered, soft chair, ran her fingers through her hair which was almost all gray now. Her eyes moved to a picture of her father. "Papa Befoe. Great Papa Befoe. My father. My love." She closed her eyes and saw her father as he had been in the past.

Carl Eustace Befoe had come south looking for fortune during the Civil War. He came to find ways to exploit the war and make money, from either side. And he made a lot of money because there were things both the South and the North needed and wanted from each other. It was supposed to be illegal for them to do business with the enemy. However, they were willing to pay for what they wanted "under the table." Both sides. Help your enemy?! But it was done, as it is always done by those who love money. Carl Befoe was good at it. He made himself and several other "gentlemen" rich.

He was tall, slender, dark-haired, with dark eyes that twinkled always with some private joke of his that he was playing on life. Or so he thought. He loved women and didn't know of any he would marry because he did not want any woman that any other man had slept with. Not because of religion or any high moral standard. He just knew what he had done to most of the women in his life and didn't want any used property.

Naturally, he attended many social events while in the South for the necessary connections for his private work. He was welcomed every-where because he was single, handsome and rich. Few people look be-yond these things. At one of these events, he met Victoria Elizabeth. She was a lovely, quiet, tender, young girl. A virgin. Everyone knew it. He turned his twinkling eyes on her and her innocent heart flew gently to him. Of course, it helped that most all the eligible men were off fighting the war. Carl and Victoria married shortly thereafter, mostly because Victoria's father knew Carl Befoe had a great deal of money and was well established in the South and North. He would not have to worry about his daughter any longer.

Carl had his virgin. Victoria had been raised to be a lady, a genteel lady. She had a soft, gentle gaiety. She had been taught sex was a duty, which, for her mother, it might have been. Carl was a healthy, lusty man. He loved healthy, lusty women. He took his quiet little wife to Paris and to Rome to make her gay and glamourous. Stood at her side and bought magnificent clothes, rich perfumes, makeup, all things that women usually love. Victoria wore the clothes, they were lovely, but in her growing unhappiness the clothes lost their glamour, some of their beauty. They just hung on her and her quiet personality. She wore the perfumes, she loved the perfumes, until she saw that they encouraged Carl to want to make love. She stopped wearing them. She never touched the makeup. She could hear her mother say "powder and paints are for whores." She never knew her mother used makeup, however lightly.

Carl was gentle, even patient, in the beginning, but in a few short months he became disgusted with Victoria, uncaring and, consequently, rougher. These were small but important things to both of them. Soon Victoria began to hate her life. She still felt some love for Carl, but she tried to avoid him. To do that she pretended to become sickly. It did not stop him. When she had her first child, a daughter who Carl named Carlene, she was just beginning to hate her husband. She requested separate bedrooms. Carl indulged her. He felt she was delicate and the birth was difficult. Besides, he was already often at the isolated house of gaiety the local gentry had built and kept for such purposes.

When she gave birth to her second, unwanted daughter, she named the child Sally. But now her hatred for Carl completely filled her frail, tired, little body. She seldom left her home.

The housecleaning and kitchen help, even her own maid, gave her no sympathy because they all thought Mr. Carl Befoe was such a handsome, wonderful man. "How can that woman be so dumb she don't know when she got the best thing!" they laughed. She was alone. Except for little Sally, whom she loved. But, now, Victoria even began to hate her daughter Carlene, because Carlene adored her father and tried to be like him always. Her robust temperament was at odds with her mother's. Victoria exasperated Carlene who laughed at her "vapors."

About a year later, Victoria had used up all the little staying power she had left. She lay in bed looking at all the bottles of medicine prescribed for her by the town physician. She did not know this medicine was practically useless. She took it all. She begged God, "Let me die, NOW, let me die. I don't want to stay here in this life. Let me PLEASE die NOW!"

She did not die. When she woke up the next morning she still felt ill, but her heart held the first rage she had ever known in her life. At last, she went down the grand stairs as they were meant to be descended. She went into the kitchen, stared fiercely at the cook and the kitchen help. "Where is the laudanum you give yourselves when you are sick? I want it now!" She went up the stairs with the laudanum the same way she had come down, but now she felt triumphant. She sat in her bed, drinking the laudanum from a sherry glass, laughing to herself. "It's the coward's way," something said in her mind. She laughed more weakly now. "I'm no coward. I'm tired. I don't belong here in this world with this man and his child. I've never liked the world since I've been grown. It is filled with lies and false friends." She lay back in the bed, the glass tilting, spilling bits of the liquid. She thought of Sally. "I . . . love . . . Sally. What am I doing to Sally? Leaving her here alone?! Poor Sally!"

They found her dead with glass in hand, one foot on the floor. She had tried to get up to go to Sally, but the confused, sad and sickened heart had stopped.

Little Sally was too young to know much about the life going on around her, but she felt the loss of her mother keenly. Carlene was very cruel to Sally, called her slow, stupid, careless and other things to make her father see that she, Carlene, was his true daughter in his image and would grow up to be the son he wanted. Carlene told others, "My mother killed herself because she hated Sally. Because she was not my father's baby. My mother was shamed." Yes, even as young as she was, the coldness, the evil grew all by itself. Satan looked forward to knowing her better.

Carl loved Sally, but the time came when he didn't like to show it when Carlene was around, so Sally suffered the loss. She was a lonely, little girl. She took after her mother—quiet and reserved, undemanding. She even resembled her. She tried always to be invisible so as not to bring herself to Carlene's attention and bring on that terrible laughter and derision that tore her heart to pieces.

Sally was prettier than Carlene. Her father liked to put his arms around her because he liked beauty and was pleased to see it in his own child. But Carlene's sharp tongue dripped venom as well as honey and she would ridicule them both until he sent Sally away. Once, Carlene took a pair of scissors and cut to pieces his new riding suit just sent from the East. She never did admit it. She blamed it on Sally. But Carl knew. He knew she was like him. And like his brother.

Alone so much as she grew up, Sally applied herself to her studies.

She was intelligent and did very well in all her work. When grown, she cried, begged, pleaded to be sent away to some college or finishing school. This was the one time Carlene helped her. Finally Carl let her go. For peace. It was not long, perhaps three years or more, when Sally wrote she had fallen in love and gotten married. She was of age and it was legal. In fact, Sally had made a good marriage. Her husband, Gentle, came from a small but prosperous, old esteemed family. She was well provided for. Sally was able to make her husband happy for many years and gave him two children, a son Reginald and a daughter Lenore. She saw her father when he came east on business. Carl did not always tell Carlene about these visits, but he always enjoyed seeing Sally. He enjoyed, somewhat, Reginald and Lenore, except they were snobbish, selfish children who seldom smiled unless amused at someone's discomfort. They were nothing like their mother. They had reached back past her to her in-laws. There were times Sally did not even like her own children. She did not go back to Yoville for many years.

Times were changing then. Most people never change, only the things they wear and use change. People did not need many of the old things. All kinds of things were being invented. New things were in demand. Technology had begun. The world was becoming more industrial. After a financial crisis, Sally's husband and his family were nearly bankrupt. It was so important to maintain a standing. Her husband had a heart attack and died, and Sally had nowhere to go except back to Yoville. Her son Reginald was just finishing college and thinking of starting a family of his own. He planned to marry rich; he would be safe. Lenore was still in finishing school. Sally's in-laws said they could continue helping their son's daughter, but there was no place for a daughter-in-law with them at that time. Reginald said, "If it had been at any other time, Mother, I could help, but, you see, I have just started getting in this new family myself. I can't have you coming in, also. It's a bad time." Besides, her children knew Sally had no money to leave as an inheritance.

They did not want her, so Sally struggled several years on her own as a governess or by keeping household accounts. But she was getting older and tired. Her spirit was breaking from the difficulties a lone, shy, inexperienced woman can have. She did not ask her father for help. He had told her to go back to Yoville, but at that time he no longer lived there himself. He had left Carlene there with her family. All their lives had drifted further apart.

Satan watched Sally, thoughtfully. He could not do much with one who gave him so little to work with. Satan wanted to see her return to Yoville . . . where Carlene ruled. He might at least make hate grow there. Satan is not able to pervert, he can only tempt.

chapter 15

In the meantime, after Sally left for school and married, Carlene had her daddy and Yoville all to herself. But through the years, Carl drank more than his usual social drinking and stayed away longer and longer on his business trips. When Carlene complained about his absences, he growled, "I've got to get away from this gawdforsaken place!" He wanted to be where there was more pleasure, more women, any place where every time he turned around Carlene would not be there. Sometimes she forced him to take her on a trip with him, saying, "It's the only way for me to meet people and learn more about our businesses." Most times he left her behind in Yoville or sent her somewhere else far away from him to visit one of her friends.

Carlene knew how to make herself attractive. She was young, healthy, energetic and gay when she was the center of attention. She had a few suitors who knew her father's financial situation was excellent. After all, he was in steel, cotton, banking and, that big money-maker now, munitions. But no suitors were pleasing to Carlene. She wanted them to match her dollar for dollar. The men who could do that had their own choice of marriage partners or brides who were chosen by their families. In any event, they did not need to marry someone who was not totally pleasing to them as possible. Carlene's mean, little ways did show, you know. In addition, Carlene wanted her husband, whoever he may be, to change HIS name to hers and become a Befoe. The men she might have accepted for social honor were more than satisfied with their own old, established names. Satan never worried about Carlene. He knew she would find some way to do something unkind or wrong.

Now, Carl Befoe had a brother Richard who had managed to marry a woman with a huge fortune inherited from her family. Richard and his wife, Marian, had one son, Richard junior. Young Richard was also of marriageable age. Carl arranged a visit for Carlene and himself. Smiling, he said, "This way we won't have to change the names on anything we have." Carlene threw back her head and laughed, happy to share a plot with her father.

$b$ut now, Carlene sat at her desk remembering those words and she did not laugh. She looked into the laughing face of her father in the picture she held. For the first time in her life she spoke these words to him, "You bastard. You ruined my life. You paid me back. You were a bastard." Carlene picked up the coffee cup which was now cold. Even the coffee in the pot was cold. She didn't feel like getting up to pull the bell for Minna. She looked at her father's picture again. "You betrayed me in the end. You ruined my life." Then she laid him on her desk, face down. The sound startled the spider who had dozed off as she waited in the dimness. Her bright, black eyes looked at Carlene and waited for whatever was next.

Carlene sighed as she placed her hand over her heart and reached for the picture of Richard. Uncle Richard. Her father-in-law, her uncle. Her mind traveled back to the days of that trip. She had been so excited to be going off with her father. The new clothes he urged on her, though she had never needed much convincing, his willingness to pay the huge sums. He had encouraged her to see more expensive hair specialists, even skin and body specialists, and had even sent her to New York with a chaperone, of course, to acquire all she needed. She learned things about makeup and beauty care she would use the rest of her life. When they finally left Yoville for their trip to Uncle Richard, she was bursting with happiness. It was like a piece of the sun had entered her and shone through her eyes. Carl was even happy. Carlene's happiness was marred only a little when her father had to leave on business a few days after they arrived at his brother's house.

Carlene was attractive with all her learned artifice. She needed to be admired, to be embraced and to touch, walk with and talk to someone who she knew cared about her, loved her.

Uncle Richard looked a great deal like his brother. It may be said Carlene was not entirely responsible for what happened. She certainly did not intend for it to happen. But Uncle Richard was so attentive to her needs to make her stay comfortable. So gallant, so charming. Young Richard was reserved, even shy, although he liked Carlene and her worldliness.

Of course, Uncle had been, and still was when possible, a great womanizer. He loved the female sex. One morning, Richard the younger was unable to attend them because of some work he had to do for his father. Was it planned? Satan was always comfortable and amused with Richard the elder. Anyway, Uncle Richard and Carlene went horseback riding. They eventually stopped to rest and enjoy the surroundings at the end of a long, hard ride over his meadows and land filled with streams and hillocks and small, wild animals. They came to rest beside the lake the streams fed into. The morning was bright and clear. The grass was slightly damp but still soft and inviting. The trees moved gently with the breezes.

The two riders were damp with perspiration, healthy perspiration. Uncle took a small blanket from behind his saddle, spread it over the grass and smiled into Carlene's eyes as he offered it to her with a wide sweep of his arm. She laughed and jumped down from her sidesaddle, unbuttoned her tight, fancy, riding jacket, pulled up her riding skirt a bit, knelt, then sprawled on her back, looking into the sky. She had no low intentions, was not trying to lure him, her uncle. But Satan passed by and saw an opportunity for confusion and possibly grief. Knowing his true subject, Richard the elder, Satan left behind his little suggestions and feelings that run through hearts and minds and stomachs. Thoughts that remove complications, that momentarily clear consciences. Satan knew Uncle Richard from the past.

Richard, puffing lightly from the exertion of riding early and long, took off his jacket and lay beside her. He reached for her hand, saying, "By gawd, my favorite niece! You are a woman of my heart!" They laughed together.

Somehow—isn't it always "somehow?"—she held his arm, hugged him and lay her head on his shoulder. She whined, "I surely love you, Uncle Richard! You are so much fun! Why isn't your son like you? He is so serious all the time!"

Richard lifted her head and put his arm around her shoulders, laughing. "He's not so bad . . . What is it you want him to do?"

She spread her arms and legs innocently, looking up to the sky. She was not thinking about what she was doing, "Oh, I don't know! Be more loving I guess. Play with me sometimes. Swim with me, walk with me more. Just not be so serious all the time."

Richard pulled her to him, laughing like an uncle. "You mean you want him to hug you, don't you?" He squeezed her tightly, playfully.

"Yes!" She moved her head back, chin to the sky, pouted, then giggled. "Yes!"

Uncle Richard raised his head and leaned over her. "And kiss you all over your sweet cheeks like this?" He demonstrated for her.

"Yes!" She squirmed and giggled in his arms. She felt safe.

"And your sweet lips!" He kissed her. "They want to be kissed, too!" And he did kiss them.

She could not answer, her lips were sealed. When he finally moved his head away from her lips, they laughed . . . a little. She rolled her eyes skyward. "He does not even touch me!"

Uncle Richard felt encouraged. "And when you say play with you, you mean chase you, wrestle you, touch you?" He began to tickle her.

She wriggled in his embrace, laughing. "Yes!" She could hardly speak, she was laughing so, and his kisses were all over her face. Her clothes were awry. In his fumbling, tickling, he had managed to raise her skirts above her knees. He could see her lovely new undergarments, white, ruffled with lace, clean and fresh, scented with delicious perfume and the natural scent of perspiration from a long ride and the warm, musky scent of the female.

He threw his leg over her and began a fresh burst of tickling over her neck, under her arms, over her breasts, around her waist. Lying on her now and again to kiss her lips or tickle her neck with his tongue. A million tongues it seemed he had! She began to kick and roll wildly, still laughing.

He raised his head to look around the lake. His land was huge, and no one was there. "Ho!" he laughed, "You are a tigress! So you want to kick your loving Uncle Richard!" He placed his knee between hers and lay his body over her, pressing his body, as if to make her lay still. She struggled, still laughing, still playing.

Soon her dress was around her waist. He was kissing her harder, seriously. His knees pressed hers apart. He raised his hips and his hands began to tickle her below her waist, firmly but gently. His hands were everywhere. Carlene still laughed breathlessly, but her eyes were bewildered, her body hesitant. When his hand cupped that part of her that she knew was her very, very private part, she gasped softly. She began to gently push him away. "No, no," she murmured. In her mind she spoke to herself, "No, I don't want him to do that!"

Her body had moistened. He laughed softly, then inserted his finger into the privacy of her body. "I bet you I can get another one in there." He spoke with laughter into her mouth. "Go on, let's see how strong you are. Get away from me, if you can!" His laughter made her relax a little, thinking this was still part of the playing, the game. But she knew you did not play games with your "privates." Her maid at home called it that. But then he was inserting two fingers in there! And moving them slowly, lovingly. She was very wet now.

She raised her body high to throw him off. He was very heavy. He made a deft movement and, when she raised her body again, the greatest tickler of them all was no longer tickling but penetrating her young, virgin body. She knew she should scream, do something! Make him stop! But violent waves of something she had never felt before were filling and moving her body. Her legs opened of their own accord, against her will even. She did not stop him, did not scream. She raised her body to meet his; even with the pain, the joy was such that she did not want it to stop. Her last coherent thoughts were, "He is my uncle, I know he loves me." She did not stop him. And the deed was done.

When it was over and done, he apologized. She cried. They both straightened their clothes. But he knew she had had an orgasm, and she knew, too. As they rode back to the mansion and the man she was supposed to marry, Carlene thought to herself, "Why couldn't his father be the one I am to marry instead of the son?" He was thinking, "My son will have a virgin . . . good!"

As the wedding plans moved ahead, Uncle Richard had something for his son to take care of every morning while he and Carlene were horseback riding. Uncle Richard almost hated to see her leave. But all had been arranged, and the young Richard and Carlene were engaged. She was not sure what she wanted to do. She appeared nervous and anxious. Uncle Richard wondered why but did not seem to really care.

Three days before Carlene was to depart, he was reaching for her as she lay on the blanket at the top of their morning ride. It was a larger blanket now and they no longer stopped in the clearing by the lake. They were lost in the shadows of the beautiful, huge trees that covered much of his acreage. The grass was thicker and softer here.

She spoke to him softly through the thrills of their embrace. "Uncle Richard." He continued his fumblings. "Uncle Richard!" She spoke, not with anger but with some urgency. He was not listening. "My monthly has not come." He was listening at last.

"Your what?"

"My monthly . . . my curse."

"You mean . . . Are you saying . . ." He took his arms from around her. "Do you mean to say . . . you are pregnant?"

"I mean I am something. Pregnant is a good word. With child, is another."

He spoke very quietly. "Neither is a good word. Both are bad words. Have . . . you . . . been with my son . . . at all?"

She grew angry. "Oh course not!! What do you think I am?! I have been only with you! With you! It is you I love. Why, I can hardly stand it when you arrange for your son to be with me every evening, every night, every afternoon!"

Uncle Richard began to gather his clothes together, button his shirt, brush his pants. It was instant distance. He spoke calmly, "Well, my dear, you better get busy on him." Satan patted him on his back, smiled and moved on thinking, "This will take care of itself without my help."

No one, except one who has experienced it, knows what it is like for the man who has made a baby in you to tell you to give it to someone else.

Carlene was deeply hurt. He did not want her! He wouldn't stand up and fight the world to have her and their baby! Then she thought of her sweet and kind Aunt Marian. She thought, "Oh, to hell with her!" Then she thought of . . . her . . . father. Then herself again. She thought of money. Uncle Richard would no doubt be kind and good to her . . . but that was not the same kind of money that Carlene wanted for her life. The elder Richard's money belonged to Marian, his wife.

She turned to Uncle Richard who was standing, ready to leave. "What must I do? Richard only walks with me, and we talk a little on our evening walks. He has pecked me on my cheek with his dry lips only three or four times in all these weeks! What must I do?!" She was almost in tears. Then she looked at him and realized he was preparing to leave. She grabbed his trouser bottoms and gripped them tightly. "Where are you going? Aren't we . . . ? Why are we leaving now, before . . . ?"

Uncle Richard knelt and gently removed her hands, speaking softly to her. "I would never think of getting rid of the little one inside your virgin womb. It is, after all, my child. Let me think today. I will tell you later."

Carlene threw her arms around his neck. "But I want to . . ."

He gently removed her arms. "Little, darling niece of mine. I was going to tell you that we must stop meeting like this. It is breaking my heart to fool my brother and . . . cheat my son of what is rightfully his. I have been having dreadful headaches because of it. In fact I have one now, this very minute. I did not want to bother you with my ailment. The . . . old . . . always have something wrong with them. But . . . we would not have made love this morning anyway. My back is also going out on me." He held her gently, saying, "Forgive your old uncle. Pray to God for me that I may regain my health enough to just enjoy the little life I have left, sitting in the sun, thinking of these wonderful last days of joy I have spent with you."

He raised her slowly as he spoke. "I believe you should cling to my son more. Stop following me around . . . dear. Oh, how I shall miss your sweetness at my side. But . . . sit by him. Do not sit by me so much." He frowned. "This pains me so, but we must be strong together. Talk to him. Kiss him when you are alone, but let him put his tongue in your mouth first. Do not do that to him first. And do not touch me so much when you are talking to me. Touch him, talk to him. Be more of a lady. And Carlene, your father had better not find out about what I . . . what you have done, or I will assure him you are a liar and I do not want my son to marry you!" He dusted and straightened his clothing. "This will be our last morning ride. I will free my son of obligations so he may ride with you instead."

Carlene stammered, "But what . . . when . . . what . . ."

He gave her a quick embrace; it lasted only a few seconds. "I will be thinking about . . . your problem. I will talk to you soon. I will have an answer."

Before she knew it, she was sitting on her horse and Uncle Richard was slapping the horse's behind to make it run on home. As an afterthought, he hollered, "Gallop!" He looked after her with distaste, no longer liking her very much. So many things had happened to Carlene so quickly, she could only ride with wide eyes as the landscape flew past on her way to Richard the second, her fiancé.

Uncle Richard avoided her that evening and the next day. Carlene became more anxious and nervous. She stayed close to Richard the younger almost all the time. He had been relieved of all duties because his fiancée was leaving, he was told.

On the last evening before Carlene was to leave, Richard senior gave a dinner party and invited several of his friends for the weekend. The ladies were excused soon after dinner, and the men sat smoking and drinking whiskey and brandy, playing cards, laughing and talking way into the night. Finally, the younger ladies were excused to go to bed.

Near dawn, Carlene was awakened from a very light sleep already filled with worry. She heard her bedroom door opening. She pushed the covers from her face and turned, looking over her shoulder to see her uncle half-carrying his son in to her. His voice rasped, "Hush! Be quiet." He spoke roughly but softly. "Pull the covers all the way back. Here, help me undress him." She moved quickly, grasping the idea like a smart Befoe. She tried to blush at the son's nakedness but forgot about it quickly as they lay him in the bed. Uncle Richard left quickly, saying, "Look sharp ahead!" as he closed her door.

Carlene pushed Richard junior to see if he really was so drunk and asleep that he could not be awakened. She wanted to feel his private member to see the size and feel of it. She did. It became hard. It was not as long as his father's. She sighed. She lay quietly a moment then decided to get on top of him. Second thoughts occurred to her, "If he wakes up and I am on top, he will never believe he raped me, a virgin."

She lay his private member quietly down thinking, "I don't like him like that anyway!"

She was almost asleep when her door opened softly again. Her uncle came quietly into the room dressed in his pajamas, saying, "We must give him proof."

She sat up. "Proof?"

"Yes. Get out of the bed." He pulled the covers back and she got out. "Now get down on your knees, bend over the bed like you are crying." She did that, too. He knelt down behind her. "Now," he whispered, "If he wakes up, we can say I was consoling you. I will have time to put myself away." He lifted her gown over her plump round hips shining in the little moonlight that shone into the room.

"No, no," she started to say, but he held the front of her body, pressed her thighs apart, holding her "rosebud" in one hand. Raising himself up a little, he eased himself forward, guiding himself to enter her. She moaned and put her head down on the bed, spreading her arms out. He worked slowly and quietly. He covered her mouth several times with one of his hands to stop her from making her sounds, she moaned so. He sucked on her shoulders to keep himself from crying out. When, finally, they were finished, he wiped himself on her gown and told her to put her fingers into herself and smear them on his son's penis. He took a small vial filled with chicken blood prepared earlier in the day and told her to smear some of that on his son, also. "So he will know you were a virgin." He wiped himself on her gown again, patted her on the head and the behind. His last words were, "Let nothing keep you from leaving here tomorrow, dear Niece. Good luck and good night!" Then he was gone.

Carlene, as clever as she was, was inexperienced. She did not know how to think of all that had happened to her. She was in something she did not understand; she was confused. Her mind had never thought of marriage with her uncle, yet . . . What did she want? Had she been used? Did her uncle love her in another kind of way than he did his wife? All these thoughts and more ran through her mind. Satan loves to create confusion; people don't hardly know what they are doing then. With another deep sigh, she did all her uncle had told her to do. "I can think about the other stuff tomorrow. Tonight I had better take care of the important things." She was a real Befoe!

The man Richard who lay beside her, who was to stand with her to the end of his days, who had made no deliberate choices, who was considered a fool both by one who had been and one who would be the most important person in his life. One of them was a fool and the other one would be a fool. But now he blindly loved and trusted his father and his future wife. He thought things in life were as they should be, not as they were. Ignorance is not always bliss.

Richard the younger was undone when he, at last, woke up. He held a tearful Carlene briefly before reaching for his clothes. She cried in truth from anxiety, confusion and fear. Embarrassed and ashamed, he apologized profusely. As he went through her doorway, he said sadly, "We better get married soon." She nodded her head in haste and smiled through the tears that disappeared shortly after he shut the door.

Later that day, holding fast to his arm, she left in a carriage for the train station. Head held straight, chin high, eyes misty, she looked back to wave to Richard senior, but he looked away as he turned to his wife and walked back into his home, the mansion. Carlene was to love him all her life.

Carl Befoe thought something was amiss when his daughter wanted to plan the wedding "right away! This month! No later than next month!" Her lips trembling, her eyes all teary. But he didn't think of the right thing amiss. "You have a scoundrel for a son," he wrote his older brother Richard.

"Yes, he is. But he is going to marry your weak and innocent daughter" was a line in the otherwise respectful answer. Actually, they both laughed at the episode—one, at the joy of young love and the other, at the joy of his clever love. "Imagine," the older Richard laughed to himself, "a child at my age!" Carlene cried herself to sleep many nights thinking of him. Her love.

And so she was married in the grandest wedding the society of America had seen in a long time, and the rich are certainly known for their grand gestures. There were twelve bridesmaids, one of whom was Virginia Michelson who caught the eye of several and later became Master Krupt's wife and Yinyang's mother. At the wedding, Virginia also caught the eye of Carl Befoe. Eventually he gave her, among other things, a diamond ring of such proportion that Carlene hated Virginia Krupt for the rest of her life, socializing with her only to keep an eye on what her father might be doing playing the fool.

But now, it was Carlene's stage. Satin, silk and lace imported from France, cut and sewn into creations "fit for an angel," said the angel's father. Finally Carlene marched down the glorious aisle with her betrothed, his father smiling benignly over it all. The baby snuggled securely in its mother's womb. And it was done. Champagne flowed all day and all night to celebrate the event.

The honeymoon, a gift from the husband's family, was a trip to Europe, the romantic isles of Italy and the clothing center of the world, Paris. Carlene made small screams and squirms on her wedding night and performed as duly expected. But her husband was not his father and, his experience being so much less, he left Carlene turned on her side away from him. She cried softly, felt cheated and began to dislike her kind husband even more. Satan, very busy all over the world, still noticed Carlene and said, "Bravo!"

Seven months later, a child was born "premature." A girl-child, properly named Richlene after her father, Richard. Everyone was pleased and relieved. Carlene had had a miserable pregnancy. She shouted out at household help, slapping them at times. She was mean to everyone, including her husband. She did not like him to touch her. He was not his father. One thing she had wanted, she got. Her name was still Befoe.

Richard senior died a few years after the birth of Richlene. Shot while hunting with his wife and friends, an accident, everyone said. It was a shame his wife had to see him like that, everyone said. Marian had found him. In his own woods where he had seduced so many lovely women while his wife sat looking through the windows of the rich house thinking of what he was doing. He had seen the child only a few times when Carlene and Richard came to visit. After his death, instead of becoming closer to her son and grandchild, Marian became even more distant by always being busy or away when her son planned to bring his wife home with him on his frequent visits to see his mother. Carlene thought with fear and anger, "If she knows the secret, she kept it to herself. Well, she is used to keeping her husband's secrets, I'm sure."

Now everyone may think Carlene was the winner in the little farce, but certain things done in life demand their price. It is a miserable thing to hate the person you are married to. To lie beside them night after night all your life, if it ends that way. Richard was not the only loser. To have a good marriage is one of the greatest things in life. To be with the one you love. You know.

chapter
16

Carlene leaned back in her chair, shook her head as if to clear it. She turned her head slightly and looked at the baby picture of her daughter Richlene. How cute, adorable and messy she had been. She had been a quiet baby. Hardly any trouble at all. Only sometimes, she cried and cried for what seemed like no reason at all. Her nanny or mammy could not find out what was wrong with her. Then, just as she would suddenly start crying, she just as suddenly stopped. She would be the sweet, quiet baby everyone loved for several weeks. Then the crying would happen again. Well, everyone became used to the situation, expected it. Carlene would make them take the baby out of her hearing and tell them to "leave her be, let her cry till it's over."

When Richlene was two years old and walking fairly well, everyone noticed you had to look deep into her eyes and repeat a word two or three or even four times before she would repeat it back to you. She didn't talk very much. They let that pass because Carlene said, "Let her be. What has she got to say anyway?" Richard was most often away on business. True business. He was handling responsibilities inherited from his father which involved a great deal of money. He was also slowly taking over some of Carl Befoe's business. Carlene studied all reports on everything related to the business, but Richard did the running. When he was home, he spent as much time as he could with his little daughter whom he loved dearly.

When Richlene was five going on six, Carlene's friends were already taking their children on outings, showing them off dressed in their little angel clothes. Carlene began trying to talk to Richlene but got no response. She looked deeply into her own child's eyes and saw nothing there except perhaps fear of her mother screaming at her. Richlene's tiny baby voice said, "Mama. Mama?" Carlene took another deep breath and said, "Mo-ther, I told you, Mo-ther!"

The child began to cry. Carlene shoved the small one away and left the room in a huff. Consequently, Richlene stayed at home and out of sight when guests came to visit, although she was always dressed as a flowery, ruffled angel in case one of the guests accidently saw her.

Richlene took ill a short time later, a throat problem. Under the doctor's care, she healed. In his final consultation with Carlene and Richard, the doctor suggested, "The child is extremely nervous. Unusually so. You should have her examined for mental health. She is a very . . . slow child, which might indicate retardation." Carlene almost screamed, "You are a small town doctor and you do not know what you are talking about!" The doctor shook his head slowly. "Mrs. Befoe, I'm sure of what I am saying." Carlene snatched her child from his table. Richard gently took Richlene from her and looked earnestly at the doctor. "Then," Carlene threw over her shoulder as she left the room, "you are a liar! Come, Richard!"

Carlene took to her bed and the bottle. Richard held his little girl, looking searchingly into her eyes. He crooned to her, petted her, soothed her when Carlene screamed at her or when she was upset in any way. He was the one who searched all over America for the finest teachers and schools for Richlene. He loved her. Isn't life strange? The one who had nothing to do with creating her was her protection, provider, a fighter for her life for her own sake.

They became very close, Richard and Richlene. She always knew when he was leaving on business and she was always inconsolable until he returned. They became close in such a way that Richlene could live around Carlene. Knowing how much her father loved her, Richlene did not depend on Carlene for love. Her whole world was her father and the colored mammy, Mana, who cared for her. She would let few others of the household help touch her. The regular ones she came to recognize. She would stare at her mother quietly for any length of time she was in the same room with her. She would not let her touch her, however. Her mother brought her to near hysterics.

Richard was always the one to take Richlene to the new doctors and teachers. All new things she shared with him. There came the day when she was eleven and they were alone in a rich hotel room in Switzerland where Richard had found a doctor renowned for his knowledge and success in his school of teaching. Richard had just tucked her into her bed and kissed her.

"Good night, my lovely, little daughter."

"Good night," she spoke softly, hesitantly, "my lovely, little dadda."

He stroked her cheek gently, "Someday you will be fine. I know it." He moved to the door of her bedroom and turned to look back at her. "Sleep tight." He switched the light off, then she spoke to him for the first time without repeating what he or someone had just said to her.

"Dadda?" Slowly, laboriously she spoke. "Will . . . you . . . pull . . . the shade . . . up . . . so I . . . may . . . see the moon . . . better?"

He held his breath and looked in the direction of his daughter. Quickly, he moved to the window. "Of course, my child."

"I . . . love . . . the moon . . . Dadda. I love . . . the sun . . . but I . . . I can . . . not look at . . . the . . . sun."

After arranging the shade and curtains so she could see the moon glistening through the night and shining into the room, lighting the darkness, he moved to the bed, taking her hands in his. "You are speaking, Richlene. Oh, Richlene. And no one has told you what to say."

"I . . . can . . . talk."

"Then, why . . . ?"

"I can . . . talk . . . to you."

"I am happy! I am glad. Everyone will be happy you can talk!"

"I . . . do . . . not want . . . to talk . . . to . . . every . . . one. I will . . . talk . . . only . . . to you . . . and . . . and Mana."

"She is only a nurse, Richlene. A Negress. There is your mother and, and . . ."

"Mana . . . is . . . my friend."

"Oh, Richlene, my child, you must."

"You . . . have to . . . pro . . . mise me. You have to not tell my . . . mama."

"Richlene, I cannot . . ."

"I will . . . NEVER, never . . . talk to Car . . . lene. I will . . . not talk . . . to you . . . again . . . if you . . . do not . . . promise . . . ah . . . me!"

"Richlene, she is your mother."

"She is . . . not . . . my mother. She . . . ha . . . hates . . . me."

"She loves you."

"She does . . . not love . . . you . . . either."

"You are a child. You cannot know . . . do not know . . ."

"My . . . my . . . heart . . . tells me things."

"Alright, Richlene. Alright."

"You . . . pro . . . mise?"

"I promise."

Richard stared at his child of eleven years. How could she know of such things? But then Carlene never touched the child unless she was drunk or some other reason known only to Carlene. Why, she almost never touched him! Almost never. He frowned, remembering. Richlene patted the place beside her on the bed. "Stay . . . with me . . . till . . . I go to . . . sleep . . . like . . . Mana." He lay down atop the covers and held his child until she slept. He did not sleep; he lay there thinking about his wife, his daughter, his life until the moon shone through the window no longer.

Now Richlene was not totally disabled. She had learned to speak, even to write, but everything was done in a slow, laborious way. She learned to dress herself and made certain chores for herself. She was never forward or aggressive. She liked to smile, and she reacted to concern or love slowly but gratefully. She could now feed herself, eat neatly, she even chose her own clothes to wear for the day. She chose them for their colors or some ornamentation on them. She was well liked by the help though not really close to any but Mana, her nurse and friend. She was a pretty child. She fared well with everyone but her mother.

Carlene now refused to sleep with Richard any longer. She moved into a suite of rooms of her own, the mansion was so large. They didn't make love, they had sex only occasionally if he demanded and pressed or if she was drunk and decided she wanted it herself. "I will have no more children who lack brains . . . if that is all you can make!" she told him one night when he was especially persistent. He returned to his rooms hurt and bewildered that his family was no family. After several days when there had been no change in Carlene, he left for the city. Thereafter he found his passion with other women during his business trips. Of course, eventually, one or two women satisfied him more than others and became rather steady. One he finally kept in an apartment, giving her money and jewels. Richard tried to make it feel like a home when he was there, but the woman didn't want a home. She wanted a sugar daddy. Richard's heart found small satisfaction.

chapter
17

Carl Befoe was away most of this time, and Richard began to take care of most of the business. Carlene hated it when her father stayed away for long periods of time. She believed, and she was right, that he was spending most of his time with his other "family." She knew he liked beautiful women, and he was getting older. She thought, "Suppose someone has a child? Or even lies to him and says that the bastard was his? The money!" But Carl Befoe had thought of all that and had made arrangements for his other "family" before he died. When he did die, Carlene knew about them at last, but there was nothing she could do. It had all been done. By his hand, from his hand, they were secure. As was she. But she had wanted it all.

Carlene leaned forward in her chair, reaching for her father's picture. She smiled down at it and then held it to her breast. "You ole bastard, I loved you more than anyone else ever did!"

Carl Befoe had died in Philadelphia in bed with his lusty, youngish wife. "That common-law whore he lived with!" Carlene screamed. Carlene was beside herself with grief. Even now, just thinking of the past, she remembered her grief. She had taken to her bed immediately. In less than an hour, she'd thought of the money, the will, and was up again. She had no time to lose. She spoke to Richard with tears in her eyes, "I must set my grief aside. There is our child and my sister I must think of. I need to see the lawyers. He died, it seems, in the house of that bitch he was living with. She probably poisoned him! I must go take care of any business. And . . . and I want to go alone. I must be alone awhile, with my grief."

She could not get out of Yoville that day. The riverbarge was gone and she refused to ride ten miles in a horse carriage. The next morning, she was packed and on her way. "Do not send a message to Sally if you know her address, Richard." Richard always tried to keep in touch with Sally for business reasons. "I want to tell her myself," said Carlene. "We will need each other at a time like this." Then she was gone, waving her handkerchief to them sadly.

Her first stop was at the eastern lawyers' offices that handled most all of her father's business and, of course, his will. They were astonished to see her, having planned to go to Yoville for the reading of the will, in view of the grief-stricken family. Her eyes sparkled with tears as she held their hands and explained she wanted to tell her sister, herself. "Please do not forward the news to her. I don't want her to be alone when she finds out our dear father is gone. And I will let you know when we are able to hear the will read. We will come here to your offices." They smiled agreement because they had not looked forward to Yoville and the disagreeable travel.

While the lawyers were looking for some papers Carlene said she needed, Carlene excused herself to go to the ladies room. Returning from the ladies room, Carlene asked the secretary who she had known for many years, "Miss Withers, do you have a sheet of paper I may use to write a few notes to myself?" Miss Withers pulled open her drawer that held all the business stationery and scratch pads. She withdrew a pad and handed it to Carlene, saying, "I am so sorry about your father, Mrs. Befoe, he was a wonderful and kind man." In reality Miss Withers had never liked him and his gruffness with so little respect, she thought, for women. At least, not until holidays when he gave such nice presents to the employees of the firm.

Carlene took the scratch pad and reached for her purse as though to get a handkerchief to dab at her eyes. "Oh! Miss Withers, I have left my purse in the ladies room." She sat down, weary. "Would you please fetch it for me?"

Miss Withers fairly flew up as fast as her age would allow. "Oh, of course! You just sit right there, Mrs. Befoe, I'll be right back." As soon as the old secretary was out of sight, Carlene jumped up and slid several sheets of their business stationery out and placed them under her coat. She was about to reach for several more sheets, just in case, when she heard Miss Withers returning. Carlene quickly sat down, holding her head in grief. Miss Withers handed her the purse, thinking, "The poor child is beside herself with grief. She is forgetting herself." "Here, dear," she said out loud, "Perhaps you would like some tea?" Carlene shook her head no, covered her mouth with the handkerchief and started back to the inner office of the lawyer. "Oh, Mrs. Befoe, you have forgotten the notebook." Carlene spoke into the handkerchief, "Never mind, thank you, Miss Withers."

Her next stop was a public stenographer. She had removed her rings and bracelets that sparkled with diamonds. She spoke to the woman, "I am a legal secretary to my husband. My typewriter is broken. I need . . . we need a letter immediately. I have the business stationery here." She handed a few sheets to the stenographer. "You will please type what I . . . we have written out on this piece of paper. It is to Mrs. Sally Gentle . . ."

Thus, the letter was written and forged telling Sally her father, Mr. Carl Befoe, had thought she would be well taken care of by her husband and so had left her nothing in his will. That, since her husband had died, her father had, perhaps, meant to change the will but had not, saying it was for the best as it was. Signed, with regrets, saying, "Do not contact us, we will contact you if there is any more information forthcoming." Carlene was elated things had gone so easily and well. She returned to Yoville and her grief. Satan shook his head at God. "To these you give free will! I didn't do it! She did!"

Sally truly grieved for her father, regretted his death and regretted that they had not been as close as they should have been. But she felt there should have been some inheritance for her. She had always felt she would, at last, be independent. Her life was crushed. The little strength the years had been using up, gave out. Then, Sally became sick. The doctor did not know what was wrong; he could find nothing, he said. Her heart was probably tired. The grief . . . you know.

Her employers of that time had two children for whom Sally was governess and tutor. The children had never liked or respected Sally because she was gentle and honest. Neither did they like their parents whom they never saw.

Her employers were rich, yet they told her, "We cannot afford two governesses, and we need a healthy one, in any event. You must make preparations to leave at your earliest convenience, of course. The new governess will be needing this room in three days. Oh, yes, the month is not ended, you know, so you will not receive a full month's check. We will see that you do get to the station or whatever rooms you may find, of course. Oh, and do let us know how you are getting on. When you have time, of course." That night, Sally was in tears when she wrote her sister Carlene that she was coming home to Yoville.

Though it was half Sally's home, Carlene "allowed" her to return, giving her rooms on the top floor in the servants' quarters since they were not used much any longer. She said there was no space anywhere else. But there was, and all knew it. Consequently, the servants respected Sally so much less or not at all. She was given keys to the household and placed in the position of keeping the accounts, being a housekeeper. She remained in her rooms in the great loneliness she had always suffered in this house. Richlene was the only person she allowed herself to relax with. She tried to teach her things and found Richlene was not so dumb and unable as Carlene and others said. So they became close. Richlene loved her Aunt Sally, and Richard was always kind to Sally because she loved Richlene. And because it felt so good to have someone around who was kind.

Carlene did not straighten out the matter of the will. No one knew. Sally, in her state of despair, never checked and gave up. Carlene could never use that money, those properties; it was tied up legally. She just did not want Sally to have her rightful share. She thought, "Of course now, when Sally dies, if she dies first . . . Well then, the money and all is mine! And her stupid children can kiss my ass!" Then there was Carlene's laughter.

When the will was read, Carlene found that her father had married "the bitch" and made her children legal. Her father had been careful though. He had willed and prepared his papers so Carlene and Sally were left with the bulk of his estate. His other family had received one very important business and many bonds and a very fine house in Pennsylvania.

Now, Carlene decided to call on the widow Arabella, the second

Mrs. Carl Befoe, her father's wife. She told no one where she was going. She dressed in her finest to overwhelm and intimidate the woman. When her chauffeur pulled slowly into the curved driveway, even Carlene was impressed with her father's "other" house. The grounds were well kept and flourishing; many trees and extensive lawns were trimmed, healthy and beautiful. The house had two stories and an attic. Carlene stepped from the automobile and saw huge glass doors with polished brass handles. They opened into an entryway to the front doors which were tall and made of the most magnificent wood. The name "BEFOE" was in large golden letters over the door. "The whore wants everyone to know!" thought Carlene with disdain.

Carlene did not really believe her father had truly married THAT woman, no matter what the lawyers said. "This whore who caught an old, sick man," she thought as she banged the knocker and waited.

A maid opened the door. "Good day, madame." Carlene was abrupt. "Is Mrs. . . . your mistress of the house in? I am Carlene Befoe and I sent a note I was coming. I am expected." The maid invited her in and left her in the vestibule, saying, "Please wait here. I will tell the madame you have arrived."

Carlene bristled at being told by a maid to wait in a hall in her own father's house, so she wandered around the large entry, looking through the doors which were open. It was beautiful, quiet and calm. "This house has had the benefit of an interior decorator, I'm sure of it!" she thought.

Mrs. Arabella Befoe was a lovely, attractive woman. She had been in a very, high-class house for rich men when she met Carl. She was young, healthy, robust and very passionate. "All for you," she told him softly. She listened to him patiently. She made him laugh. He grew to care for her a great deal. He paid the madam so that no one else might use Arabella's body. He soon set her up in a house of her own . . . truly for him alone. She was soft spoken and a gentle woman. One of the kind that is all reserve on the surface, but, being healthy, she was a wild, passionate, imaginative lover behind closed doors. She knew men well. She knew Carl Befoe. She soon became pregnant—with his child or not. We never know. They did not marry then, but he stayed with her more. When she bore him a son who there was no doubt he adored, he named the child Carl Befoe junior and he moved in. It was popular knowledge he rushed home in the evenings and stayed home on weekends and holidays. She never changed her loving ways. When she became pregnant again, they moved into a much more respectable and rich neighborhood, and he quietly married her. She bore him a daughter, then she bore him no more. Still, she never changed. In fact, that is how Carl died. Atop her, clinging to her body, her breast in his mouth, his eyes looking into hers but not seeing her at the last, because he knew he was dying and he had not planned to.

He had arranged things for this family. She was secure for the rest of her life and their children, beyond.

Now, today, Arabella came down the magnificent stairs he had planned for her. She came down beautifully dressed and beautifully poised. Carlene looked up at this woman Arabella with hard disgust, even letting it show on her face. Carlene spoke first, "Mrs. Befoe, I do presume."

Arabella smiled, "And you are Mrs. Befoe? Or someone she has sent with a message of condolence for me?"

Carlene now smiled with sarcasm. "I AM Mrs. Befoe AND Miss Befoe. I have been a Befoe all my life!"

Arabella was now level with Carlene. "How wonderful for you. I'm sure you are quite pleased." She smiled pleasantly. "Ahhhh, Mrs. Befoe, may I be of some service to you?"

Carlene looked around her. "Do we stand here in a hall to talk? Surely my father taught you better manners than this."

"Your father, my husband, taught me many things. But I always do what I decide to do. Yes . . . I will invite you to sit and talk a moment. Follow me, please. Would you like some tea? . . . or coffee? I have no hard liquor in the house, I'm afraid." She led the way to a nearby sitting room where a small fire was burning. Carlene knew that she or someone had been expected. She thought to herself, "This bitch expected me. So she knows how to play a game, mmph. Well, she's playing with the wrong woman now. My father may have been a fool for her, but I am not my father."

As they made themselves comfortable, Carlene spoke, "I do not care for anything. I simply wanted to see the woman who had . . . taken advantage of my father."

Arabella laughed, startling Carlene. "Taken advantage of your father?" She continued to laugh with gentle gusto. "You think your father was a fool then! Oh, my dear, my dear, it seems your father took advantage of you!" Her body was shaking with her laughter. "You do not know your father!" Suddenly the laughter stopped, but she continued speaking. "Certainly not as I do."

Carlene was getting angry, but could think of nothing to do or say that would upset this woman and still leave herself a lady more highborn than Arabella. "Yes," she finally said, "I am sure I do not know him as you do. Where are the . . . children?"

Arabella smiled. "The children? They are too old to be called children. My son, our son, Carl junior, is away at school. He will be going to college very soon. My . . . our daughter, Heda, is upstairs attending classes with her tutor and governess."

Carlene's voice was very low as she asked, "You have named your son, Carl junior."

Arabella still smiled. "Yes, after his father . . . at his father's request."

Carlene could hardly stand being where she was, hearing what she was hearing and looking at this horrible, horrible woman. She spoke in a tight voice. "You took everything you could from him, didn't you?"

Arabella still smiled. "Dear, ladies never 'take.' Ladies never have to." She laughed that gentle, infuriating laughter. "And don't forget, I didn't take you from him." Suddenly Arabella stopped smiling and became serious. "But, yes, where is your sister, Sally? Carl lost touch with her. She was moving so much and you . . . said he had not received any mail from her."

Carlene was taken aback. "What do you want with my sister Sally?"

"Well," Arabella answered, "Carl left something very special to him . . . for her. I wish to give it to her."

Carlene thought a moment. "What is it? What special thing did he leave for Sally?"

Arabella leaned back in her chair. "I cannot really say what it is. It is wrapped and has been for years. He said many times, it was for Sally . . . when . . . he . . . passed on."

Carlene sat forward in her chair. "Give it to me. I will see that she gets it."

Arabella thought a moment. "No . . . I would rather give it to her myself. I'm sure you won't mind. Carl's request was to me, you know, dear."

Carlene's voice became hard, "You are very rude to tell me I cannot take a . . . gift from my own father to my own sister."

Arabella stood up. "And you have been trying to be rude to me since you arrived here in my house. I cannot see what further need you have of me . . . and I have some very important things I must do. So if you will excuse me . . . I will have the maid show you. . . ."

Carlene stood up, enraged. "How dare you! To try to put me out of my own father's house!"

Arabella's voice now became hardened. "This is MY home, Mrs. Befoe. I tolerate no one here I do not wish to."

Carlene turned to leave. "I was ready to leave anyway, but," she turned back to Arabella, "this house may not always be your home. I have lawyers, excellent lawyers. I am going to contest the actions my father took. He was old and obviously sick."

Arabella's voice did not rise. "Then you will have to have his will examined where you and Sally are concerned, also. Perhaps he did not know what he was doing there either. And Mrs. Befoe, he DID talk to me a great deal about you . . . and Sally . . . and what he wanted for her . . . and you."

Carlene could only stare at Arabella, wondering how much she knew. Had she talked to the lawyers? Were they friends? Did she know? Did they know? They were always wondering why Sally had not come in to see them.

"Something is wrong here," Arabella thought to herself. "I will find Sally on my own." She turned to the door where the maid had suddenly appeared. "Please, show . . . Mr. Befoe's daughter out." She turned to go up the stairs and never turned back to Carlene until she had reached the top. Carlene was still standing, stupefied, staring up at Arabella. Arabella knew the grandness of a stairway as her late husband had. She turned her head to look over her shoulder at Carlene and said, "It would please me, dear, if you do not return to my home until you are invited. Good day." Then her skirts swished as she disappeared from view.

Carlene, blinded by tears of anger, was soon out the front door and being helped into the automobile. She looked back at the house until she could see it no more. When she did turn around, her first thought was "Perhaps I had better leave well enough alone. I won't contest my father's provision for her." A wave of anger swept through her then. Her heart raged with the question, "But what is in that package from my father to Sally?" She hated Arabella and Sally.

The devil, Satan, had much amusement with what had happened to Carlene. Even though she was a faithful subject of his, he didn't like her at all. Satan cannot love, you know.

c h a p t e r

18

Carlene's thoughts on this early morning were tearing at her nerves. She sat her father's picture down and reached out to her liquor tray which always sat on the edge of the desk. She poured a brandy. She thought as she sipped, "My father would have been overjoyed to know he had well-balanced grandchildren." She forgot Sally's children were also what could be called "well-balanced." However, they had proved with the treatment of their mother that they did not know much about love.

She frowned into her glass. "He never did spend much time with Richlene. Never." But Carlene had spoken so disparaging of Richlene and had taken so little time with her herself, he had just followed suit. She had done the same with Sally's children. Belittling them, ridiculing them, laughing at them, she had colored his vision. As she had about Sally. She had been abrasive. Carl was not a complete fool about Carlene. He had hidden his new family. He never let her meet them or told her about them. But she had heard about them anyway. And hated them, as he had known she would.

Carlene stopped reminiscing a moment, looked out at the sunny morning and took another drink from the crystal glass, thinking, "But he couldn't always leave me behind. I began to travel myself!" She smiled, but it was not a pretty smile. "I went to all the great capitals of the world. I shopped in Paris and Rome. I have been dressed by the greatest. I have been served by the best!"

Carlene had traveled almost to the point of maternal indecency while Richlene was growing up. Richard stayed home, handling the huge financial structure and seeking help for Richlene. Carlene always saw that she received statements and reports because she knew about keeping watch over your kingdom. She did buy beautiful clothes, jewels, furs, carriages and even some art. To show, to have, more than to enjoy. She entertained, huge parties in Befoe homes all over the world. She received many invitations, although not many people really liked her. She did not entertain much in Yoville, it was so far out of the way, and she had not wanted the railroad spur to come there. She had arranged for a large, richly outfitted barge to be built to carry her along the river from the Mythville railroad station ten or so miles from Yoville. She came home only to rest until it was time to go again.

She had lovers. She was a passionate woman. But she was a liar. A liar is also a sneak and sneaks do many things we never know of. Carlene was one of Satan's people. But since Satan cannot love, he did not love her and he always took the people she loved from her in payment for his gifts. However, she always made the first choice. Her life was the result of her choices. And I suppose he was pleased because she could do so much more harm as an unhappy lady.

She replaced her father's picture on the desk and reached for Richlene's. She did not hold it to her breast. She stared at it and, unusual for her, tears formed in her eyes. She was thinking of the past again. But who was she crying for? Richlene? Herself?

The sun was moving across the sky, the weather was glorious, but Carlene saw none of it on this morning. All her thoughts were turned inward.

chapter 19

a fter Richard learned Richlene could speak from her own mind, they became even closer over the years. She was almost fifteen years old. He devoted much of his time to the business but came home often and spent much of his time there with his daughter. He often tucked her in at night. He always kissed her good night. She would often ask him to stay with her until she went to sleep.

He was a man lonely of soul. Yes, he had his women, but he really was a family man. He loved his home. He had begun to drink after arguments or hard words with Carlene. He wanted more children, Carlene wanted neither him nor more children. Then he would be angry and sulk until he went to see his daughter.

One evening he returned late from a business trip. The day had ended with a few drinks to celebrate a business success with his associates. He left these friends to go visit his current lady, who was not in because she had not expected him. He felt no special tie to this woman so was not disturbed at her absence. He would have stayed the night had she been in, he paid the rent. Instead he chose to go home, a two-hour train ride.

He had a few private drinks on the train, feeling sorry for himself.

He was so alone. The house was dark when he arrived. He went in to see his daughter, his love. He lay beside her, loving the child in his heart. He kissed her brow, smoothed her hair, smiled down at her, then lay his head upon her pillow and fell asleep. During the night he woke up cold and, lifting the covers, he got in beside her.

Now perhaps he was not an evil man, this man. Maybe he thought he was with his city woman, but that woman was certainly not a virgin. Or he just what . . . ? He made love to his daughter sometime during that night. Why did she not scream out? This man was her father. In her own heart, was she grateful to be in his arms? Did she know the loneliness, the need in his soul, that would make him do this horrible thing? What were her thoughts? This child who was also lonely. In need, not of this kind of love, but to be touched, held by someone she knew loved her? She did not understand just what he was doing, but she knew if someone came in, it would be wrong. She cried, but softly. During his orgasm, he became wide awake. He could not stop himself, but he froze in his position, staring down at her. Her eyes were open, filled with tears, but there was no look of accusation on her face. He stealthily arose, cleaned his daughter with his shirt. Then she spoke, softly, through her tears. "Dadda, you hurt me. I hurt."

His tears came. "Dadda is so sorry, baby. So sorry, so sorry. Hush, now, hush. Don't cry." He looked around the room, bleary eyed, saw her pills her mother kept for her when she was getting hysterical and found the one he wanted. He gave her some water, she took the pill. He stayed with her, talking her to sleep. "Dadda so sorry, my baby. This will never happen again."

"You . . . you pro . . . mise?"

"I promise from the bottom of my heart."

"I hurt."

"I know. Oh, I know. Go to sleep, baby, go to sleep."

He stole away to his room. He lay in his bed, alone, crying quietly in that deep hoarse way men have, until the sun came up. Then he fled quietly away to the train and the city. And left Richlene . . . alone.

Richard went directly to his mother's house. He sent a message to Carlene that his mother Marian was ill and he would be staying with her until she recovered, taking care of his business from there. His mother was happy to have him there and was pleased Carlene had not come with him. She could tell he was disturbed about something, but she did not ask any questions. She took it for granted his wife made him unhappy. "I hope my dear son is planning a divorce," she thought. "I cannot bear the thought of that . . . woman spending my money after I have gone from this earth." Even though her husband was dead and she was alone, she simply continued maintaining the schedule she always kept in the huge mansion. Chapel in the mornings, full breakfast and dinner services at the long, formal dining room table with the crystal and gold-laced lemoges plates, chandelier or candles lighted. Servants served and waited behind her chair as she quietly ate the several courses prepared every day. So she was pleased to have her son with her for a while.

Richard's conscience bothered him a great deal. He could not sleep, tossing and turning all night, every night. He walked and walked over the acres of land. He sat staring into space. Finally, one night, after a dinner he had hardly touched, he spoke of his problem to his mother as they sat before the great fireplace that crackled with flames. His remorse bore heavily on him. In self-degradation, he told her what had happened, what he had done to his child, Richlene.

Marian continued staring into the fire but said nothing for long moments. When, at last, she turned to him, she looked at him for a long time. Her eyes made a slight, inner shift and she was looking beyond him. When she rose to leave, she passed him and placed her hand on his bent shoulders, pressing his shoulders for a long moment. "You are my son," she said. "You did not intend to do it. It was not done with . . . evil intent. You have not done as much wrong as you may think." She began to walk away then stopped, turning back to him. "We shall never speak of . . . this . . . again." Then she was gone.

Richard sat until the fire burned down, shaking his head no when the servant indicated putting logs on the fire. He sat until twilight was gone and the shadows darkened the huge mansion where two bodies, mother and son, stayed in opposite ends. Only the servants, unobtrusive, moved about, quietly doing what was necessary for the two lonely people in their strong city of wealth.

Satan thought, I give those people everything! Why aren't they happy? Busy as always, he flew off to finish giving suggestions to the scientists he was helping to discover something in the earth that might finally destroy the earth. He went happily.

When Richard returned to Yoville, Richlene was shy of him but so glad to have her "dadda" back home. Everything seemed the same as before. But Mana, the Negress, Richlene's second mother, knew something had happened in the way people who love you know things about you. Mana had told Sally because she trusted her and knew her love for Richlene was honest. They both talked to Richlene who, in her simplicity, saw no reason to hide anything. Mana was angry; Sally was confused, could not understand. However, no one told Carlene.

One day, soon after his return, Sally passed Richard in the hall as she went about her house inventory chores. She looked into his eyes trying to see deeply into his mind. She saw pain . . . and fear. They said nothing at first. Then Sally spoke, "Richard, you must never, for any reason, place yourself and your daughter in such a circumstance again."

"Oh, Sally," he began anxiously. His voice was full of remorse.

She did not let him finish speaking. "No one ever 'intends' to, they say. But you, her father, must never lose your self control again. She is your child. She is not responsible. I thought you loved her. The only one who loved her. You were all she really has. You ARE all she has. Let us pray her mind will survive the memory and may God have mercy on you. Now, let us put these thoughts away, forever, if possible." She started to move on.

"Oh, Sally," he began once more.

She swung her body back to him. "No one ever prays in this house! They know no god but themselves and gold and stocks! Build us a chapel or a place we may pray . . . together! Everything in this world, this house, can be lost. Wisdom is needed in this house." She moved away hastily.

Later, when Richard was telling Richlene about the little chapel he was building, Mana told him, "Build it a little way from this house so people can go in privacy if they want to and won't nobody be laughin at em for goin!"

Richard looked at her, "You think someone would laugh at a person going to church to pray?"

Mana put her hands on her hips and asked, "You ever been to any church?"

He shook his head and said, "No."

"Then just do what I ask you, please." And so it was done.

Mana and Richlene used the small chapel. Sally went there daily, even if only for a few moments. Richard would go there occasionally and sit very still as though he were waiting for something.

Several months later after another business trip, Richard went to Richlene's rooms to visit her. He was hugging Richlene and happened to look over her head, finding himself looking into the angry eyes of Mana. He smiled anyway and said, "Good evening, Mana."

"Good evenin, sir." She pursed her lips as if she was willing herself to speak or not to speak.

He held Richlene away from him; she was laughing up at her father. "Richlene, you are gaining weight!"

"She sure is gainin weight!" Mana's hands went to her hips.

"I have seen how much more she is eating. Good! She has a healthy appetite." Richard laughed.

Mana patted her foot. "Yes, suh, she's eatin aplenty . . . now."

Richard sensed there was something else Mana wanted to say. He smiled, thinking, "Darkies are so strange. Why should she be afraid to speak to me?" Aloud he said, "What is it, Mana? Why does her appetite worry you? She is still a growing young girl of fourteen."

Richlene said proudly, "Four . . . teen and a . . . a half, Dadda."

Mana lowered her voice but still spoke with anger, "She is eatin for two, Mr. Befoe."

It took a moment for the words to sink in. His smile drained from his face. "For two?" he asked vaguely.

"For two, I 'magin. Only God knows just how many for sure."

Richard sat down clumsily. "Oh, my God, I don't know . . ."

Surprisingly, Mana's voice softened, "You do know . . ."

He looked into Mana's eyes. He could see she knew all that had happened. He moaned, "Oh, my God, my God."

"No, Mr. Befoe, not your god, your little chile. This little chile here."

He wiped his brow. "How long, how far along . . ."

"Too far, Mr. Befoe, she is already showin. One of them operations could kill her. Betta she have this baby and you all can do what you wants to. But she could have her life over again. One of them operation things might take her on away from . . . us. And I know she sho don't deserve that."

Richlene sat at her father's feet, looking up at him. "I am . . . miss . . . ing my monthly, Dadda." She smiled. They did not think she really understood.

Richard could only wipe his brow, shake his head and say, "Dear Lord."

Mana continued, "She got bout four more months to go. You got to think of something fore her time comes. You know, she can have that baby here at home. Most all these womens round here do. We got Ma Lal and that daughter of hers, Ma Mae. Then . . . I'll take care it, I'll raise it at my house."

Richard stood, "Don't be absurd, Mana." But he was thinking about what she had said.

"Scuse me, Mr. Befoe, but I am not the ab . . . surd person round here."

Richlene looked from one to the other of the people she loved. "Dadda? Why you fuss with . . . Mana?"

"Daddy is not fussing, sweetheart. Mana is right." He seemed not to know which way to turn. "I, Dadda is going . . . right now. I'll be back to . . . tuck you in bed." He looked at Mana.

Mana spoke softly, "You know she gettin too old to be tucked in bed, but you come on back, Mr. Befoe, and tuck your chile in bed like you been doing for years when you home. I'll be here."

Richard went to find Sally. Anxious, distraught, and almost in tears, he told her that Richlene was going to have a baby. "MY baby," he whispered in agony.

"Oh, Richard, Richard," she whispered back as her back bent with the news. Sally was quiet a moment, then she straightened up. "We will do nothing now. We will see that Richlene is healthy. I shall take her one day on a train ride and we shall go to Pittsburgh or some large city and see a doctor. If you tell Carlene. . . . Don't tell Carlene. Don't tell Carlene, yet. Let her, just let everything happen naturally. She will see . . . soon enough." And so they did. And so Carlene did, two months later in Richlene's eighth month.

Satan had not liked Sally, now he did not like Mana. She was not without her wrongs, but she didn't help him much at all. But then, Satan does not like anyone. He was amused at the situation though, as usual.

chapter

2 0

ℳana and Sally had dressed her in wide, loose clothes and Carlene seldom really looked at Richlene anyway, but, one day, she did.

One morning, Richlene was out in the gardens helping Joel Jones, the gardener, dig and place the plants and bulbs. She was laughing and playing with Joel's little son, Lucas. Carlene came out of the house to go to the horse stables. She looked and paid attention only to the fact that Richlene always seemed to be around a Negro. She thought as she stopped, "She likes niggers! It's because of that Mana of hers that I can't seem to tear her away from!" Then, she thought of Joel being a man. "Richlene is almost fifteen now, she is too old to be alone with Joel so much." Joel was her best horse man and had been for several years. He gardened because he liked it and it brought in a little extra money for his new family he was beginning with his wife Ruth. "Or," Carlene thought, "because he has his black eyes on Richlene because she is so dumb!"

"Richlene!" she called, "Richlene! Come here! It is too hot for you to be out here doing work like this! Go inside the house. Take a nap . . . do something else!"

Richlene rose from the ground slowly, wiping her hands on the apron Mana had given her to wear for yard work. She said nothing as she walked toward her mother, her face half-turned to the side, looking at her mother. The extra weight and size of her stomach made her walk a bit wide-legged.

Carlene's eyes slowly moved down Richlene's body. The thought took a moment to materialize. "Why does Richlene look so funny? What's the matter with her legs?" Then her eyes slowly moved up Richlene's body and the bulging stomach stopped her eyes. Carlene opened her mouth to speak then stopped, then started again. "What's the matter with your stomach, Richlene?"

Richlene looked down, saying nothing. Then, she looked back into her mother's face, still with her own face turned to the side as she reached Carlene. Carlene snatched the apron to the side and up . . . and there Richlene stood, her pregnancy large and so obvious. Carlene gasped, her hand flew to her mouth.

"Richlene!" Her voice was harsh, "What has happened to you?!" She threw the apron tail at Richlene and looked at Joel. "Joel! What have you done to my daughter?! Why, you black nigger bastard!" Then she screamed for help. "Mana! You black bitch! Sally!" She screamed louder. "Joel, don't you move! I'm calling the sheriff! I will have you killed for this! She is a white woman. A child!"

Mana had come. "Mrs. Befoe, Joel ain't done none of that! Joel is a good man what got his own new family. He love Richlene like a chile!"

Carlene was livid. "Then who the hell did it?! And how do you know what Joel does? Call the sheriff! I pay you to watch my daughter and look at her! She is going to have a baby! A baby! Or it's the biggest tumor I've ever seen! A grandmother! I'll be a grandmother! Call the sheriff, I said! Don't you move, Joel! I'll kill you myself!"

Mana only raised her voice a little, "Call the sheriff if you want to, but Joel ain't done this." Softer, she spoke to Richlene, "Come here Richlene, come here, baby."

Carlene snatched at Richlene, "Keep your black hands off my child. You are fired! All of you niggers are going to get off my land. You are all in this together somehow!"

Richlene raised her hands in fear. "No, no . . . you . . . can't make . . . MMMana go. My Mana . . . is . . . mine. You . . . cccan't make MMana go!" Richlene spoke so seldom, everyone turned to her. She held their attention for only a moment though.

Carlene became even more angry. "I'll see about that! You just go into the house. Joel, don't you dare move from here till the sheriff comes." Sally was hurrying to the little group of screaming and crying people.

Richlene seemed no longer afraid. "You can't make Jo . . . el go. I will tell my dadda! Jo . . . el is my friend."

Carlene's voice was ugly. "So I see. Look what your friend has done to you."

"Jo . . . el didn't . . . do . . . any . . . thing to me."

Sally moved into the circle. "Joel didn't do anything to her."

Carlene ignored everyone except Richlene. "Then what is wrong with your stomach, you little fool? You are so dumb, you wouldn't know what anyone was doing to you!" She turned to Sally, "Send for the sheriff!"

Richlene looked down at her stomach. "It just . . . grew out."

Sally spoke quietly, trying to quiet Carlene. "She is going to have a baby."

Carlene was still shouting, "I can see that! Whose baby is it if it is not Joel's?! She never goes anywhere or sees anybody! The only people she's around are Mana and Joel, you and me and her father!" It became suddenly quiet. Everyone was silent. They all looked at Carlene sadly. Mana held Richlene protectively. Joel stood there, but he was shaking with fear, thinking, "White folks can do whatsomever they wants to . . . and rich white folks can do more than that! They can kill me! What will Ruth and my babies do? Oh, God, Oh God, help me please. I ain't done nothin to nobody!" He reached for his son, Luke, who had begun to whimper as Carlene kept pointing and screaming at his father.

Carlene looked around at all of them, one face at a time. Then she gasped, her eyes grew wide. Her voice low and menacing. "Are you trying to tell me . . . Richard did . . . You lie! All of you."

Mana spoke, "We ain't told you nothin, 'cept Joel didn't do it."

Sally reached for Carlene's shoulder. "Let us go into the house. Go on about your business, Joel."

Carlene jerked her shoulder away. "Don't you try to act like you run this house. I told Joel to stay!"

Sally took Carlene's shoulder again. "He did not do it, Carlene, there is no need for the poor man to be frightened to death!"

Mana was leading a crying Richlene into the house. Sally followed. Carlene threw a last look at Joel then stomped to the house behind the others, speaking to Sally, "Don't you think you are taking over here! I'll get to the bottom of this."

Sally still spoke quietly, "Let us go into the house. Other people who have nothing to do with this can hear you, and this is Richlene's life."

Remembering this on this morning, Carlene clenched her fists as she looked through the windows at the hills beyond the river, not seeing them. Today, as always, she remembered that day so clearly.

She remembered how, when at last the truth was understood, she had raged and wept, then raged again. She seemed a distraught mother concerned for her child, but she was not thinking of Richlene. She was thinking of herself and how all this would reflect on her family name. How it would look to people. Her social life. If she could dislike Richlene more, she did.

"I will have her operated on. I will get rid of that . . . that . . . thing!"

But, later, Richlene placed her arms over her stomach protectively, and she didn't stutter but once. "N . . . No, this is my baby. I want my baby. This my baby. I will not let my baby go away. This my baby."

Sally moved to stand beside Richlene. "It is too late. She might die. She must have the baby. Then . . . you can give it . . ." Sally frowned at the thought she could not complete.

Carlene turned in anger, "You're goddamned right I can! And I will!" Then she left them, flinging herself away to her rooms.

c h a p t e r
2 1

There had been a great sadness and even pain inside Carlene as she threw herself across her bed. Her beautiful, lacy, satin, plush bed. She cried from anger and sadness. Alone all her life, whether she admitted it or not, this was another pain of life. Not being together with anyone. Unused to admitting and facing pain, she was in turmoil over something that could not be hidden or paid to go away. Her mind turned to Richard senior, her lover, the love of her life, she thought. She raised reddened, tearful eyes to the heavens and cried, "Look what he had done to us. Oh, where are you, when I need you so much! Why didn't you live!?" She tossed her body, turning to face the ceiling, tears in her eyes. "He has violated, abused our love child. OUR child. The only thing you ever gave to me, from the few short weeks of happiness we shared. Oh, if only our love could have been fulfilled. I have never felt anyone like I felt you. I have never loved anyone as I love you now. Oh, Richard, I could welcome you to my arms, my bed, my life and be damned to everyone else! Richard, Richard," she cried aloud, "I cannot forget you!"

She raised herself from the bed, sniffling, her face red and puffed. She went to the brandy decanter she kept in her bedroom even then.

Pouring herself a large drink, she continued talking to herself, only this time with a little anger. "What did you do to my body? You pressed your penis into me and drove it all the way into my heart, my very soul . . . And I cannot get it out! I can . . . not . . . tear . . . you . . . out . . . of . . . me." She laughed an ugly laugh. "And now, your son, YOUR SON, has done this to us. He has ruined our child. Our love child."

Carlene poured another drink. One more of many to come. She continued thinking out loud. "But he cannot ruin our love. Let him take her then. I have you." She sat slowly on her bed, her head falling over her breast. "What's wrong with me? I am a full woman. I have a heart. A soul. I need love. First, my father loved a whore and not me any more. And you died. I'm left with nothing." She threw the glass across the room. "I don't want to live!" She cried from deep within her breast for a long moment, then, "But, I won't die! I'll live and make them pay, Richard and Richlene. She has betrayed me, too. No one but you ever really loved me." She took another glass and poured another drink. She smiled to herself as she planned her payment to Richard for the pain he had given her.

When Richard had come home and she had torn him with every vile word she knew, he had left. She did not feel better, but more alone. She blamed him for that also. Holding Richard senior's picture to her breast, she swore on the name of god, her god, she would kill him. The woman even prayed, "Please God, please give me some way to kill him that no one will ever know. Please, please."

Well, Satan was right there listening all the time. He was so pleased with Carlene. He laughed, and it takes something to make Satan laugh. "You will find a way," he smiled at her. "I will help you. You have prayed to the right god for murder. Me." See, until you open your mouth, Satan does not know what you are capable of. He cannot always read your mind, only your words and actions. He made his suggestions to Carlene. She listened and planned all night.

Early the next morning, Carlene left for Philadelphia to see her husband's doctor. Richard was taking medication for blood pressure and a few other minor things. Practically in tears, she explained how concerned she was for Richard. That he did not always take his medicine as he should, that she wanted it sent to her so she could see that things were done as they should be. That the dosage should be stronger, relax him more, slow his heart down so it would not stop or hurt itself. "And," she dabbed at her eyes, "What is he supposed to eat, what should he avoid?"

"I think salt is the worse thing for him," the impressed doctor replied. "We are not completely certain."

"Then he shall have none!" the concerned wife affirmed. Taking a bottle of the new prescription, Carlene walked jauntily away. She stopped at a pharmacy and picked up empty capsules, explaining she had to take a purgative sometimes and hated the taste. Everything was so easy for her.

When she returned home she went to the kitchen, took the salt package and went directly to her room, saying to the cook, "Get more of this salt." Then she took the empty plastic capsules and filled them with salt. She put the new stronger medicine and the salt capsules away, "until the time is right to begin." She smiled to herself and to Richard senior's picture. "I need him to do some things first. But . . . it won't be long." Did it not occur to her she was speaking to him of killing his son?

Satan smiled with a "tsk, tsk, tsk" at Carlene.

c h a p t e r
2 2

The baby, a son, was born, named Carlton and disposed of within a week of his birth. Richlene knew nothing of what was going on around her. Her mother had the doctor keep her full of sleeping medicines. Carlene told him, "because Richlene is so young and has no idea of all that has happened to her, we want to protect her."

Richard insisted on taking over the matter of the baby. All he would later tell was that "it is taken care of." What he had done is secure a small house in Philadelphia, staff it with the necessary people to take care of and raise a child. Mana, older now, was sent with the baby to see that everything was done right and that the child would have love. Richard also changed the baby's name from Carlton to Phillip. "I am going to break this family farce up. Start new." Later when the time came, he would see to the education and continuing needs of this child of his daughter. His son. His grandson, to the world. He would never let Phillip come to Yoville until he was old enough to protect himself from cruelty.

There was never a month that Richard didn't see Phillip. Often he visited several times a week. And after he became ten years old, Phillip accompanied his "grandfather" on many business trips. He was loved by

Mana and Richard and he knew it. Richard even told him of his mother, Richlene. He told him she was ill but that Phillip would see her one day.

Carlene did not know all these things had happened, but she remembered that when Richlene was allowed out of the stupor she had been kept in, she raged and cried and cried, and cried. "She will make herself ill," Sally told Carlene. "You must do something to help the poor child."

Carlene began to think about a suitable husband for Richlene. "With our money, someone will marry a retarded woman. I think a . . . man is what she needs, now that she has known one." No one agreed, but Carlene would not be stopped. She finally talked Richard into finding someone, "an innocuous person, to be sure. Someone who would not mind changing their name to Befoe and becoming a husband to Richlene, who will be a billionairess one day."

That is how Richlene married Arthur, once Corruthers, now Befoe, who worked in one of Richard's firms. The young man, a rather trenchant one, poor, having worked his way through a community college to become an accountant, was in no way going to let this opportunity pass through his fingers without squeezing it with all his might. Richard was heartsick but had no power now with all that Carlene held against him. Richard now stayed away almost completely, as Carlene's father had done. Carlene was unable to start Richard on the pills she had put away until such time as she would be able to use them for her purposes.

Life continued at the Befoes' just as though nothing had occurred. When Richard was home in Yoville, he hardly ever saw or spoke to Carlene except if she asked to speak of business and reports. He withdrew further into himself, giving vent to his passions by making more money and keeping two lonely and greedy women. One was young, one older, so whichever mood he was in could be satisfied. If he wanted to be a boy, he saw the older. If he wanted to feel as a man, he saw the younger. This continued several years. His happiest hours were those he spent with Phillip and Mana, staying where they lived or traveling with his son, his grandson.

When Phillip was old enough to enter a university, Richard stayed in Yoville more so he could be easily reached if needed. A malaise settled in his soul. He, finally, began to go less to the cities on his business. Reports and business visitors were more frequent. He stayed close to his rooms.

Richlene had two children by Arthur. The eldest was a boy, Carlton, because the first child named Carlton did not exist to Carlene, and she had to have a Carlton after her father. The second was a girl, Emily. Carlene liked the boy a bit but did not care for Emily. She finally tired of Richlene's husband Arthur and his groveling ways. "He is making too many children. They may have the name of Befoe, but they are still his! He is not one of us! Get him a divorce and send him away." It had cost a pretty penny; as they said, Arthur was no fool. He remembered why he was there in the first place. Money. He left with quite a bit of it. Richard had been more than kind.

Half the time Richlene did not care about anything that went on around her except for her children. She had liked her husband Arthur but did not love him. He had played games with her and held her in his arms sometimes. He was often gone to some city. In truth, he had cared for Richlene, but he did not like to stay where Carlene was. Richlene did not like her oldest child Carlton very much; he reminded her of her mother. She loved him with reservations. She adored her daughter Emily. The sweetest child in her world. When Arthur left, divorced and sent away at Carlene's instigation, they told Richlene he was gone on business. In time she grew used to him being gone. No one ever said he was never coming back.

Richlene was the only one who ever thought of him and asked about him when she thought of it. Finally Sally said he would not return. "You have divorced him, dear." Richlene never asked again. Carlton did not care about his father; he had his grandmother who did not like his father anyway. Emily was too young at that time to really know much about anything.

As time passed, the malaise of the house spread. Richard seemed to stay even closer to his rooms or his favorite people, venturing outside sometimes to lay back in the cushioned furniture and rest in the sun, looking toward the river for hours.

Mr. Creed, a Negro man who had once worked for Richard, sometimes passed by on his way fishing. He would stop to talk with Richard about politics and Wall Street. Mr. Creed did not know much about these things, but he was interested. He amused Richard Befoe. The acquaintanceship grew. Richard's servant Baily attended his needs, bringing a glass of liquor or a meal to him outside. Baily frowned when he was asked to bring a glass for Mr. Creed. The servant didn't like "uppity niggers, don't know they place!" When the day was over, Richard would retire to his rooms again.

He was a desperately lonely man. All he had was money. Yes, he had his grandchildren. But he didn't like the oldest one, Carlton. He seemed so sly, always to be laughing at you behind his clever eyes. He did like the girl, and often Emily would come to sit with her grandfather, suggesting now and again, "Don't drink so much, grandadda." Then she would help him back to his rooms. He leaned on her and smiled. He would not feel alone for a little while.

Richard didn't drink because he was a drunk. He drank because he was terribly lonely and bored and a drink seemed to help a day pass. That is why when Mr. Creed asked him to go fishing with him one day, he went.

Mr. Creed had retired himself. He was one of those who, as a child, had found and hidden a cache of gold with his father who had sworn him to secrecy. But they had kept their gold buried and continued living as they always had. Working as they always had. The father died and young Creed was guardian of the gold. He married, had three children but only one, a son Lincoln, who lived. When his son became old enough to enter school, Mr. Creed had insisted he go and go and go. Most had laughed at him, thought he was a fool for working hard as he did and spending on that boy to go to some school far off some place. But Mr. Creed persisted, even sending the boy to college when his grades proved to be good. All this was done with some of the gold. By then his son knew about the gold, how to transfer it and make transactions, and Mr. Creed never suffered the calamity of Joel and Ruth. He had trusted no one but his father and his son.

When Creed worked for Richard Befoe, he always worked around to where Richard was and talked a little bit of crops, weather, hunting and horses. Making an acquaintance. Until now, they had come to speak of life and money. Came the day Richard spoke of investments, lacking the usual companionship of men like himself, and Mr. Creed listened avidly, sending the advice to his son. So his money had grown. He continued to visit with Richard when he saw him sitting outside. Not just because of the money, but because he felt sorry for this man who had everything . . . and nothing. Mr. Creed's wife had died of something money might have helped, but Mr. Creed did not bring his gold out in time to save her. That bothered him sometimes. He had held on to the gold longer than he had her. He didn't like to think of it in that way.

Mr. Creed was lonely also, but not the same kind of lonely Richard Befoe was. Except for not saving his wife in time, Creed had good memories. Memories are blessings when they are good.

Mr. Creed liked Richard sincerely. He wanted to do something for him to alleviate his sadness, his aloneness. One day he suggested a walk to the river. They did that several times. Then he suggested an overnight fishing trip, it was so beautiful on the river at night. They went finally to stay overnight in a place Creed knew. Richard had little interest in fishing, but he lay back on the thick soft grass, surrounded by berry bushes and tall, quiet trees outlined against the sky. He stared at the clear, bright, glittering stars. His heart filled up until his throat hurt him; he cried. Creed heard him, but thought it best not to say anything. It was a harsh, quiet, hacking cry. The sound of pain. The sobs finally dwindled into the sounds of the wind rustling. Richard fell asleep under the stars to the sounds of the night, only to awaken to the same barren life. Though he found, somehow, he had been comforted a bit just by feeling free a little while.

On the way home, Creed tried to find someway to speak to Richard, to console him, to give him some kind of hope. They were passing through the shadows of the tall trees, listening to the sounds of all the life around them, hearing the sound of the river rushing past them as if eager for its destination. Mr. Creed ventured, "Ain't it somethin! All this here beauty out here just for us! God sho is good to us!"

Richard smiled indulgently. "Do you really believe in all that? I thought you were an intelligent man, Creed." He bent under a branch in his path.

Creed smiled back. "It sure must'a took a lot of intelligence to do all this here, don't you think? God ain't no fool, now, no suh!"

Richard, still smiling, looked at him, and shook his head, "Just what does God do for you, Creed. Look where he left your people so long. Look where you are now, for that matter. What good does He do you?"

"Wellllll, suh," Creed rubbed his near-bald head and smiled again, "You got to put the blame where it be due! I blive there is a devil, and God say he is mighty busy separating people with hate. It's been some mighty mean and evil people in this here world. Still is, and always will be till the end of these times, Bible say. Life, somebody else's life, don't mean a thing to them. You got to blame them."

Richard brushed a cottontail weed stuck to his pants leg. "That's what I mean, Creed, what did God do for you all with people like that?"

"Why, we survived, Mr. Richard, we survived. Now, we free. Pretty soon, ain't no tellin! This's just 1914. Times is still hard, but they ain't as hard as they was. We can get education now. Best thing is, we free!"

The indulgence stayed on Richard's face as he continued to smile. "It takes a mighty little to make you happy, so I guess your God is good for you."

They were almost at the clearing, the road to the Befoe house was just ahead, here is where they would part until next time. Richard looked at Creed expectantly, so Creed answered, "Mighty little? Oh, I know. You mean I ain't got much. You mean money? Big houses? One of them new-fangled automobiles? Well, He gave me something nobody can't take away. He made me so I can see all this beauty. EVERY day, every season. He make me know something is way bigger than me. Another thing He let me know, ain't nothin a man can think mean a damn-gone thing to me, lessin he got my life in his hands. But the best thing? Was love, suh. Oh, yeah. He teach me bout love. I loves everything. See, like, one of them fish I catch ain't got a mean look in his eye and be too young to die, I throw em back. I love them, too. Mr. Richard, you can't beat love. Ain't NOTHIN better than love . . . for anything. Make you feel good, make you beautiful inside. God gave me that." He stopped a moment, took a deep breath. "And Mr. Richard, I don't mean no harm, but . . . I ain't cryin at night fore I goes to sleep. I smile and thank God for another day." He wiped his head again, smiled gently and looked serious. "Now you let me know when you wants to go fishin again. I'll be ready. We ain't seen all the beauty yet!"

But Richard stopped him. "If that's how you feel, why do you take up your time with me, try to get information from me about stocks and such?"

"Well, Mr. Richard, it ain't the stocks and such what makes me come round you. It's cause . . . I think you got some nice . . . things inside you. I think you don't mean no harm to nobody, though God knows with that bullet makin factory you got, somebody gettin harmed. But . . . I don't think you thinks of that. I . . . just . . . think you a nice man. And you don't find too many nice people in this world sometime. So I comes to see you. That's all is why." Creed could not, would not, say he felt sorry for Richard. So they parted. Richard was not smiling, nor was he angry for more than a minute. He was thoughtful.

Now Satan knew these men were talking. He knew Creed, and he knew Richard certainly. But he did not care about two old men talking about life and him. He knew the munition plants Richard was invested in would run long after Richard was dead. Satan was busy with other thoughts. He was bored. He had ravaged life long before Babylon, Greece, Rome, China and Egypt. He had helped create wars all over Europe with greedy and envious, rapacious hearts. Inquisitions. Asia, India, Spain—where had he not been busy? Adolf, with such persuasive powers, now had to be prepared, his mind to be groomed and twisted. The large expanse of Russia. Alllll those people, what a war they could make! He loved Vatican City, because they loved gold. There were a few sincere people in all that mask of righteousness, but they were not enough to count. What, or who, can stop hatred and greed in mankind? Even for no gain, a little malice can work wonders.

"Show me," Satan laughed up at God. "Show me I am wrong!" But now . . . now . . . he was bored. He was working on scientists, inventors. He had led many who were once peaceful in the country to desert their old homes and families to find their ways to cities. Even whole families were led there by those who promoted poverty. Satan smiled, "More temptations. Where they would prefer money to peace." He was working on a device that would bring strangers with their strange ideas into the homes of everyone in the world. Oh, they could do good with it, but, knowing mankind, he knew the liars and thieves would use it, too. And this land was new! It is time for wars to begin. The slaughter of the sons! And those left to have the burden of paying for that slaughter. He was tired of wars that killed one or two men at a time. It could be hundreds! Thousands at a time! He had been working on that a long time now. So they had abolished slavery, let there be a new slavery—be free, yet work for the government. Income tax must, would pass. Something must pay for these new inventions and wars. Satan was too busy to stay with such little people as Richard or Creed, or even Carlene. He had so much to do, and he was bored. And so . . . he flew away on his business. God looked down upon this. He shook His head, for He had a plan, and He knew Satan knew that plan, and He knew woe would be heavy on the earth. The people would be laden with woe, but they would laugh at the way out of that woe. They would not believe God, they would continue to place their trust in governments, and the governments would fuck them to death with lies.

c h a p t e r
2 3

When Richard reached home, there was a message that his mother was dying and he must come to her house at once. He made arrangements to go immediately. The message also stipulated that if he came, he was to come alone. As he packed and gave orders to Baily, he wondered why his mother disliked Carlene so much. But there was no time to think now. He sent a message to Carlene by Baily that he was leaving and why.

Now though Carlene hated Richard and his mother, she knew Richard would be inheriting many millions of dollars. There was no other heir. She nodded her head quickly to the message and went to his rooms. Richard was astonished. Carlene had not been in his rooms in years. She took his hands, pressed them to her breast, then reached up and drew him to her body, patting his back with loving concern. "Oh, Richard, I do not know what to say at such a terrible time as this." She already knew the message had asked that she not come with him. "I will go with you, it will only take me a moment to pack a few things."

Richard stepped back from her, shaking his head, and said, "No, no, I will be alright. No need to disturb you." But Carlene persisted, know-

ing she was not going. "But I am your wife. I should be at your side."
Richard assured her, "I will be alright. I will let you know what is
happening." She, reluctantly, gave in to him, going sadly to her rooms.
She did wave good-by to him from the door when he left.

When at last Richard arrived by train, he rushed to his mother's
home, the mansion. He had not thought of the money, the property he
would inherit. He had so much of that. He was truly concerned for his
mother. In a moment he did not understand, he wished for Mr. Creed,
but that passed quickly. His thoughts returned to his mother. He rushed
past the servants to her room.

She was lying back on the finest cotton and lace pillows, the yellow
satin quilt covering her added a sicker color to her already dying gray
skin, her frail body was hardly a lump in the bed. She seemed to be
dozing, her breath rasping lightly. When Richard came quietly into the
room, she turned her head, slowly, to face him. He could tell she was in
pain. The lines were etched deeply in her face.

"Mother, I am here. Oh, are you in much pain? Why didn't you tell
me, send for me before now?"

"I cannot remember when I have not been in some kind of pain. Sit
down, Richard." He had to bend down to hear her.

"Should I call your nurse or the doctor to give you something for the
pain?"

"There is no medicine to stop my pain. Let it be."

Richard lay his head on the bed beside her, holding her hands, pressing them to his lips.

"Stop, Richard, stop. There is not much time. Let me just . . . be
. . . and enjoy your visit."

"Oh, Mother. I have been so busy with my own life. The banks, the
plants, Richlene. I have not given you enough time. Perhaps I could have
found . . ."

"How is . . . Richlene?"

"Your granddaughter is . . . doing much better. She has her own
family, you know that. She can talk, Mother, she can talk. I plan
to . . ."

"Richard . . . Richlene is not my granddaughter."

"What are you saying?" He smiled gently. "She is my child, she loves
you. She always wants to visit you."

His mother tried to raise her head and shoulders from the bed. She began to gasp a little from the effort. "I said . . . she is not my grand-daughter."

"Mother! Please lie down. Rest. Do not exert yourself. I don't want you to die!"

Her voice was little more than a whisper. "I am not going to die until I tell you what I want you to know. I don't want . . ." Anger, disgust choked her, she coughed, then continued, "that harlot to control you and your fortune for one more minute." She reached out to him. "Lift me, raise me up. I cannot speak well."

Richard assisted her hesitantly. "Mother, Mother . . . it can wait. You must try to live. Live."

She shook her head ever so slowly. It took all of her strength. "It cannot wait, I have already waited for more than forty years. From the time I knew what your father was . . . waited for this very day."

"Mother, what are you saying? Lie down please."

"You are my son. I believe I love you. But . . . you are a fool."

"Why, I am taking care of everything, Mother. I have lost nothing of ours. I have added to our fortune by a great deal."

"Business and property are not all of life. I know now. I have had nothing but things. Things. You can weigh gold, but you cannot see . . . life."

"But I have a family . . . like you always . . ."

"Hush . . . be quiet, my son. You do not have a family. I did not have a family from the day I left my father's home . . . with Richard . . . until you were born. You do not have a family."

"Richlene is my family."

"Richlene is not your child."

Richard drew back from the bed. "You are ill indeed! You are losing your mind."

"Richlene is your father's child. You were blinded. Made a fool of." She took a deep wavering breath. "Don't you remember the beginning of your courtship? And who Carlene was with most of the time?" Her illness forced her to fall back on the bed. Spittle gathered at the corners of her dry, parched lips. "Richlene is your father's child."

Richard stared at his mother, dropping her hand without being con-scious of it. She was gasping for breath, the sound of her rasping filling the quiet, darkened room. Her eyes were open wide, staring at her son, desperately trying to say all she had held in her heart for so many years. She was not thinking of the pain she was giving her son, the misery.

"He made my life meaningless. He destroyed my womanhood, my vanity, my joy in being myself. He loved other women so, he made me feel ugly, unwanted and useless. No matter what I did for him, he always had someone else to give the love he should have given me. He had my mind, my nerves, my love . . . so . . ."

They were both silent. Richard staring at her with horror, her eyes closed in exhaustion. A sob tore from Richard's throat. "But, why, why tell it now, Mother?"

Sweat from her efforts had dampened her gray hair and it clung in tendrils around her darkening face. "Because . . ." She reached for his hand, weakly. "Because you ARE my son. Because you DO love me . . . not just the money." Her last gasps hung on the heavy air of the room and stayed there in the silence, screaming. "I mean to help you. Would you rather have made . . . love . . . with your daughter than with your sister?" She lay her head down slowly, breathed once more. She was dead.

Richard sat there, tears streaming down his face. Crying. Crying for what? His daughter who was not his daughter? His father who had betrayed him in the worse possible way? His mother who hated his father more than she loved him, her son, or she would not have hurt him like this . . . now? He was human. He cried for himself.

Later, at the family plot, the private cemetery on their land, Richard's eyes were red, puffed but dry as they lowered his mother into the ground beside his father. Not too many people were there. The few who came had known Marian many years. Had worked for her or were truly her friends. Richard had cried all his tears. He was now thinking of his life.

Carlene sent many messages. She wanted to come "be in my place at your side," she said. But in truth, she wanted to roam through the house, look at the things that had belonged to Richard the elder. Take and keep something of his. And, of course, to take any of the many treasures the mansion held. Weren't they hers now? she thought. Richard sent the final message, "I think you had better not come. Thank you." So she waited.

Before he left that home he planned to return to one day and live in, he finally decided what he would do about what he had been thinking about. He had his father's grave dug up and the decaying casket moved to a place in the chicken yard that was kept thriving on the estate. The gravediggers thought he was "going off his ticker." But he paid them well and, after a few drinks over the shovels, they laughed him away. He left the gravestone off. His farewell words to his father were, "You will have chickenshit for a gravestone. I will see that you have it for all of my life, until it is forgotten you are here."

Then, he went home to Yoville and Carlene.

Though Richard did not change his way of being after he returned from his trip, Carlene knew that he knew . . . something. There was a difference. The distance now between them was made by him. This did not make her feel ashamed or hurt; instead, she became angry.

Carlene had been planning his death for many years. She still held the capsules, but time had passed and she had never used them. Either he had bought his own medicine while on his travels or he was gone so often she could not set up a regular system. But now, he was home much more often for longer periods of time. Now she wanted him gone . . . for good. She bought a new supply and prepared them once more.

She had, for the last eight months or so, taken charge of his medicine. Sending for it, issuing it to Baily, who did not see the necessity for any change from the old way but who questioned nothing. Richard held up well, but he was tired more often now. Carlene thought, "If there was just something, anything, to excite him, scare him, shock him, I believe it would kill him. He is dying on his feet! What is taking him so long?! Maybe that doctor lied about that salt, that medicine!"

She was too cautious to ask any other doctor or person. "I have time, what the hell!" So she waited.

She was still waiting this morning as she sat before her pictures, thinking over her life, the past, the present, the future. The spider slept and waited. And Yinyang was on her way.

·   ·   ·

The sun was getting warmer as the day moved on. Yin had not found the little shack Josephus had told her about. She would need rougher clothes and shoes. She planned to go back again, soon. She was not giving up. She had to make her life.

Now, Yin held her head high with a serious, little hat perched on it, stepped firmly to the main road and turned in the direction of the Befoes.

When she reached the walkway of the Befoes' huge, immaculate house with its manicured lawns, she almost hesitated, but her feet went down to the ground and forward as if of their own will, and she started the walk of 150 feet or so to the wide front terrace-porch. She could see a man sitting there—a white man with a Negro man sitting sideways on the porch steps. They both watched her as she came toward them. She did not smile. She looked what she thought was businesslike, serious but pleasant. Her heart beat wildly. "This is my life," she thought. Mr. Befoe didn't turn his eyes away; he smiled slightly as she reached the house.

chapter
2 4

The picture of Richard, her husband, lay face down on the desk, and Carlene's thoughts returned to herself. She caressed the picture of Richard the elder, her lover. She was about to pick his picture up again and pour herself another drink, when she heard voices floating lightly on the air coming through her window. "Why it sounds like a woman's voice. A young woman's voice." She leaned forward to her window to see who Richard might be talking to. She saw a pretty, young woman, not too young, but young. Very neat, crisp white blouse beneath a navy blue, well-cut suit of the latest style. The dark shining hair was pulled severely back and topped with a small but charming hat. Carlene leaned closer to the window, not caring whether she was seen or not.

"Has one of his bitches come here to find him? No, no that is not a whore, she looks like a lady. What does she want with Richard? Oh, the bank, maybe. Or a lawyer, that dumb man Syntoll. But what is she doing here?"

The spider awoke and moved further back into the corner as the movement and sounds came close to it. "I don't like all this light," the spider thought. "I need the darkness. My own home." She moved cautiously out of the corner of the window as Carlene reached for the bellpull to call Minna. The spider's legs rushed over the sill and down, down beneath the top of the desk until it found shadows shading into darkness, then she rested briefly. When she had adjusted to the darkness, she could take her time finding her future home, her nest for her babies. "There are so many wonderful places here." And she began to spin the web she would need for sustenance. After long hours it would be connected to several things which gave her more avenues for search. She rested. And waited.

Carlene rang for Minna and waited, and as she waited she could hear the voices through the open window, but not clearly.

Yinyang was arriving.

She had watched the men watching her approach; Yin spoke first, "Good morning."

Mr. Befoe nodded, saying, "Good morning." Mr. Creed just nodded.

She stepped up on the first step. "I am . . . my name is Yinyang Krupt. I am here to find . . . inquire about," her voice grew strong, "my house. I understand . . ."

Mr. Befoe nodded again, "Yes, I know the house, certainly. I think we've been taking care of the place, taxes, yard work."

Yin thought, "You know you haven't." But said, "Well, sir, I intend to pay you . . . all you have spent on my house and the land." She decided to smile, thinking, "Hell, what does a smile hurt?"

Richard Befoe smiled. "Mrs.? Krupt."

"Miss."

"Well, Miss Krupt, I have a law office here in town, I keep my records there. There is an attorney there, Syntoll. He will help you find out . . ."

Yin continued to smile in what she thought a business manner, "I've already spoken to him, he said I must see Mr. Befoe because he keeps all the records here at his home."

Richard frowned, he didn't care for Mr. Syntoll anyway. He talked too much without knowing what he was doing. Richard already had an older, more settled and experienced man in mind, a recent widower, who would be willing to take Syntoll's place and live in such a place as Yoville. But now, he said, "Did he now?" looking at Yin's clear and lovely smile.

"Yes. I have looked at my place, Mr. . . . ?"

"Befoe. Richard Befoe."

"Mr. Befoe, I have looked at my place and there does not seem to have been a great deal of money spent on it."

"Well, ten years is a long time."

Yin looked down for a moment, then up at Richard, still smiling agreeably, "I don't count money in years, I count money in dollars."

Richard Befoe laughed, his laughter surprised him, and Creed. "What do you intend to do with the place, Miss Krupt? Do you wish to sell it?"

Yin stopped smiling. "Do you wish to buy it?"

Richard was indifferent, "Well, no, there really is quite a bit too much wrong with the place, and then what would anybody want with it?"

Yin smiled lightly. "Good! Because I plan to live there again. It is my home. And since you know it needs so much, then I can't owe too much to reimburse you for all you have spent."

Creed looked down at his foot and laughed silently. Richard glared at him and then laughed out loud. "The early bird gets the worm."

Creed shook his head, "Yea, but the worm was early too, what does he get? Sides gotten?"

Richard looked back to Yin. "I don't think it will be too much, I'll look into it and let you know." His eyes appraised her. Satisfied and curious. She smiled fully, feeling a bit relaxed.

Minna came out of the house and approached them, saying, "Mrs. Befoe say who is the visitor?"

Richard answered, "Yinyang Krupt, her old friend's daughter." Minna left, but returned shortly. "Mrs. Befoe say have Mrs. Krupt come up to her, please."

Carlene was still sitting at her desk going through her mail when Yin was ushered in by Minna. She looked up briefly, nodded, looked back at the mail and said, "Have a seat, Mrs. Krupt. It is Mrs.? Or Miss?"

Yin sat in the seat across from the desk instead of the one beside it. "Miss."

Carlene lay her hand on the desk, "Such a handsome young woman and still unmarried? Or widowed?"

Yin said nothing. She crossed her hands on her lap and waited. Carlene Befoe put her mail down with a sigh. "Invitations. Everyone seems to be having fun."

Yin smiled slightly. "It is nice to be included in their pleasure."

Carlene sighed again. "I probably will not go. The yacht trip sounds interesting, but . . ." She looked directly at Yin. "I remember your mother. We were . . . friends. She met your . . . her husband here in this house. Oh, and I have wondered for years whatever became of a very beautiful diamond ring I . . . loaned her, which she never returned. And then she passed away and I never got my ring back. Do you know of it?"

Yin was a little angry but controlled it. "I seem to remember a ring my mother wore sometimes, but the one I remember was hers."

Carlene picked up the invitations again. "Are you sure?" When Yin did not answer, Carlene looked at her again, smiling. "Yes, the yacht trip sounds good to me, such a beautiful way to travel."

"You should go. It is a beautiful time of year."

"Oh, the date is almost a year away. You know how you have to plan that sort of thing early, there is so much to do to prepare for it. But . . . I'm sure I won't go. I have a bad hip. Gives me problems. Rocking on a boat for two weeks would not be attractive to me."

Yin thought the pain might be what made Mrs. Befoe so discourteous, she felt sorry for her. "You look very well. Surely the hip will not hurt long."

Carlene said dryly, "It hurts almost all the time now. Even if I stay in bed, off my feet."

"To stay in bed is not the best thing for that, I don't think. You should use it, exercise it."

Carlene looked up, interested, laying the mail down again. "You sound as though you are a nurse . . . or something."

Yin smiled. "I know a bit about it. I . . . once nursed a . . .

friend with similar problems." She wanted to change the conversation before this woman started with her crude questions. "Mrs. Befoe, I am here to acquire information regarding my house."

"The Krupt house?"

"Yes, my house."

Carlene was silent a moment. "You resemble your mother. I knew her quite well, before the questionable death of your . . . the Krupts."

"Questionable?"

"Yes, questionable. They could both die of their . . . ailments, but at the same time?"

Yin looked down at her hands. "I know nothing of that. I was a child. I was . . . sent away before their deaths."

"Oh? Where on earth to?"

"New Orleans."

"So, Virginia had relatives in New Orleans?"

"I was sent away to school."

Carlene was silent again for a moment. "Yes, school. There are certainly none worth attending here in Yoville. You've been gone about fifteen years or more."

"Yes. And I would like to know about my house and land. What is the amount required to pay you back?"

Carlene mused, "The bank is the lender."

"I understand Befoe is the bank. How much to pay to the bank then?"

"Did you speak to Mr. Befoe about this?"

"Yes, that is what I was doing when you . . . when I was brought up here to you."

"What did he say?"

"He said it would be checked into. It couldn't be very much."

"I don't know why he said it couldn't be very much." Carlene turned to her mail again.

"Because it is obvious that very little has been done to the house or the yard . . . in fifteen years."

Carlene's face was serious when she turned to Yinyang. "Well, then . . . it will be looked into. Where are you staying? Will you be going back to New Orleans until the matter is cleared up?"

"No. I intend to be here, to help clear it up. I intend to live in my home. I am presently staying at the . . . hotel? with Mrs. Whitman."

Carlene laughed a little. "That must be charming," she said with sarcasm.

Yin smiled but did not laugh. "That is why I am impatient to move into my own house."

"It needs a great deal of repair. Do you . . . work?"

Yin hesitated. "I can . . . teach."

"And . . . you can nurse."

Yin shook her head. "No, there are just some things I know."

"Doctor Dont might need someone like you."

"I am not seeking employment."

Carlene smiled. "Tell me more about my hip. What is better for it?"

Now Yin smiled. "Well, massage works wonders for bones and muscles."

"Do you do that also?"

Yin's smile faded. "I have done it . . . for my friend."

"Was your friend a man?"

"No, I hardly think I would do it for a man. I have never been married."

"But you would for a woman?"

Yin fidgeted with her hands. "If . . . she were my friend."

"Well, then . . . we shall try to be friends . . . at least friendly. I did know your mother, you remember. And you will be needing some funds, if you intend to fix that old house up. I can pay you."

Yin's voice was a bit strained. "Simply help me by giving me the information about my house, and I will pay you."

Carlene's voice hardened a bit. "You seem not to want to help me."

"What I really want, Mrs. Befoe, is to acquire my house, repair it and move in."

Carlene ignored that. "What else have you been doing all these years?"

Yin spoke clearly. "Someday, when I am all settled, I shall come for tea and we can chat. Now . . . I am solely interested in . . ."

"Your house."

"Yes."

Carlene was silent a moment. "How do I know you are the heir?"

"There is no other. Of course, you know."

Carlene looked at Yin a long moment, taking in the clothes, hat and shoes. "You have certainly not suffered."

"Was I supposed to?"

"You are impertinent."

"I am impatient. I do not wish to remain where I am any longer than I have to!"

Carlene tilted her head, saying, "We have a guest room. Upstairs near my sister Sally's room. You could stay there."

"Then you do not think it will be long before my business is cleared up and I can get settled in my house?"

Carlene laughed lightly. "What I am thinking of is my hip . . . and what you may know to help it. The massage. The exercise."

"Mrs. Befoe, there are doctors all over the world that can help you."

"I do not like to travel in pain."

"They would come to you. You are rich."

"One trip. One short trip at a time. That would hardly be significant enough to do any real good. You, on the other hand, will be here."

"Will I?"

They looked at each other a moment. Carlene thought, "This might be the one who can excite Richard to his death."

Yinyang was thinking, "It would be so easy for us to conclude our business. Did she dislike my mother so much? Why? What is it this woman wants from me?"

Yin was not foolish enough to believe that Carlene liked her for herself or that Carlene really wanted to help her, even in return for help with her hip. Yin thought of her last experience with Miss Will and concluded, "It is not sex; Mrs. Befoe nor I are lesbians. I don't think." She looked in Carlene's eyes and saw Carlene studying her in return. "But she wants me for something. Well, I want a rich husband. And a yacht trip. Who will be on that yacht?"

Finally Carlene said, "I see you can only think of your house. I can understand that, although I have never been without one."

Yin spoke softly, "The cost . . . please?"

"Two hundred dollars. That's less than twenty dollars a year for keeping the brush back and other little sundry things that have been done."

"That was not all done for me, that must have been done for you. I will give you one hundred dollars."

"You are indeed impertinent. And you are asking the favor!"

"Mrs. Befoe, I will have a great deal to do to prepare the house for living."

"That is for you. Not for me." Carlene was enjoying herself. She laughed.

Yin laughed, too. "I will give you, if it pleases you, one hundred dollars plus a massage for your hips. I will even teach your maid how to do it for you."

"Accepted. There, see, my soft heart ever defeats me. I can not be hard, no matter how I try."

"Your heart knows."

Carlene looked at Yin to see if she meant more than she said. Then, "You may go now to fetch your things."

Yin rose from the chair. "I have not decided I shall live here as a guest. I will think about it."

"Nonsense. It's all settled. I will have Minna arrange for your things to be delivered."

Yin, standing, said, "Mrs. Befoe, I appreciate your . . . kindness. But we must understand, I do all the decision making for myself. I am not seeking employment. I was not seeking a room. I am doing a favor in kind. I will not be a servant here."

"Why certainly, of course. Whatever makes you think I would want to run anyone's life? Or make their decisions? I've enough to do already. So you will direct your life yourself. But . . . I direct this house. I will have rooms prepared for you upstairs near my sister. It will be ready . . . if you decide to be my guest."

"Thank you, Mrs. Befoe. Now, while I am gone to take care of more of my business, would you arrange to take a very long, hot bath? Soak in it for at least an hour. Then I shall do my best for you with a massage."

Yin left, led by Minna. She passed the gentlemen, Mr. Befoe and Creed, still on the front terrace. Richard smiled at her, saying, "Ahhh, you have met my wife."

Yin smiled back. "I have met your wife. I have seen your lovely home. I have much to do to my own home."

Creed spoke, "I am right handy with hammer and nails and paint. I know a good yard man, too."

Yin laughed. "Will they work for slave labor?"

Creed smiled. "Ain't none of them around now. But we'd give you a good price. Fair price."

Yin smiled down at Creed. "Mr. Befoe will know how to find you?"

Richard said, "He will give you his address himself."

At last, Yin smiled and walked away, haughty and sassy, head held high. Both men watched her. Creed was smiling. Richard was not. He was thoughtful.

Yin saw the lawyer Syntoll on her way back to the rooming house. She told him she had taken care of her business and to prepare papers stipulating payment of the one hundred dollars and medical assistance to Mrs. Befoe. He blinked his eyes in surprise as she continued, "I will pick them up in about one hour."

"Well, Miss Krupt, I can bring them to you."

"I will be living at the Befoes and I can pick them up on my way back there."

His lip dropped. Mouth open, Mr. Syntoll watched her walk away briskly. "Well! That is that!"

If Yin had stayed alone at the rooming house, he might have visited her in the hope that a relationship would create itself. But her being in the Befoe household stopped his plans cold. She would now be occupying a space that would be too large for him, and it quite put him off.

She told Mrs. Whitman she would be moving. Mrs. Whitman placed umbrage on her face until the Befoe name came through her consciousness. She had thought the lawyer Syntoll and Yin had made some headway toward a close relationship and that Yin was moving in with him. In her day, getting her husbands, Mrs. Whitman had done that several times. She was above that now, being too obviously old for it to work any longer. Now, her religion forbade anyone else to do it. The Befoe name stopped her thoughts. She immediately became obsequious.

Yin continued talking, "I do not wish to give up my room, though. I want to leave most of my things stored there." She smiled and looked the woman in the eye. "I have inventory of everything I brought with me, so if anything is ever missing I will be able to let you know just what it is and we can retrieve them. I am sure your help is honest, I was rather thinking of other guests you may have. Now! That reduces the cost for meals and hot water. So I will pay you for the room only, by the week. Occasionally I may sleep here in my rooms."

Yin packed a few things in a smaller bag and Tillis arranged to take her to the Befoes' great house. As she rode in the wagon-carriage Yin prayed, "Please, God, let me work a miracle. Let my fingers remember."

Satan smiled in amusement. "I will be there with some suggestions to make, little one."

c h a p t e r
2 5

minna brought the refill for Mr. Befoe's prescription to Carlene, who closed her door herself and settled down to emptying the real medicine out and replacing it with the salt. It was a tedious job, time consuming. When Minna knocked on her door to say the hot water was ready, Carlene gave a sigh of disgust. She did not want to keep the hot water waiting so she covered the vials and packets with a towel. No one used her bathroom but herself, the medicine work could wait a little while. Then she told Minna to prepare her bath. She intended to hurry the bath soaking only a little, but the water felt good to her aching hips and legs. In fact, she lay there so long that Yin was already settled in her new room and ready to do the massage.

Yin had met Sally briefly; they had smiled and were prepared to like each other, then Yin started down the narrow stairs to go to Carlene's rooms. "Mrs. Befoe must not like her sister very much to put her up in these quarters. Hell! She must not like me either! But this house does not half belong to me like it must her sister. If I was the sister, I wouldn't stay up there. Of course, I'm not going to stay up there long myself."

Richard Befoe was nowhere to be seen.

Yin passed Minna in the hall near Carlene's rooms. "Minna, will you bring an extra sheet to Mrs. Befoe's rooms?" Minna sighed, "Yes'm" and was gone. Yin knocked on Carlene's door and heard the answer, "You wait a minute, Minna!" Yin did not knock again.

When Minna returned with the extra sheet, the two of them stood in the hall, waiting. Minna spoke first, smiling, "My gramma say she was there helpin when you was born."

Yin smiled back hesitantly. "How does she know that? I have not seen her." Minna made a little laugh. "Oh, Miz Yin, this such a little ole town, everbody know when someone new comes here. Everbody know a strange pretty lady is in town. She members your name is Yinzang."

Yin smiled thoughtfully, then, "It's Yinyang. Yinyang Krupt. I will have to meet your gramma. There are some things I would like to know about." Minna smiled, said, "Yes, mam."

Then they heard Carlene's voice calling them in. Carlene stood frowning as Yin spread the sheet across the bed. "Will we really need that? This is not a hospital."

Yin continued her preparations. "This is how I do. Please lie down." Carlene started to lay down in her underwear and nightgown. Yin laughed and said, "You must take that gown off and all those clothes. Leave your underpants on if you like."

Carlene bristled, "Well, I say! I don't like being naked without clothes."

Yin put her hands on her hips. "Oh! Pish-posh! I am a woman, you are a woman! It is not a pleasure of mine to look at naked ladies. If I am to relax and work on your . . . body, I must be able to touch it!" She reached for one of the extra sheets, "Here, wrap this around you and lie on your stomach across the bed."

Carlene wrapped the sheet loosely around herself, saying, "This had better be good!"

"Mrs. Befoe, you demanded this. I did not force it on you."

"Well, continue then. And what must I do now?"

Yin settled the sheet, lightly pushed and pulled Carlene's body in place. "Now . . . just relax. I have a lotion here Minna was good enough to heat for me. It is warm and will be relaxing to your muscles and bones. Which is what we want." Yin moved firmly about the business of massage. "We will have no talking unless I am hurting you, which I am sure I will not."

Carlene's face was buried in a pillow. "Certainly not!"

Yin had removed her suit when she settled in her new room upstairs. She was wearing a long, cream colored skirt and crisp blouse with the sleeves rolled up. Her hair was still pulled back in a severe fashion. She warmed her hands at the small fire in the fireplace and began at Carlene's neck. "Now . . . we begin," she said.

Carlene's muffled voice came, "It is my hip and my legs, not my neck!"

Yin was becoming aggravated. "Do you want me to continue?"

"I'm not sure." Muffled.

"I do not have time to waste or time to coddle. I have other things I must be doing!"

From deep in the pillow, "I am not accustomed to being talked to in that manner."

"And I am not accustomed to giving massages."

"You've never told me what you are accustomed to doing."

"Mrs. Befoe, I have not heard your life story either." Yin pressed down hard on Carlene's shoulders.

A gust of breath flew from Carlene's mouth, "Whooff."

Yin smiled, "We begin again."

Still Carlene complained, "I am sorry I allowed this to happen."

"I can stop. It is your hip." Yin did not stop the smooth movement and pressure of her hands. It did feel good to Carlene.

"Well, we have gone this far . . ."

"Alright then." She smoothed Carlene's shoulders and back with the warm cream and firm touch. She took a long time rubbing the shoulders, spine and sides with a steady, long stroke, sometimes a short, firm one. Carlene was soon totally relaxed. The begging, stiff muscles were slowly letting go, not fighting stiffly anymore. As Yin moved down to the buttocks in firm round strokes and more warm cream, Carlene moaned with pleasure a few times. Yin began to think of the pleasure Carlene was having. An idea came into Yin's mind. She spoke softly, "Mrs. Befoe, you must know allll these muscles, nerves and bones are connected. Related. You have . . . certain nerves that must be touched."

Carlene sighed with relaxed pleasure in answer.

Yin continued softly, "Your body is very private and there are places I will not touch . . . but you must."

Carlene roused herself a little, said with a muted voice, "What private places?"

Yin smiled. "In the front of your body, where the pelvis bone is located, place your hands in that area."

"What?"

"Do it. For your hip. I want to teach you something that will help you." Carlene hesitantly did as she was told.

Yin continued, "Now . . . feel the bone?"

A muffled reply, "Certainly."

Yin smiled. "Now, move your hand slowly in the direction of your feet to the lowest part of the pelvis bone . . . stay in the middle of the bone . . . until you feel what feels like gristle."

There was silence.

Yin waited, then asked, "Have you done that?"

Muffled, "Yes . . . what is this for?"

Yin answered seriously, "That is the center muscle, bone and nerve between your hips. If you hold down on that, not hard, but firmly . . . my massage will communicate to the bones and muscle pains better, with more balance. It is like a conductor."

Silence. Yin waited, then said, "I am going to occasionally touch another place. Don't jump. You have your underpants on." Still massaging with one hand, with the other she touched between Carlene's legs at the center between the buttocks and her vulva. She explained, "This spot here is also a conductor. That is why they are as well protected as they are. You can't reach this spot so I will have to help you, not too much, just a little.

Carlene's voice was still muffled, "I . . . don't know if . . . I want . . ."

Yin interrupted her, "It must be done right for the greatest effect on the pain in your hips. Now, hold on to that spot." She continued to massage with long, firm strokes. Carlene's body moved slightly, involuntarily under the pressure. Yin moved to the thigh slowly, returning at regular times back to the buttocks, stopping only for more warm cream. A half hour passed. Carlene said, "I do feel this in my hips. The pain is not so sharp."

"Good! Now turn over. Keep the sheet wrapped around you where I am not working and keep your privacy. Oh! You can't let go of that spot, can you? Here, I will hold it until you finish turning. Now, use this towel to cover your eyes for complete relaxation. Mrs. Befoe, I simply can't keep holding this nerve. I have to use my hands to rub you. Here, take your one hand and spread your fingers . . . you have to open your legs more, dear, to get the right spot again. You have panties on."

Carlene spoke, unmuffled, "I feel like a fool."

Yin soothed, "The medical profession is not always decorous, Mrs. Befoe. This is a massage." She covered Carlene's eyes completely with the towel as she started at her chin, working slowly to her shoulders and breasts.

"Do you have to touch my breasts?"

Yin answered softly, "Your body is a whole piece . . . all con-nected."

Carlene spoke from beneath the towel, "I will not subject myself to this again."

Yin smiled to herself, "As you like." As she stroked and rubbed the old, drying skin, withering from age and no exercise except malice, the muscles responded gladly to the soothing, firm pressure of Yin's warm, moist hands. Carlene relaxed even more. The nerves over her body were stimulated, awakened. Beneath Carlene's fingers the nerves were also stimulated by her own pressure and Yin's strokes on her body. The pleasure moving out from the center of her body to all points. Yin's hands moved in circular motions on the unloved bulge of layers swelling her belly. Yin watched the muscles beneath her hands. She pressed . . . and pulled . . . with soft firmness as she rounded the thighs, moving frequently back up to the dried breasts and around the now glistening belly, soft with compliance. Carlene's fingers held firmly in place as Yin did the lower limbs and finally the feet. Carlene made small sounds of pleasure. Yin heard a mixture of tones in Carlene's sounds now. She watched the stomach muscles contract. She stopped. "We are near the end. Turn over, for the last time, on your stomach. Then we'll be through." Carlene did as she was told without a whimper. Her fingers never moved from below her pelvic bone.

When Carlene was settled on her stomach, Yin said, "I must put the greatest pressure on your hip bones. I am going to straddle your legs for better leverage. No, no, keep them open. You see, I am too small and do not have the weight to place the proper pressure on your hip bones which we must do for the greatest results." She crawled upon the bed, placed one knee between Carlene's legs and leaned with both hands on her lower back, then raised and massaged the round buttocks.

For the next ten minutes the massage continued in silence. Then Yin leaned close and could see Carlene straining, unaware of Yin any longer, straining to keep from having an orgasm and straining to have one at the same time. Perspiration broke out over her face, her lips parted. The feeling gathered, swirled around her body, went back to the points and gathered, swirling again. At last it swirled faster, faster, faster, so that she could hardly keep it down. With Yin's knee between Carlene's legs for balance, Carlene's feelings could be held back no longer.

The feelings ran large, huge, back and forth over Carlene's body, then gathered and drifted throughout her. She wanted to squeeze her legs shut, but Yin's knee was between them. She held to Yin's leg with her own. Hating the feelings in her body even as she held on to them. Frustrated that it had happened to her in such a manner and situation. She did not allow herself to make a sound, burying her face in the pillow at the end. But her body was fully spent, relaxed, soothed, and she lay, smothering her ending gasps as Yin got up to cover her and go wash her hands.

Looking for a towel to dry her hands, Yin lifted the one Carlene had placed over the pills, salt and packages. Yin picked up the original prescription container and read that it was for Richard Befoe. She saw that some were empty. She tasted the medicine and then the salt. Yin knew something was wrong. She took one capsule still in the original bottle and one that had been opened and refilled, put them in her pocket and placed the towel back over what was left. She finished wiping her hands and came out, unrolling her sleeves.

At that moment, Carlene remembered the pills and jerked her head up, looking around at Yin to see if she had noticed anything.

Yin spoke first, "You need to rest. I am going to rest. Minna can clean up when you are ready." She stood at the door. "May I do anything for you before I go?"

Carlene, satisfied there was no question in Yin's face, relaxed and turned away from Yin, saying, "I don't believe you."

Yin was confused. "What?"

"I don't believe you have to . . . press down on those two . . . places."

Yin did not smile. "In any event, I will not be able to do the massage

again. It is too hard on me. It takes too much out of me. Perhaps I will
teach Minna or whomever you say . . . how to do it for you when you
are in pain."

"I don't believe you have to press those two places."

Yin sighed heavily. "Then when you next have it done, don't touch
them. Leave it out. See if there is any difference. Now . . . is there
anything I may do for you before I go?"

Still looking away from Yin, Carlene replied, "No . . . no."

As Yin turned to go she said, "We can settle our business later
tonight. I have had the papers prepared."

In a low voice, Carlene said, "I know that you are half Negro."

Yin turned back to face the woman whose face was turned away
from her. "Not that it makes any difference what you know, you were
not in my mother's womb when I was conceived. I was. How could you
KNOW anything?"

"I know your . . . alleged . . . father was too old . . . too
drunk, to make a baby. I'm sure he was impotent."

"How sure are you?"

"I have brains."

Yin stepped closer to the bed. "Might there not be something to
know about you?"

Silence. Both of them wondered about the same thing. But Yin said,
"Do you know who was in your mother's womb when you arrived
there?"

The face Carlene now turned to Yin was filled with malevolence.
"My mother was a pure woman. I know my father was white."

Yin was suddenly more tired. Taking a deep breath, she said, "You
were not born knowing everything. Everyone can have a . . . secret.
Did your parents tell you who put them in their mothers' wombs? You
THINK they were white."

In a softer tone, for she had too much to lose, Yin said, "We are
here. Red, yellow, black, brown, white, whatever. According to the Bible, you are even supposed to be my sister, at least my cousin." She
turned back to the door. "I don't care what you or anyone else knows. I
am me." Before closing the door behind her, she said, "Sleep now,
madame, sleep now. Your body has been set to rest and heal. Heal your
mind."

When Yin had gone, Carlene relaxed and stretched, smiling, feeling her body which had been quiet for so many years. She had loved the massage. She wriggled her old toes and ran her hands over the satin pillows. Finally, placing her hands on her stomach, she slept more soundly than in a long time.

While all this had been going on, by instinct the black spider had chosen this time to cross the white walls to the corner where lush plants were placed to their best advantage near the windows. The spider smelled and reached the moist dirt, scampering hastily, for this was where she prefered to live. The decaying wood, the moist dirt, the cool plants for food. She backed in, watching the movements on the bed, and made herself a permanent home.

Yin sat in her room, looking out the windows of the tall house. "Now . . . why did I do that? I hadn't planned to do that. I want to go on that yacht trip. Surely there will be rich men there." She sighed, looking at the beauty of the sun setting. Then, remembering, she took the pills from her pocket. The beauty of the sky pulled her back with its radiant colors. Moments later, she regarded the pills in her hand again. She sat there a long time. Until the sun was gone. Thinking.

Satan almost smiled.

The papers were signed, the money paid by Yin (which Richard gave back to Yin), repairs and cleanup work on her property began. Mr. Creed did much of the carpentry and hiring of laborers for the cleanup and yard. He was good at the job, having been Richard Befoe's estate carpenter for years. In their daily talks, Yin learned that Richard had helped to get Creed's son admitted into a law school which had at first declined him because of his color.

"My son didn't want to be no lawyer or doctor," Creed laughed. "He want to be a farmer! I tole him he be a fool to waste a chance like this. I saved my own money, so Befoe didn't have to help wit no money. But he still takin agriculture on the side though. Just ain't got no complete sense in that boy of mine. But this war here now, what's startin up. I hope he don't go."

Yin smiled at Creed as she moved about industriously, lifting, wiping, shifting things. "Well, I certainly hope you are right. It is good to have something you can be that will make you independent. And this war should not last long, Mr. Befoe said."

Yin liked Mr. Creed. He made her think of Josephus, but she never mentioned Josephus to him. She had not made up her mind about her half-sister's family yet. And now, with all the work to do in apron and head cover, washing, cleaning, planting bulbs Luke gave her from the Befoes' garden, time passed quickly. Soon she would be able to move into her own house or part of it. She sighed. There was so much to do and she didn't want to spend all her money until she knew where she would get more. And . . . a colored family could not help her now.

In the evenings when she had quit working for the day, Yin sat in the back garden at the Befoes, watching Richlene and Luke working there. Richlene loved the earth and flowers. She seemed to adore Luke, also. She had known him since he was a little boy coming to work the gardens with his father Joel. When Joel had died several years later, Luke was young, but he knew the work and needed the money desperately, so Richard had let him take over the job. Yin imagined it was innocent because Richlene seemed so innocent. Luke did, too, she decided. Emily, the young daughter of Richlene, sat and watched her mother, sometimes bringing a tool to her or a glass of water. Yin liked them, all three. She also liked Sally, the quiet efficient woman who always seemed to be writing letters to her children who seldom answered except to explain why they could not have her visit at one time or another. She tried to talk to Sally, but Sally seemed wary of others' closeness even while she seemed to need a friend. "She is a handsome woman even though she must be over forty," Yin thought of the slim, neat, sad but truly attractive Sally.

Yin tried to keep as unobtrusive as possible in this household so that she could stay as long as was needed. So many things seemed to be happening in this house with the melancholy feeling in it. Yin wanted time to think about them, but now she was absorbed with her own house and eager to move there. She thought of Richlene. The child-woman was slow but not dull witted. She seemed to have such common sense. Reasoning.

Evening meals were formal for the most part. Richard and Sally talked a little. Carlene spoke the most, complaints, and she was seldom answered. She was not ignored, there was just nothing to say to whatever she said. Richlene did not speak unless spoken to, her father often patting her hand. Emily, naturally quiet, ate and watched her mother, hastily reaching to help when she felt her mother wanted something. When Carlene rebuked or scolded Richlene for little mishaps, Yin saw hatred in Emily's eyes toward her grandmother.

When the new attorney, Russell Goode, came to replace Mr. Syntoll, he was invited as a guest in the huge house until his own place would be ready and his things brought in from Philadelphia. Richard had bought a large, outfitted boat to make travel on the river from the train more convenient to himself and it would be used to bring Mr. Goode's things from the railway station. Mr. Goode was a settled, middle-aged man, tall, graying hair, slim, polished and well taken care of. He was a recent widower, which made his leaving Philadelphia easy. He was alone and lonely but was not seeking a wife. He turned to books. His dress was impeccable. He was quite intelligent.

Yin looked at him thoughtfully. Then, at last, seeing that Sally also looked at him when she thought no one would notice, Yin decided he was too old for herself. So life went on in the Befoe family home.

One night before turning over to go to sleep, it popped into Yin's mind, for no particular reason, that she had not had a monthly in a couple of months. "Since I have been in Yoville! Since I left New Orleans!" She sat up in her bed, sharply, mouth opened as she remembered the porter on the train leaving New Orleans. "My God! Not that! Not pregnant! By a colored man!" The night was ruined for sleep. Yin's mind turned over and over but could get nowhere.

She was very subdued for the next few days, wondering, worrying. "Minna's grandma. Ma Lal. Would she know a way to get rid of it?" But at night in her bed, she held her stomach and thought of having no family of her own. And here was one in her own belly. "It would be a family! I could find a way. I would find a way to keep this child. Leave again? Back to New Orleans? Where to go?" "Oh, no," her mind spoke back to her, "Oh, no. I have a home of my own now. I must think of a way. I just need money."

c h a p t e r
2 6

When Carlene discovered her hips really were helped by the massage, she wanted them on a steady basis. Yin refused to do them herself but assisted and taught a maid, one of the several in the house. Carlene complained, "I need an expert!" Yin answered, "And you will soon have one." She smiled as she left Carlene's rooms. "And that takes care of that!"

Another thing happened to add to the confusion of the times. Occasionally Carlene invited Yin in for a glass of sherry and a small talk before going to sleep. Actually it was to check on what Yin was doing with herself. Carlene had been thinking of Richard and his heart . . . and his death. She knew any strong exertion could kill him, along with the fact that he had not been getting his prescribed medicine. She had pinpointed Yin for that exertion.

This chilly evening, Yin was settled in the deep satin-cushioned chair near the lit fireplace. It had rained that day, and work had been slow at her house. Carlene was staring into the fire, thinking, planning, scheming. Suddenly she spoke, "What do you think of Yoville now?"

Yin sighed. "It is a nice little town. Peaceful. A good place to live."

"What do you think of my sister, Sally?"

Yin sipped at her sherry. "I really have been so busy . . . But I think she is very nice. Quiet, but very nice."

"What do you think of my daughter?"

Yin held her glass up, looking at the amber liquid. "I think she is a lovely person. Kind."

"What has she given you?" Carlene asked sharply.

Yin smiled, saying, "Nothing."

"Why did you say 'kind'?"

Yin took a moment to think. "There is something about people, whether they give you anything or not, that makes you know they are kind. That they mean you no harm. They are not seeking . . ."

"What?"

"Something. Anything! I don't know. Why all these questions?" She smiled at her hostess.

"What do you . . . think of Richard?"

"Carlene, what is this? You know Richard is very kind, nice. He is very quiet, also." Yin took a sip of her sherry. "What is that medicine he takes? He does not seem . . . quite well."

Carlene took a sip of her wine. "Yes . . . he is not well. I hope he is taking his medicine. I must ask you to help me see that he does. That ole Baily does not have a thing on his mind, but . . ."

"How could I see to that?"

Carlene waved her hand. "Well, not see to it. Just, perhaps, ask him, now and again." After a moment, she continued, "He does not seem very happy, does he?"

"I don't know. He just seems quiet."

Carlene smiled. "When he was going to the city often, he was gayer." There was silence, then Carlene laughed, "I imagine he misses his . . . friends."

Yin smiled slightly. "I imagine."

"I mean, his female friends."

Yin was silent, staring into the fire.

Carlene spoke softly, "You know it has been years . . . years . . . since Richard and I have . . . been husband and wife . . . in that sense."

Yin was still silent, taking a sip of her wine.

Carlene continued, "I love him, of course . . . but I do not have . . . that kind of love for him . . . any longer. I . . . I am old, I guess." She tried to laugh lightly, but the laugh was a bit bitter. Yin remained silent. Carlene continued, softly, "I think . . . if he had a female friend . . . a pretty, younger, female friend . . . he could be happier. I . . . I don't know what to do to help him. There is no one here in Yoville." Then, as if it had just occured to her, "Well, yes . . . there is you, you are here in Yoville."

Yin looked over at her. "What are you saying?"

Carlene laughed. "Have another glass of sherry. It's such a cold night. It will make you sleep warm."

"I have no problem sleeping warm."

Carlene leaned her head back on her pillows. "I wonder . . . How is your house coming along?"

"It is coming along. I shall be moving soon."

Carlene waved her hand again. "I didn't mean that. I just wondered . . . if it was costing . . . more than you had anticipated."

Yin laughed lightly. "Indeed it is."

"Are you running low on funds?"

Yin tilted her head at Carlene. "Why do you ask?"

"Because . . . there is a way to solve your problems. Any problems."

"How is that?"

"I could lend you . . . or . . . give you a certain amount of money to complete your project."

"Why would you do that for me?"

Carlene made a great sigh of exasperation. "Well, if you must have it straight out . . . This must be in the strictest of confidence! Or you may regret it. Now Yin . . . I have said . . . Richard needs a friend." Now, this may seem as though Carlene Befoe was taking a step down to Yin's level, since she truly felt Yin was her inferior along with everyone else. But it is the one in need of something who usually does most of the talking to persuade the other, unless the one seeking help is very, very smart and then they can make the one they need beg them to let them help. Carlene was not that smart.

Yin removed her smile. "Carlene, are you suggesting I am a whore?"

Carlene waved her hands frantically. "Heavens, no! Whatever . . . No! No, I am not. I am only suggesting . . . It would be a favor in kind, perhaps. I am helping you . . . and . . ."

"It would help you for me to be . . . Richard's friend?"

Carlene tried to cry, but couldn't. "I feel so sorry for him and there is nothing I can do. That has long ago, long ago, been off my mind, but Richard is a man . . . and men . . ."

"That is what I would be . . . a whore, if I did what you are suggesting. And anyway, what makes you think Richard would want me?"

Carlene looked up quickly, because those last words of Yin's indicated there was a possibility. She did not smile though, she continued to look sad. "Ahh, you are a pretty woman. Very attractive. You could make him want you." A strange note crept into her voice. "You could be his Lilith."

Yin tilted her head again. "Isn't she a demon from the devil's lair?"

Carlene realized her mistake, "Oh! You don't believe in all that superstitious fiddle faddle."

"I didn't bring it up, you did, when you said Lilith."

Carlene continued, "I would never believe you to be so unintelligent as to even think of gods and devils." Far off, Satan smiled.

"I . . . don't . . . know," Yin said thoughtfully.

Carlene hastened to get off that subject and back to her plea. "In any event, I will tell you this . . . If you should decide to help me . . . help Richard, I mean, I could be of considerable assistance to you . . . now . . . and always."

Yin laughed and held her glass up as in a toast. "Would we go on that yacht trip together? And would I have beautiful, new, seagoing clothes to go with you on your yacht trip and perhaps catch a rich husband?" She laughed as if joking.

Carlene did not laugh, she narrowed her eyes at Yin. "If that is what you want. And the . . . war does not interfere."

Yin continued as if she were joking, "War? There is no war. But, yes, that and money enough to finish my whole house and landscaping . . . and, of course, enough to take care of me for all the years of my life!"

Carlene softly said, "Yes."

And then Yin knew what it really was that Carlene wanted. Not to help Richard but to kill him. Her laughter stopped immediately. "You are serious?"

Carlene, still softly, "Yes."

Yin, thinking there may be danger in Carlene knowing she understood too much, said, "But you can't be. A wife asking another woman to make love to her husband?"

"I don't presume to ask for you to love him. I just . . . want him to be happier."

"What is wrong with Richard? His illness, I mean. Isn't he supposed to . . . avoid any sudden exertion?"

It was Carlene's turn to laugh. "Oh, pish! Doctors don't know everything! Happiness! Satisfaction! That's what keeps many people alive."

Yin looked down at the glass she held in her hand and said, "It also kills many people . . . getting there."

Carlene felt so close to getting what she wanted, she leaned toward Yin. "Think of your own happiness and satisfaction. Think of your house. Think of your future. You will be satisfied at last."

Yin stood up, looking for somewhere to put her empty glass, "Carlene, I refuse to continue this conversation. I am not a whore or courtesan. I am a single woman, educated . . . and with a future . . . of good family and . . . and . . ."

Carlene laughed lightly. "Well, think of it. What will it hurt? You will give satisfaction to two old people. I will be satisfied if he is satisfied. And . . . no one need ever know. You will soon be in your own house . . . and if he visits you . . . after all, you have become friends. People are used to seeing him looking over your progress."

"On that note, I repeat, I will not, cannot do it, and I will say good evening to you. I am tired." Yin walked to the door.

"You are too young to be tired. Your life is just beginning . . . perhaps."

"Good night, Mrs. Befoe." The last words she heard as she closed the door were "I will write a tentative acceptance to the yacht trip."

c h a p t e r
2 7

The next time Creed worked at her house, Yin spoke to him of Richard. "Mr. Creed, what exactly does the poor gentleman have wrong with him?"

"Welllll, I don't rightly know, but I do know it is around his heart. He was much better before his mother passed away." The thing Yin liked about Creed was he could talk while he worked. He continued, "Soon after he come back from that trip, he went by hisself, you know, he just seemed to slow down. Didn't feel like doin much of nothin at all. Stopped mostly all his travels on his business. Now gets that lawyer here to bring it to him, and things like that."

"How long ago did his mother die? Had Carlene been to see her?"

"Bout nine, ten months now. No, she didn't go none."

"What medicine does he take?"

"Oh, I don't know all that. He gets it from the drugstore man here. Sent down from New York or Philadelphia, I don't know." He stopped working and looked at Yin. "You sure worryin bout him."

"I think he is a kind man, and someone should worry about him. Carlene seems . . . distant."

He started back to work. "They is distant. It's been years since I even seen them talkin together. But I ain't with em all the time, so I don't know. His daughter can't look after him, so he look after himself."

"What would happen if he didn't get his medicine?"

"I blive when you don't get your medicine . . . and you got a bad heart, you can die . . . easy."

"Then he really should not do too much, exert himself in any way, I mean . . . ?" She looked at him in just the way he could understand.

He understood. "That can kill people . . . if they heart and pressure is real bad."

"Even making . . . love?"

Creed blushed, then laughed. "Miz Yin, you going too far for me. I 'magin it would! What you thinkin of?"

"Nothing, just talking to a friend." She took herself off to work somewhere else alone.

for the next week or so, Yin was very quiet, thinking about the pills, the request, Richard and the new baby. Everything was so big, so confusing, it hurt to have to think of everything. But finally she did think, "If I do this with Richard, I can say my baby is his. That gives me seven months to get as much money as I can. And I'll cheat that ole bitch. I'll get him some real medicine and switch them on her. Wonder should I tell him? He's got plenty of money himself! Oh, there's got to be a way! There is a way! I will think of it." She struggled in her mind. "But the yacht trip! I want that yacht trip. But I won't kill him. I don't want that on me. And I won't give her the satisfaction."

That evening, Yin went to Carlene and said, "I need five thousand dollars. to do some work I must have done."

Carlene looked at her thoughtfully. "Does this mean . . . ?"

Yin cut her off, "Just leave it be. I don't want to talk about it. Give me the five thousand dollars. I will not fool you or cheat you. I will . . . help him in your way."

Carlene smiled a strange smile. "You are a wise . . . and kind woman."

"I don't want to talk about it."

Carlene nodded her head. "As you like." And soon, in a day or two, the money was given to Yin.

. . .

When Yin next saw Richard, she spoke to him thus. "Dear Richard. Are you a fool?"

Richard looked at her as if she were a fool. "What do you mean?"

"If I tell you something that would hurt me, will you tell the one who could hurt me?"

Richard liked Yin, so he smiled. "I don't think so."

Yin thought a long moment. "Your wife wants us to have . . . an affair."

Richard laughed. "How do you know that?"

"She has told me. 'For your happiness,' she said."

"My happiness?" He sounded incredulous.

"Yes. And I will tell you this," She took a deep breath. "You need to get your own prescription filled and keep your pills with you."

"Oh, I have never done that. Carlene always . . ." He looked at her, then away, thoughtfully. He sat down heavily, looking back at her, placing a hand on his chest.

Yin jumped up, reaching for him. "You certainly must not die now!"

"What has she promised you?" His voice was strained.

"The money I need to complete my work here . . . in entirety."

"How much is that?" His breathing eased.

"Ten thousand dollars."

"Yin, you don't need that much now."

"I want that much. I want a lovely home to live and grow old in. And raise my children in . . . if I ever have any."

"I would rather give the money to you."

"Oh, Mr. Befoe, Richard, when?"

He made a small laughing sound. "Before I die. In a few days."

Yin smiled deeply, her sexiest smile. "But . . . what will we do about . . . the affair?"

"Why, we shall have it, of course." He smiled sadly.

"In a little while, a week or so, after you take some REAL medicine."

When they did make love, Yin insisted on being on top. To her surprise, it was good. Richard was gentle and very tender. Afterwards, she lay in his arms in a sort of wonder. What was wrong with Carlene? Why would she not want this man? She asked Richard those questions.

In his mellow, relaxed mood, thinking of all this relationship could be, he told her. He told her everything about his father, Carlene and Richlene. Even Yin was filled with disgust for Carlene, but she was thrilled at the information she now had.

Yin did not fool herself. She did not intend to love Richard. He was married and married to a veritable bitch. No, she did not need that problem. She insisted on never doing it again because she cared too deeply for him and it would be too painful to love a man who was married and would never divorce his wife. She looked at him questioningly. He simply nodded and said, "She is my wife."

As usual, if it did not involve business, he tended to believe people. In a few days, however, he gave her only five thousand dollars. She was too wise to pout. "Hell, it was a gift," she thought as she smiled up at him.

Yin anxiously waited another month, then she went to Carlene.

"I have done what you asked of me . . . I want the money you have promised me. I am suffering for what you had me do. I am made pregnant by your husband." Carlene stared at her, unable to say a word. She did not believe it, but she could not disbelieve it either. She knew Yin had no lover in Yoville. Unless it was Creed. Carlene shook her head no and looked with wonder at Yin. Yin just quietly closed the door and left Carlene sitting there staring at the door.

Then Yin went to Richard and told him she was pregnant. To her surprise, he seemed happy about it. Then she said as soon as she could she was leaving to move into her old home made new. He thought it was a good idea. "But I will need more money," she smiled. She received more than she asked for. Richard was happy about the baby. With Richard's financial help, she shopped and shopped for her own home. The next few days she gathered all her belongings from Mrs. Whitman and the Befoes. Anxious, joyously, she was on her way to her own home, which she had lied for, stolen for, loved for. It was surely hers now. She had done some good too though, hadn't she?

c h a p t e r

2 8

She was settled at last, all her belongings neatly put away in her own home, so many new things to have and enjoy. Settled. It had taken time, but it was done. Yin smiled to herself as she looked over all she now owned. Her home. Her child's home. A family with a home. She frowned, thinking, "My child better not be too dark. But I can take care of that. I will cross that ocean when I get to it."

Very soon after Yin moved into her own house, she was sitting on her veranda looking toward the road. It was lonelier now. She had enjoyed some kind of closeness with Sally and Richlene and Minna in the Befoe house, and now there was no one. Sally came sometimes for little short visits. Yin didn't encourage anyone to come, really, because her pregnancy was showing, and she didn't want anyone counting the time and perhaps mentioning it to Carlene.

This morning she was looking at the main road some distance from her house. Someone, a woman, bent a bit and walking slowly, turned into her entrance. Yin watched the woman as she slowly moved closer to her. She felt a bit comforted that people would be stopping by, even though she didn't really want company. She fluffed her dress over her stomach. And waited.

When the figure was closer, Yin could see it was an older woman, but she did not recognize her. "Maybe selling eggs or something," she thought. Yin went into the house to get a dipper of water for such kinds of company and was holding it for the visitor when she finally arrived.

Smiling an almost toothless grin, the woman spoke as she reached for the dipper, "How do?" As she drank, Yin looked her over. The old woman was not in rags; in fact, her clothes were rather nice and clean. Yin thought to herself, "Someone she worked for probably gave them to her." Aloud she said, "How do you do? What can I do for you this morning?"

The woman returned the dipper to her, still smiling. "Oh, that was good! An old body like mine surely needed that there water. I done walked a long way, least it sure seem like it. I ain't use to it. I don't get out much no more." Yin smiled, waiting.

The woman came up on the porch and sat down without being invited, breathing heavily from the walk. Yin sat down slowly, waiting. Still smiling, the woman said, "Oh, you don' need to treat me like no compny, I done known you since you was a born baby."

Now Yin smiled. "You have?"

"Sho have. I was there the day you was born. I was helpin the midwife what tended your mother. My name Laly, they call me Ma Lal. I'm the colored mid-wife roun here. The oldest and the best one." She laughed; it was like a cackle.

"You knew my mother? I mean, you saw her? Helped her?"

"Yes ma'am! She was a mighty fine woman. Didn't have no easy time wit you gettin here." She cackled again then looked slyly sideways at Yin. "I knew your daddy, too."

Yin leaned forward. "Oh! You did? You knew my father?"

"Yes mam. He was a fine man, as men go." She cackled softly, never taking her eyes from Yin's face.

"Well." Yin sat back. "It's very nice of you to come by to see me. How did you know I was here? Oh! That's right, Minna is your grandchild, she must have told you."

"Tha's right. She a good child. I hate to see her over there workin for that ole Miz Befoe, but when you ain't got no money, you got to do what you got to do! That ole Miz Befoe can be mean though." Ma Lal fanned herself a moment with her big rag handkerchief. Then, "I reckon you gon be needin some help here in this big ole house. Sho is pretty agin. You doin alright, chile!"

Yin did not say anything. The woman continued speaking, "We colords sho do poorly here. Ain't no place to get a real job what pays real money. We all poor, Miz Yinyang." Ma Lal laughed her cackle again. "But you already know colords have a hard time in this world."

Yin looked down into her lap. "Yes, poor can be very hard. I know."

The answering cackle jerked Yin's head up. Ma Lal was laughing, saying, "Wasn't talkin bout just bein poor, darlin. What you know bout being poor anyway, Miz Lady? I bet you ain't gone without too much!"

"Well, you are wrong. I have."

"Well." Ma Lal looked around at the house and grounds. "Well, it sho don't seem like it. You sho is doin alright for yourself now."

"I try." Yin was deciding she did not quite like the old woman. The cackle sounded. It irritated Yin and she frowned. Ma Lal said, "I try, too, daughter, I try hard, but it don't do me no good like it done you."

Yin waited a moment while Ma Lal fanned again. Then Yin stood. "Well," Yin said, "I have a million things to do. It was awfully nice of you to . . . stop by and visit, but I must go now."

"Wait a minute, daughter, I ain't tole you why I come by here to you."

"No, you haven't."

"Well." The old woman bent her head and placed a gnarled, dry, wrinkled old hand up to her brow. "Well, I don't need to tell you I'm old and I got a fam'ly to watch out for. I don't have no money . . . and I need some. I come here to see could you find it in your heart to help a old woman who done helped your mama . . . and your daddy." She looked up at Yin and smiled.

"I . . . I have a . . . dollar . . . or two I can let you have."

"A dollar or five ain't gon help me . . . none!"

"What did you want . . . need?"

Ma Lal still smiled. "I need a hundred . . . or two."

Now Yin laughed. "Ma Lal, I don't have that kind of money to give away. I am a single woman . . . now. I need everything I have."

"Not as much as me."

Yin shook her head. "You are not my responsibility. You have children. And please stop calling me 'daughter'."

"I think if you think on it, you will find your way to give me what I ask for."

"I don't think that will help."

Ma Lal looked sly again. "People roun here don't know bout you what I do. If they was to know . . . everythin . . . well, everythin just might change on you."

"What do you mean?"

"I tole you, I know your daddy."

"So?"

"Josephus was your daddy. Jus like he was Ruth's daddy. He a colored man. I knowed him and all he done. You got plenty relations round here is black as me. Luke, Lettie, Lovey and that un that went away. They's your natural blood kin. I knowed Bessel when she had that baby for Josephus! He didn't know it, but tween her mama and her, I knew it. Ruth! Ruth was what she named that chile. See, I know! I know bout that gold, too. I know bout that diamond ring, cause Ruth had it on evertime she gave birth to a baby. She didn't have no money to pay me! I told her, 'Sell that ring, you have you some money!' But she was a damn fool, wouldn't sell it. Stayed poor! Died poor! Now, she gone, he gone, but that ring still somewhere! Glittering, shining, alive! I always wonder where she got that ring, but I blive I know. Your mama was dead when Josephus took you away. You! You ain't no white woman. Now . . . I ain't tole nobody. But I know you passin for white, but you ain't white. Now this little money ain't gon hurt you. And I needs it! You can get you some more."

"You certainly know a lot about my money and me, Miz Lal."

"I know a lot bout a whole lot of things, daughter. I know how to keep my mouf shut, so people can run they bi'ness like they want to."

"I'm running my business like I want to, and I don't include you in it. Now . . . I think you had better go."

Ma Lal did not rise. She choose to look sad and try again. "Daughter, I'm a old woman, done wore myself out livin and doin for other peoples. Just help me this here one time, I won't never come to you agin."

"Miz Lal, you had all those years to plan ahead and do for yourself. You didn't even know if I was coming back here or not, so you do not count on me. I have to look out for myself . . . and that's what I'm gonna do."

Ma Lal stirred herself to rise. "If I tell . . . the right people . . . bout what you really is, you might not have no bi'ness to run."

"I am not afraid of anything you might say. Look at me. No matter what I have in my blood inside me, my outsides are white. I don't care about being colored, cause I am me. I'm not hiding . . . anything. Now you tell whoever you want to. I'm still me and I still look like I look. I am not ashamed. And . . . as a matter of fact . . . you weren't in my mama's womb, so you don't know who put me there. Now . . . I have asked you to leave. Now . . . leave my home. And do not come back. You are not welcome here."

Ma Lal slowly stood, brushed and straightened her clothes. "I'ma leave, daughter. I'ma leave. But you should have listened to me, helped me. I sho would'a helped you."

"Just help yourself."

"I tends to, daughter, I tends to." She slowly made her way down the steps onto the path leading to the gate. She turned back once. "You a fool, daughter. You could have the world on a hook. But you gonna need a fren. Everbody need a fren."

"Miz Lal, if I need a friend, I won't look your way. Good day to you."

Ma Lal frowned a smile, then moved on.

Yin watched the old lady make it to the road. She was thinking, "When I have my baby, I will deliver it myself! Women do it, I can do it. Nobody is going to know anymore of my business."

And that is how her months passed, preparing and getting ready for her child. As life moved on.

chapter
2 9

Life was moving slowly in Washington, D.C. for Hosanna, who woke up one morning in her employers' house, their room and their bed. She even slept in a nightgown her employer, Mrs. Doll, had given her. She lay there a while thinking, "I am so lonely. Oh, God, I miss somebody who blongs to me. Are you up there, really? God? I don't know who You are, but from what all I have heard of You, You are a mean, jealous man. You let little babies starve. You let there be wars. You call people to die. My mama and my daddy are dead. You left us kids all alone. By ourself. Then they say You are a God of love. I don't know what to believe, but most all the people I hear talking about who and what you are, they wasn't nothing themself! They didn't do all those things You ask Your people to do. They did the opposite. Even on a dollar bill it says 'In God We Trust.' That's a lie. They don't trust nothing but that dollar bill. Now I know it's SOMETHING up there, cause this world too big, the sky too big, oh, everything is too big for SOMETHING not to be there. And I notice the sun and the moon rise on time. Winter, summer, spring and fall get here, right on time. I seen a seed grow to a big ole plant from nothing but a little bitty seed. I watch the birds, see the trees. I feel the wind, the rain just coming from nowhere out the sky, washing this earth. It's something so great and special on this earth, something special got to have put it there. Now . . . if You are there, will You help me? I want to go home. I got a home. I got sisters and a brother. I am so lonely, God. These people don't love me. I miss love. Butler's alright, but I miss having my own." She thought a moment longer, then jumped up, saying, "Soul, let's go home. We got a home!"

She didn't have any suitcase so she went to the store, got two, medium-sized cardboard boxes, took them home and packed them with all her worldly goods, as they say. She found some thick rope in the attic, wrapped and tied the boxes so one could follow the other as she pulled them along holding the long piece of rope on the end. She didn't know exactly which way the railroad station was or just how she would get there, but she knew she could do it. She would not leave without talking to Mr. Butler first; he could tell her, she thought. She didn't want to carry the boxes all over town, so she left them in a corner of her little attic room and walked over to Butler's.

She had saved EVERY dime she had made except for a little money she had sent home now and then and the money for stamps to mail the letters. Wouldn't even buy a stick of candy or a book, and she loved books. Anyway, Mr. Butler let her read his. But she loved fairytales. The family she worked for had a daughter, so they had some fairytales and lots of other kinds of books, too. She read all of them she could, after she read the homework given her by Mr. Butler. Anyway, she had all her money. It came to about $103. Big money to her. Saved in only almost a year. Back then in 1914.

She reached Mr. Butler's house and knocked because he didn't expect her. She would remember to leave his key. He answered, surprised, but welcomed her in.

"I'm going on home, Mr. Butler." The words burst from her smiling face.

Mr. Butler looked down into the bright, dark eyes set in the honey brown face, the small full lips smiling open, showing white even teeth. He raised a hand and placed in on the head of thick dark hair that ended in a fat braid that reached just below her shoulders.

"So . . . my little friend is going home to Yoville. You smile so, I won't ask if anything is wrong there."

"No, sir, I don't blive so."

"Well, come in, come in, sit down. The old gentleman is home so we won't go upstairs. Let's sit in here by the fireplace." When she was settled, he looked at her with pleasure and respect showing in his eyes. "Hosanna, I have not known you very long, but you are very dear to me. Like a daughter I will never have."

"Thank you, sir. I am so glad I had you for my friend."

"Yoville is small. What will you do there?"

"Oh, there some places to work, I guess. I'll find something."

"Remember, Hosanna, you know a lot of things now. You have learned to embroider, knit, cook special foods, gourmet foods. These things are worth money. You can go into business for yourself. All you have to do is to do things well, as good as you can, and you are very good at these things. You know how to handle fabrics, clean and care for them. I am not saying you should be a domestic all your life, but money is made from the things people need. And . . . your work is special."

"Thank you, Mr. Butler."

"Go into business for yourself as soon as you can. You don't have to start in any big way, you can start at home. Your work will advertise for you if it's good, and I know yours is." Hosanna grinned, happily. "Ask more money than people pay a sloven worker, because you are extra. Charge for it! And save!"

"I done . . . have . . . saved $103."

"In all these months, that is all you have made?"

"That's good. My aunt never even had that much."

Butler smiled. "I want to give you a going away present. While I am gone, write your address down for me. And be sure you have mine where you will not forget it." He left the room.

"Yes, sir." She got busy with the pencil and paper. When he returned, he handed her an envelope.

"Now, Hosanna, do not think I am a fool. However, I do think of you like a daughter." Hosanna looked into the envelope and saw a hundred dollar bill. She burst into tears and reached for him. He held her until she was only sniffling. "It may help you in a start. Buy things that will make money for you. Try not to be dependent on anyone until you are married." He held her face, wet with tears and snot. "You'll probably be getting married soon. A small town like that can be lonely. Take care. Let him come get you. Don't go after him, it won't end up being what you need."

"Yes, sir, Mr. Butler." She moved away, preparing to leave.

"Write me if you need anything, you hear?"

"Yes, sir."

"I may surprise you one day. I may drop in and see how you are doing."

She opened the door. "Oh, Mr. Butler, you are fooling me."

"You can never tell. I'll think of you often." Then he told her where she had to go and how to get there. They held hands a moment. When she was out on the porch, the tears threatened to come again and there were tears in his eyes, too. She ran before she would cry and he watched her slim, little brave body until she turned a corner . . . and disappeared.

Hosanna returned to her job and got her boxes. She wrote a note to Mrs. Doll. She didn't mind leaving this way because the lady of the house had done her wrong in so many little ways, knowing she had nowhere else to go. "I worked twenty-four hours a day with NO days off, cept to go do another job somewhere, so I will just say good-bye and thank you or thank you and good-bye."

Then she wrote Aunty a nice letter to thank her, also. "For nine years she gave me a home. I might'a slept on a cot and had to put my bedroom away every morning, but still I had a roof over my head and somebody that cared for me enough to see to me eatin and goin to school. She didn't have to do it. I was a motherless child and she taken me in. I know now, people don't HAVE to do anything for you! I did appreciate it. Wasn't her fault bout that mess she had for a husband. And if it was her fault, it wasn't my business. It was my business to get my own place if I didn't like hers, and I did."

She wrote Aunty a nice, long note thanking her and telling her what she was going to do. "I know she gonna look for some money in this envelope, but I can't put no money in it. I put some love in it. I hope she finds it. She needs it."

She packed herself a little lunch bag. Stuck her money to her oversized bra the lady had given her, with three safety pins and a tiny bell from the playroom that had broken off of something so she would ring if she happened to fall asleep on the train. She was a little frightened. She was alone again. Then she left, pulling her two boxes down the street, holding her purse and her lunchbag tightly in her hand. Going home. Her heart was soooooooo happy!

As Hosanna pulled her boxes along, she thought about what Mr. Butler had said to her. "I know a whole lot of things I learned from Aunty and the ladies I have worked for. I know bout how to keep a house! I can set tables pretty as you want to see! I can cook things I never had no idea people ate before. Cook em good, too! I know how to keep a lady's clothes up. I even learned how to dress a little from watchin other people select their clothes. Oh, they hadn't meant to teach me cept what I needed to know to help them, but I love learning all kinds of things to help myself! Some things they didn't even know how to do, just fixed it so I could learn. See? I don't plan to do everything I know how to do for somebody else all the time! I plan to do it for me! My boxes are packed and my brain is too!" Hosanna smiled as she talked to herself, pulling the boxes on her way home.

She reached a bus stop mostly used by domestics in that area of the wealthy. When the bus came the driver let her pull and struggle with the boxes until he got tired of waiting, then he helped her lift them on the bus. That done, she sat back and smiled. People smiled back and asked her, "Where you goin with them things?" Still smiling, she said, "Home."

They ask, "Home up here in the city?"

She said, "No, home down there in the country where I come from. Where my family lives."

One lady asked, "You sure ain't gonna walk, draggin them boxes, is you?"

Hosanna answered, "No mam. I'm gonna buy me a ticket and ride home in style. I ain't walkin!" They laughed. She didn't have to say any more. People started smiling with her and giving her information on how best to travel alone. When she got where she was to change buses, a few got off and stood with her so nobody would bother her. Even helped her get her boxes on the next bus before they went on to their jobs.

The next stop was the train station. A man helped her get off the bus, setting her boxes on the ground because there wasn't much of a sidewalk there. Then he hugged her and got back on the bus, waving as it drove away. Hosanna dragged her boxes again through a muddy dirt. The boxes were beginning to look kind of weak, but the rope held. She got inside the railroad station with them and parked them by an old lady, smiling as she did so, then she went to get her ticket, thinking, "Sweet Jesus! Goin home!"

She was mad at herself when her turn came at the ticket window because she had not had sense enough to separate her money when she was at home by herself. She realized she could not take all her money out and was embarrassed until she realized she could find out how much the ticket cost, then go to the restroom and get out the right amount. She looked at the old lady sitting beside her things, and thought, "She just a old lady. Surely she ain't gonna take my things." Then she changed her mind, got the boxes and pulled them into the restroom with her. It was dirty and crowded. Toilet paper and towels all over the floor. She had to drag her boxes all through that then try to get them to fit in the small cubicle with her. It took her awhile, but she did it. Then it seemed like that little bell was a great big ole bell! It rang and rang and rang as she struggled with those safety pins. She finally got everything out, separated and done. Went to the toilet since she was in there anyway. Dragged her boxes back out, washed her hands, ignored the funny looks from people with raggedy, cardboard suitcases laughing at her boxes. "Hell, I'm goin home!" Hosanna thought and held her head up higher. She went back and bought her ticket, sat down and waited for HER train. When it came, a nice, smiling, old black man helped her get her boxes on and her to her seat. She sat back, still smiling, dreaming of the faces of her family she would see when she got HOME!

She reached for her lunchbag. "Oh, oh! I have done left it somewhere!" She was a little hungry, but she didn't care. She did not intend to spend her money. Something was telling her she was going to need every dime she had.

Hosanna was near starving in a little while. She had not known it was as far as it was. She thought of stealing something, and she didn't want to. But if it hadn't been for that nice, old black man and a white lady with a baby, she might have stolen something. They didn't have much, but they shared a few crackers, some cheese and a little tiny chicken wing. It tasted so good to her! Hosanna thought to herself about her money, "I ain't cheap! Just thrifty! And I can't be pullin my money out and ringing that bell all over the place." At last, after a long, long day and a night, the train finally got to where the next stop was hers. She was so sweaty, tired, uncombed and unwashed and just plain sick of that train. She snatched her now raggedy boxes by the rope and flew off that train with tears in her eyes, she was so glad to get almost home.

Now Hosanna didn't know just exactly which way to go to get home because she had left when she was five years old. Naturally she had sense enough to ask the right questions and make her way. There was a war going on so nobody paid much attention to her with her boxes. She started out walking. It wasn't hard walking to her because she was getting closer to home. What was hard was keeping the bottom of those boxes from coming apart. So besides the ticket, she spent the only money of the whole trip on a little red wagon with a pull handle, loaded it and started on down the road. Thirty-five cents. Her and her little red wagon!

c h a p t e r
3 0

Sweat soon poured from Hosanna's face as she trudged the long, unpaved road to her home. The sun in the middle of the sky shone down relentlessly. It was only about eighty degrees, but she was not used to walking in such heat for so long. Trees bordered the road but lent little shade for any length of time. Now and again she would see snake tracks across the road. She was afraid of snakes so she looked carefully ahead. The little red wagon became heavier and heavier with each mile.

Far ahead, Hosanna saw a figure resting, it seemed like, on a log or something on the side of the road. She watched the figure until she saw it was an older woman, dark of skin, large boned but rather thin for her height, with a look of weariness and patience in the tired lines of her face. Having felt so much loneliness in her own short life, Hosanna recognized or felt the aloneness of the older woman.

Hosanna wiped the sweat from her face with her arm as she reached the woman and smiled. "Sure wish I had brought a hat." The woman smiled back, saying, "Take mine."

"Oh, no, I can't do that."

"Where you goin to?" the woman asked in a pleasant low voice.

"Yoville. Home."

"That's jus wher I'm goin. We can walk together and spell the hat off. I'll wear it awhile, then you wear it awhile."

Hosanna smiled. "Only if you let me put your sack on my wagon and let me help you carry it."

The woman smiled. "I sho be glad of that! I's tired, chile. Sit down a minute. You been to town?" She waved mosquitoes away.

Hosanna tried to laugh, but it dwindled away in the heat. "I sure have been to town. I been to Washington, D.C.!"

"Oh! You must'a come in on the train, I saw it comin in."

Hosanna wiped her brow again, enjoying the shade. "You been to town?"

The woman shooed the same mosquitoes away again. "I been to Pittsburgh in Pencil . . . vania."

Hosanna turned to her. "Oh, you came in on the train, too. I don't remember seeing you."

The woman laughed wearily. "Tha's cause I was'n on it."

Hosanna still looked at her. "What you took?"

"I walked."

"You walked all the way to Pittsburgh?"

"There and back."

"My Lord!"

The woman laughed softly again. "Tha's what I say. Well, we best be gettin on our way." They got up and adjusted the bags and boxes on the little wagon. Hosanna shook her head. "You musta walked near three, four hundred miles."

The woman sighed. "One step at a time. I been gone a month. Be glad to get home . . . if it still be there."

Hosanna persisted. "What possessed you to walk like that, that far?"

They started walking—Hosanna pulled the wagon, the woman fanned with the hat then handed it to Hosanna who now refused to take it.

"Well," the woman continued to fan herself, some of the breeze reaching Hosanna who held her face up to it, "Well, I had a brother had a daughter. She live in Pittsburgh now, wit two childrens. Her husband dead now. My brother dead, too. I be her onliest family and she be mine. I got to look on her ever once in awhile, for my brother, you know. She poor, I'm poor, so I got to walk. Oh, she don't know it. She think I got a train ticket. I don't tell her no difference. Cause then, she feel bad for me . . . and she already got nough to feel bad bout. Two childrens and no daddy to help. I don stay long cause I don't want to cost her nothin."

Hosanna nodded, "Oh, Jesus."

"Oh, it ain't so bad. I'm old, but I'm strong. The Lord helps me along. I sing to Him and I walks, one step at a time. I gets there. And now, I done got back. Be a year fore I hafta go back and see bout em." They walked in silence a little while, each thinking their own painful thoughts. Finally the old woman spoke, "What's your name, chile?"

"Hosanna."

"Oh, your mama gave you a right pretty name. We sings that name in church. My name is Ellen. Ellen Mae Bell White. You can call me Ellen."

"Thank you, Miz Ellen."

"I be happy if you say, Aunt Ellen."

"I be happy too, Aunt Ellen!"

So they met, so they walked and talked . . . and the time passed quickly. They spelled the hat, but Hosanna would not let Ellen pull the wagon. They had to stop often to let Ellen Mae Bell White rest her swollen, sore feet. They finally came to the outskirts of Yoville.

Ellen stopped, "I lives down this here road, do you ever want to find me."

"How far down that road?"

"Oh, chile, I'm so close to home that don mean nothin. I guess it still my home. The rent is due."

Hosanna turned off the road with Ellen. "Come on, I'll walk you there and carry your bag. You rent your house?"

Ellen took her raggedy shoes off and let her sore feet touch the dirt which was cool because the little worn path wove through the trees. "Me and my husband was buyin, but when he died, a white man come wit some papers say I got to move or pay rent. Said I can't keep the little house of mine what we had done worked for so long."

"Where the papers? You still got em?"

"Chile, it been so long, bout fifteen years now."

"What the papers say?"

"Lord, chile, I can't read none. He say it said it ain't my home. So

. . . I pays rent. It's bout to fall down, but it house the few things I got left in this here world. I wants to send the few little things blonged to my mother on up to my niece for her to have. Got to plan on how to do it."

"How you gonna pay the man the money if you ain't got none?"

"Oh, I been late befoe. They give me time. I find some piece work to do."

"What you gonna eat today?"

"Oh, I blive I still got some taters and cabbage in my garden. Some onions."

They reached the little leaning house soon. Hosanna helped Ellen haul up water from the well and had a long cool drink. Someone had been in and gone through her few poor things, but there was nothing to take. In anger they had poured water on her bed with the homemade quilt and coarse, threadbare sheet. Hosanna got angry, but Ellen just sighed and took them out to hang up and dry. Someone had been in the garden, but she planted it to grow things in waves so there would be something always. "There be some things in there that I can eat. I'll be full. You go on. Go on home, chile. See your famly."

Hosanna left, pulling her little red wagon, looking back at Miz Ellen who stood leaning against the leaning fence, waving farewell. She felt the tears in the tightening of her chest. "Life ought not to be like it is, Lord." Then she moved her thoughts to her own home. "What will I find there?"

Waves of emotion pulsed through Hosanna as she continued on her way, walking the rough, long, main road that went into her town. She wished that her mother would be there, there in the house. Her mama and daddy. "Oh, mama," she moaned to herself out loud, "Oh, Mama, I'm coming home, I'm coming. Oh, my sisters, my brother, I'm coming. Home. Home." Her tired feet hurried. The wagon was light and heavy at the same time. Tears were in her eyes. Tears of pain and happiness. Home. Home.

The road was paved now with a black tar type of material. Soft in places from the steady heat. She passed the bank, the small market, the post office. She saw the people. She did not know them. She hurried on past the other buildings she did not even see. She passed the Befoes' house, knowing it only by the sign over the huge gated archway. It was far back from the road down a long path. She saw three people at a distance in the yard, two grown and one young. One was a colored man. She did not know it was her brother Luke. She hurried on. Her eyes straight ahead, looking for her house, her home. The paved road became smooth gravel again. Hosanna still stared forward. She moved steadily, pass the main part of Yoville. The trees, the thickets were thicker, wilder. She came upon a very pretty white fence bordering about two acres of the road. She saw a woman in a white dress standing, bent over, at the gate. Hosanna's pace was steady, the wagon behind her. The woman waved. Hosanna looked behind her, there was no one there. "How she waving at me?" she thought. When she reached the woman, she saw the woman had been crying. Her stomach was swollen with child. Her eyes were red and wild, the face streaked with tears. The woman shouted at Hosanna.

"My name is Yinyang Krupt! I live here." Yin threw her hand back over her shoulder, pointing at the house. "I need you! I need your help! I am about to give birth and I have no one! Help me! Pleeeeeease, help me!"

Hosanna stood there helplessly, wondering what to do. She did not know anything about childbirth. "Tell me where to go." She was breathless, "I'll go find your midwife for you!"

Yin bent over with another pain. "I don't have no damn midwife! I meant to go away to have my baby. But it's coming too early! I didn't have any chance to go! I need help now! Don't want no midwife. I'll pay you! Come in here and help me. Right now! Please, please, please." Her voice broke as another pain took her body.

Hosanna turned her wagon into the gate entrance with a bewildered, tired sigh. "Well, you better get in the house. You don't want to have it out here on the road. I think I know somebody who can help us." She thought of Aunt Ellen and her rent.

"No!" Yin's voice startled Hosanna, coming back so sharply. "No, no, no! I don't want anybody from around here!"

"I'm from around here." She led Yin to the house.

"I've never seen you. And, and you're colored."

Hosanna could not understand what Yin meant. She continued to support Yin while pulling the red wagon behind her.

Yin gasped, stopping her already slow walk. The back of her gown was wet. "Listen, I don't know what I was going to do, I thought I could do it alone. I'm frightened, scared. But you are here now. God must have sent you. Oh, listen to me, I'm going crazy. But I need a friend. We have to become friends right away, right now! I have to trust you. Are you kin to Miz Lal? Or Miz Mae, or Minna?"

"No, not as I know of." They were getting closer to the house.

"Good. Minna cooks for the Befoes. I don't want anyone, you hear me? ANYone to know about my baby until I am ready. You hear me?! I'll pay you!" Yin was wildly distraught.

Hosanna was tired. "Lady, I got enough in my life now to worry about. I don't need your problems, too!"

Yin nodded, "Okay, alright. Help me in the house, in to my room. I have put water on already."

Hosanna helped her up the steps and into the house. "Lady, I haven't said I can stay and do nothing for you. I'll go get somebody. I want to go home." Yin pointed upstairs, toward her bedroom. They kept moving.

When they reached the bedroom, Yin ran to a beautiful chest of drawers and snatched it open. She had placed fifty dollars there earlier, separate from where she hid her money in the house. "Here! Here is some money. Whoever you are, you need it. Ain't you ever had any family who needed you?" Her anxiety made her revert to the speech of Josephus days.

Hosanna looked bewildered but remembered her mother's child-birth tragedy. Yin pressed on. "Well, I need you. Now. As God is my witness, though why he should be I don't know. I will pay you another fifty dollars when we are finished. Girl, I know that's a lot of money! Take it!" She thrust the money into Hosanna's hesitant hands. "Now . . . I already put the water on." She bent and held her stomach as the next pain took her. Her voice was getting weaker, strained. "But, please, help me." She screamed from the pain and fell onto her bed.

Yin had put out towels and sheets. When Hosanna returned, Yin raised her head and said, "I read everything I think we will need. There's a knife and some scissors for the cord and some oil for to rub me with, down there. For the baby to come easier." She pointed. Hosanna backed up and frowned. Yin screamed at her. "You can do it if you're a woman!"

"I'm a child," Hosanna almost whimpered.

"You colored, you're a woman!"

"I'm a woman." Hosanna's voice was stronger.

Yin gasped and nearly screamed again from the last pain. The pains were coming quicker now, more often. She opened her legs wide and placed her hands on her belly, said, "Now, come on, my baby, I'm ready." She gave Hosanna a small, pitiful smile. "You ready?" Hosanna nodded and began to like the able, young woman. She smiled back, "I'm ready."

Yin sweated, swore, tossed and nearly squeezed Hosanna's hands off. Hosanna sweated and cried from exhaustion and ran for more water, more everything Yin called for. She blanched and hesitated at rubbing the oil "down there," but she did it. Hosanna marveled at the baby's head showing. She admired Yin even more. Yin's lips were bleeding from being bitten, but she kept her consciousness, her wits. Then the baby came out, slowly but steadily. Yin screamed, "I don't want to tear myself! Gotdammit, I'm too young! More oil."

Hosanna reached for the oil with bloody hands, screaming back at Yin, "I ain't got no way to put it in there, and the baby's almost here!"

"Ohhhhhhh, what is it?" Yin voice was now full of love.

"Can't tell yet."

"Don't want no girl. Life too hard." Then the last pain circled Yin's body and the baby came in the midst of her last scream.

Hosanna laughed a little laugh, "Well, well . . . It's a . . . boy!"

Still gasping, Yin asked, "What color is it?"

"Like coffee and cream."

Yin collapsed in a spent silence, the sound of her panting the only sound in the room. Finally she raised up a little to say, "Get the knife . . . and the silk string there."

Hosanna was staring at the little, wrinkled, red and coffee-with-cream colored baby.

Yin spoke more urgently, "The knife! What's your name?"

"Hosanna."

"Hosanna. Good. The knife."

"This baby is . . . colored."

Yin was concentrating on the task at hand. "What? What's that got to do with it? Take the knife and cut the cord."

That done, Yin leaned back, wiping her brow. "Take those towels there and that oil and bathe him, clean him up." Hosanna observed,

"He a cute, little ole ugly thing. Just think, I have helped bring a baby into this world!"

Yin smiled weakly, looking at Hosanna. Then Hosanna turned to her smiling and they looked into each other's eyes for a long moment over the baby's head—one wondering who this woman was and what she was, and the other wondering if she had made a mistake in sharing her business. Yin shook her head, thinking, "There was nothing else I could do!"

Yin spoke first. "You have to be my friend now. You have to be a friend to my son. Our son." Hosanna started to shake her head no. Yin continued, "He is your son, too, because you were the first person he saw. You helped him be born, you helped me, his mother. And he has no father . . . and . . . I have no friend. So he has no friend unless you agree to be our friend . . . and mean it."

Hosanna spoke as she continued stroking the baby with the oil. "I have a friend in Washington, but . . . I don't have a friend here." She smiled a big smile. "I have a family here though. You have a family? Your mother and father?"

"They are dead. I have no friend."

"Yes . . . I'll be your friend."

"And I will be your friend. Do you need a job?"

Hosanna's exhaustion came down on her. She had been already tired and now the birth had taken several hours. She sighed. "Not right now, but . . ." she brightened, "I know someone who does and she is a very good person."

Yin moaned, "Not Lal or Ma Mae, I hope. They talk so much and . . . I must keep my child a quiet secret for . . . awhile."

Hosanna handed Yin her baby and stood up. "No, her name is Ellen. Aunt Ellen. And she needs a home and some money. And some help. But she is strong and good and kind."

"Alright, I take your word." Yin started to say something else but stopped herself. "Will you get her for me? Soon? Right now? I can't get up. My body is starting to hurt again, but I can take care of that."

Hosanna felt like crying. She wanted to go HOME. These were not her problems. Here she had been held up so much already. Everybody needed help and she was in the middle. It was getting really dark outside. Hosanna left her wagon and walked back to find Ellen who was eating a yam baked in ashes, her head bowed, her feet wrapped in cool, wet, ragged towels. She looked surprised when she saw Hosanna. "What's wrong, chile?"

Hosanna stumbled into the little, leaning house and sprawled on the floor. "I got you a job . . . and a home. You be making money and can see bout this here house of yours."

"A job?"

"A job, Aunt Ellen."

"A place to live? I got to live there?"

"And eat, Aunt Ellen. Listen, I'm tired. I ain't been home yet! I came back out here for you cause I know you need it. Now . . . let's go." She struggled up from the floor as Aunt Ellen dried her feet and pulled her old dress over her head, saying, "I ain't got nothin else to wear. Lord, it's a shame to go in this. They won't want me when they see me."

"They'll want you."

"How could you find me a job when I been lookin all the time and everbody sayin I'm too old?"

"You just have to be a grandmother . . . or a Aunt Ellen. You ain't too old for that. And you can use some of all that love you got in your heart right here at home, widout walking all the way to Pittsburgh. Lawd, all my good english I learned is gone to shit. I'm tired."

Aunt Ellen was dressed with a bulging, tied handkerchief in her hand. "I'm ready now."

Hosanna took Aunt Ellen to Yin, who was trying to feed the baby and kept falling asleep from exhaustion. The baby wanted to sleep, too. Yin was so happy to see Aunt Ellen, she cried and laughed at the same time. "I've got inside water. You take you a bath and wash that dress. Put my robe on, and then come get the baby. I've got to get some sleep and some food in me when I wake up." There was a neatly wrapped package, tied. Yin pointed to it. "That has to go out to be burned, please."

Hosanna was looking at the baby, "What you going to name the baby?"

Yin smiled, "Joseph Richard Befoe Krupt."

And so the little baby, with frowning face and waving his tiny hands, was crowned with two names he would never, hopefully, understand.

Joseph was after his grandfather, Josephus. The other two were after a fortune.

Satan just smiled and went on because there was too much love and friendship in the room. He does not like those things at all. He had looked at the baby, though. It was going to be in a nice situation for problems. Then . . . Satan laughed at Yin.

chapter 31

The little house Hosanna was so desperately trying to get to was the house Bessel had lived in, Ruth had been born in, Joel had married into, all their children had been born in. The same house Hosanna had been taken from so many young, sad years ago still stood sheltering Luke, Lettie and Lovey and was the house Hosanna's feet could not get to fast enough. The house sat back from the road. A few trees on the west side shielded it from the afternoon sun, while a garden kept for the purpose of feeding those that lived within grew around the house for an acre or so. Luke was a good gardener and Lovey, even on her knees, helped. Lettie worked there in her time off from the regular jobs she tried to keep to bring needed money into the house.

The family was happy being together and holding on to their parents' land, but individually they were each sad.

Lettie did housecleaning and child-care work. From her early youth, and she was still young in years, she had worked with Luke to keep themselves a home and a family. Luke took over his father's work at the Befoes as a gardener and horse-handler helper, even as young as he had been. He had tried hard to make his farm pay, but, little by little, they worked less land each year as the profits were too small and they did not want to have to borrow from those who loaned and could never be completely paid back. Those who, in the end, took the land. So they did outside work and kept the taxes paid and bought little necessities as they could. There was no money to waste on anything they wanted. They could only have some of what they needed.

There was a school, built by the Befoes years ago. They said you could come there, colored or white, but they discouraged you if you were colored. Not just by sitting you in the back of the room, but by ignoring you. There were never enough books to go around. Old books the class no longer used, you could have. So some of the colored population, if they wanted to learn, took the books, if possible, and went home to try to teach themselves and their families. It was usually given up in a few years as the demand for money to survive became more important than a book or school.

No industry came into Yoville. The Befoes did not want it there. It would have meant jobs for the poor. Having no jobs gave the Befoes more control over the people there. Black, white and Indian. The Befoes provided most of the jobs. Cooks, cleaners and farm labor. They had their choice of all the help they needed themselves.

Lovey was willing to do anything to help her brother and sister, and tried, but her legs were useless and she had to walk on her knees. The flesh of her knees was hard and calloused from her efforts to work in the field. Even the rags she bound them with didn't help much; they were always coming loose and were already mostly ragged from the beginning of their use. But she tried.

Lovey had tried to go to the school, which was just up and across the road from their house. She didn't ask anyone, she wanted to surprise them. She got up, got dressed and started out on the first day of school. She was excited and happy, thinking, "Readin and writin! Somethin in my life. I know I can do it!" She was seven years old at the time. She dressed in her only good dress, handed down, already old. She had washed and ironed it on a cloth on the floor two weeks before. Her knee rags, too. She wrapped her knees in the clean cloths. She had no socks, but it was still kinda summer, she could go barefooted. Luke and Lettie were already gone. Her little soul was happy, her heart was light as she picked up her pencil—she had no tablet—and struggled down the steps to the ground.

There were light gray clouds in the sky when she left for school, a great big smile on her face. She trudged to the road, shooing her friend, the dog Pap, to go back, to stay home. Pap curled his tail beneath him. He was not used to her leaving him behind. He sat and watched her make her slow way to the road and then across it.

The road was a little rocky, as country roads are where the colored people live, and the knee wraps began to unravel. She looked down at them, but her heart was too full to stop now. Across the road, she walked the quarter mile or so to the little school house where, she thought as she walked, "The whites maybe sit up front, but I could sit in the back. I want to go. I am goin!"

The sky grew darker, but she was almost there now. "Only a little ways more," she said out loud to herself. Then the first drops spattered on her pretty cheeks, then a few more. Then more. She trudged on. The dress she had ironed so painstakingly was getting wet. Lovey wanted to cry because she could not run. She thought, "Never mind that, I'm goin to learn to read! Books and things!"

The rain was heavier now. One knee rag had come loose and was wet and dragging behind her. She could not stop to fix it, she was already too wet and the rain was coming down harder. She finally reached the school, slowing down, tired from her efforts to hurry. Her dress clung to her little body. Her pretty hair was stuck to her face and neck, sparkling with the water. The mixture of mud and clay clung in lumps to her knees and her hands from trying to grab the tail of the rags as she walked. The children were already inside when she got to the school door. Lovey struggled up the steps to the red door.

Somehow, her heart was still thrilling as her hand reached eagerly for the handle to open the door to her little life. The handle turned and she opened the door and the whole class turned their heads to see who was late and looked at her. For a moment, the room was hushed. Then the blue-eyed teacher gasped, "Oh! Oh, my!" The teacher rushed over to Lovey who was about to say, "I'm alright, I'm here," smiling because she thought that the reason the teacher gasped was because she was wet from the rain. But the teacher said, "Oh, my dear, my goodness! You can't come in here with all that mud on you! Look at you! Wipe your . . . You have to leave that mud . . . and those filthy rags! Outside!"

Still holding the handle of the red door, Lovey looked up into the teacher's face. Water dripping from the little face and body, the rags surrounding her legs on the floor. The teacher's words did not penetrate. "I am at school!" was in Lovey's wet smile. Then somehow, she felt the tone and did not let loose the door or move forward. The teacher reached to remove Lovey's hand from the handle and pressed her own hand to Lovey's chest, pushing her backward, back into the rain, while with her other hand she waved Lovey out. When Lovey did not seem to understand, or move, the teacher pressed Lovey harder, it became a push. "You must go out now, little girl, you can't come here wet like that."

Lovey looked down at herself and saw the clinging dress and the bungled rags. She thought, "I'll let em dry. I'll fix em. What that got to do with school?" She forgot to say it out loud, she was looking with longing and joy into the other children's faces. Lovey moved forward, dragging the rags. The teacher pressed harder and snatched the door from Lovey's hand. "Go home, little girl! Go home to your mother! She should not have sent you here without consulting me! We have no place for crippled people here! And you can't bring dogs!"

Lovey looked around and there was Pap, standing in the rain. She wanted to cry. She wanted to remove the hand from her chest and go in to the bright, warm room with the books on the desks. The children in the class were giggling and even laughing at her.

An Indian girl of twelve years or so got up from her seat way in the back of the room, went to the cloak room then came to the red door. She placed a hand on Lovey's shoulder and removed the hand of the teacher from Lovey's chest and said, "I'll take her home, Miss Small, I think I know where she lives." Miss Small was relieved as she held her own throat with her lily white hand, "Well, then, good. Tell her mother she can not come here."

Lovey spoke up, "I don't have no mother. I want to come to school myself."

The teacher waved them out the door. "Well . . . well, thank you . . . ahhhh . . ." The teacher did not remember the girl's name.

"Little Wisdom is my name," the girl said as she turned Lovey around. Lovey was still looking back at the seated children who were laughing at her, with a mixture of desire and pain on her small, wet face. She looked back until the door closed loudly, sharply in her face, then she stared down at her legs. Little Wisdom pulled gently on her hand, "Come on, little girl, I'm a take you back home to your house."

Lovey answered softly through the rain, "But I want to read."

Little Wisdom pulled her gently, knowing the pain that must be in Lovey's knees. "Come on, I'll carry you." She lifted Lovey, placing wet clothes and rags against her own well-worn but clean dress also carefully prepared for school, though prepared by her mother who believed in education by the white man if you were ever going to beat him at his own game. The mother had had to fight for Little Wisdom, a girl, to go to school. But the mother won, so Little Wisdom got to go to school.

Little Wisdom trudged through the mud and clay of the school yard, then across the road. Pap followed, his head down as if in sorrow. Then Lovey said, "Me and Pap can go on from here. I'm already wet. You go on . . . back . . . to school."

Little Wisdom put the girl down. The rain was letting up. She asked, "You want me to come and teach you how to read?"

Now I don't know if you have ever seen love in anyone's eyes stare out at you, but Lovey looked at Little Wisdom with all the love in the world. All the gratitude Little Wisdom would see in her life for a long, long time. Little Wisdom smiled from her inner warmth and asked, "What's your name?"

"Lovey."

"My name is Wise Flower, but I just say Little Wisdom because it is easier for people to take. My family lives in the hills over there on the other side of the river. I cross it in my canoe every morning. I'll come to you, Lovey. I'll come when I can." Little Wisdom thought of a book she could steal. "I'll bring you a book, too! From Miss Small. It will be easy to find you. I will find you." She had been going to school without a book ever since she started two years ago, but she would steal one for Lovey.

Lovey hugged her and Little Wisdom turned back to the school. "I'm goin in, wet as I am!" She ran on her way. Lovey decided to run, she tried, her little legs slapping the earth beneath her, Pap trotting at her side.

Back at home, Lovey cried as she took off and washed her dress and the rags, standing in her little hand-me-down panties, pinned so they would stay up. She would cry awhile, then laugh a little, thinking about her love of Little Wisdom and learning to read. Pap laying not far from her knees, slapping his tail on the floor happily when Lovey was laughing. He wasn't often allowed in the house until snow was on the ground, so he was happy. Happy, until Lovey cried, then his tail stopped wagging and waited until she smiled again, then it wagged and slapped the floor again and again . . . and again.

Lovey never told Luke or Lettie about all that had happened to her. Though they finally heard about it, they never talked about it. But when Little Wisdom came, they treated her like a most welcome member of their family. Luke brought books from the Befoes that Richlene gave him when she heard. Young as she was, Little Wisdom began to fall in love with Luke because he was so kind and generous. Always giving her a chicken or something from the garden to take home. Luke did not really see Little Wisdom at that time, she was not a woman to him. He did go over to the hills to go fishing or hunting with her brother and uncles. He liked that and it saved money for food. He would not kill what he did not intend to eat.

Lettie took the opportunity to learn to read and count a little, too, when she was home. This is how their life went. Accepting the bad and the good of life. Satan never bothered with them. They were already sad.

Hosanna had sent small sums of money home to them now and again. The money always coming in the time of need, no matter when it came. They had small Christmasses. Only church for Easter. But if a holiday was about food, they had plenty. The old chicken house that had belonged to Ruth was full of chickens they kept more for laying than eating.

They were satisfied together, but unsatisfied and lonely in each of their own lives apart. They loved each other but did not know what to do with life. What COULD they do with life? They were already working with every tool they had.

chapter
3 2

On this night, Hosanna finally left Yin's and was making her way home at last, pulling her little red wagon filled with her boxes, bringing her hope, pain, need, anger and loneliness and love in it, too. She walked down the main road, looking through the darkness all around her, searching for her home, that little house she had left but remembered so well.

All the lamps and candles were out and each of them, Luke, Lettie and Lovey, were alone in their rooms with their thoughts.

Luke, in his underwear, lay on his side, staring through the little window at the night, the stars, the shapes of the trees. His breathing was soft, though he was tired from a hard day's work with the horses. Now that Mr. Befoe was getting sicker, wasn't nobody to talk to bout the horses and what they needed, cept Creed, and what could Creed do? Anyway, he had other problems. Luke looked past the trees up to the dark sky.

"I'm a man, Lord. I'm a man and I can't even take care of my sisters enough so one can go to school and the other one can rest some and go be with that man she love. Lettie scared to get married and leave us cause what can Lovey do? She try, but what can she do? Can't take over the garden by herself and we needs that little money the Befoes pay me. Lettie tired, too. We all need to get on way from here, but where we goin? We poor. Ain't got nothin but this house. And I can't even always afford to fix it up when it need somethin. It need a roof right now. This the one my daddy put on here. It's bout gone."

There were no tears in Luke's eyes. They were in his heart trying to get to his eyes, but he wouldn't let them. "What I'm gonna do, Lord? I could make more money somewheres else. I know aplenty to do. But I can't leave. What would my sisters, my family do? One young and tired. One with no legs? Lettie need to have her own life now, she bout grown. I know she loves that boy Boyd. And what Lovey gonna do alone? Die? Everybody else done left, could they help it or not. I can't leave them, Lord, they mine. My re-spon-si-bi-lity. I loves em, Lord. I loves em, but I miss my papa and my mother. Why they both had to go, Lord? Why you take everything? And why I love that lady Richlene like I do? I know she not sposed to be no real grown woman, but I know she a real woman. I love her like she a real woman, Lord, you know I do. Ain't no use in thinkin of that. Lil Wisdom try to think she love me, but she a chile. I ain't thinkin of Lil Wisdom either. Nobody but Richlene. A rich, white man's daughter. Lord, Lord, what I'm gonna do? I ain't done no livin either. All my life I been livin my daddy's life. What about me, Lord, what about my satisfaction? I ain't sayin take the cross off my back, I love my sisters. I'm just sayin give me a cane, a wheel, I'll do somethin with it. Just a little help, Lord. A little help. I blives in you."

The moonlight moved through other windows of the little house, faintly lighting up the kitchen and the little sitting room that was next to Lettie's room. She was turned, facing the wall in her little bed. Her strong, healthy body was wrapped in the big, poorly fitting gown the white lady at one of her jobs had given her instead of throwing it out in the trash.

Lettie put her hand out through the darkness and placed it on the wall as though she would push the wall away. Her other hand smoothed over her ripe, full body. "Young, strong, full of come and ain't had enough of nothin! And none of somethin!" Then she shook her head to chase those thoughts away, but she couldn't, they would not leave.

"Lord, I been seein and I been readin and I know there is romance and love and satisfaction in life. Why can't I get any? I loves Lovey, I loves Luke. But I loves Boyd too. I always got to choose. I got to choose them cause I can't leave Lovey on her knees and Luke on his behind tryin to make out a life for everbody. But I needs . . . Oh Lord, I needs . . . somethin! I ain't happy. I ain't unhappy, cause I love my family, but Lord, I ain't got no satisfaction in my nights. I wants to be married. I wants my own chilren . . . after a while. But Jesus, is this all there is gonna be? Is this all they gonna be for me? Lovey can't never change. She gonna be here forever. Do I gotta stay with her? Oh, I love her, Lord, don't blame me that, but I love me too and I wants somethin for me. Lord, other girls, other women, gonna give Boyd what he want. He be hangin roun down there at Choke's ole juke pool joint. They have real, live musicians sometime. Women always be hangin roun there, too. They sho gonna give him what he want. I can't. Spose I get pregnant? Sides, You done said not to. But you ain't here, Lord, You ain't me."

Satan loves those words. He smiled.

Tears moving slowly down Lettie's face, she continued speaking to God, "You in heaven. I wants to be in heaven . . . on earth. Boyd make me feel like I could be in heaven on earth. Oh, I ain't bad, God, I'm just . . . lonely . . . and ugly . . . and poor. And I hurt. My heart hurt and my body hurt, cause I ain't got no pleasure, no satisfaction out of my life. I know they love me, but they ain't enough, Lord, they just ain't enough seem like. Is this all I'm gonna get? What I done already got? I don't want much, just a little somethin. A little somethin. Can you see your way to send me a little somethin, God? You don't know. It's awful lonely down here. Somethin be empty inside you. Somethin be gnawin away at your insides. Somethin hungry . . . and you ain't got nothin to feed it. I wants to be full, Lord. Oh, Jesus, I want to be full of food and joy and happiness, not all this empty. Boyd say he can satisfy my life. Well, I want . . . I neeeed some satisfaction, God."

Satan moved away. But God didn't.

The moon moved through the windows of Lovey's room. She was sitting up in an old slip Lettie had given her from one of her jobs. Lovey looked down at her knees. She rubbed them a moment, thinking, "Don't you worry. I love you. You mine. You all I got to move in this world with. I just wish we could walk away and let my famly go. I know Luke could leave and I know Lettie love Boyd but just don't let go and leave us. It's me. Cause if they was alone, they could both go and live how they want to. I want to live a life, too. Thank you, God, for givin me books. Books is my whole world. They take me way from round here. I done seen Spain and China . . . a little bit. I done seen some of America. Hosanna done seen it, sure nuff. If I could walk there to that Washington, I would. Sure would, Lord.

"I know I ain't never gonna have nothin but my brother and my sister. Hosanna ain't never comin home from that city. I don't blame her neither. But I ain't never gonna have nothin but me and Pap. But you know, God, I got a heart. I am a soul. You gave everybody else legs so they could search for their satisfaction. But . . . I ain't got none what works. What I'm sposed to do? Crawl to mine? I ain't mad at you, God, but I want, I want, I want and I need, I need, I need . . . everything. I want to help my brother and my sister, too. But . . ." She began to cry. "I can't do nothin! Nothin!" She whispered out loud, "I ain't nothin. I ain't got no satisfaction. I keep them from they own satisfaction. I ain't nobody's satisfaction. Who gonna ever, ever, ever love me? And what I'm gonna do with all the love I got carryin round with me?"

Lovey reached through the darkness for the flower she had taken to bed with her. "Everythin so pretty, Lord. But not me. Who want to look at these legs? Legs ain't but a piece of my body, but legs can do so much, God. You made em, and you know. Oh, I dreams of love. I dreams of bein held in somebody's arms some day. I'm too young now, but I'm gonna be grown. Like Hosanna, like Lettie. I dream of my own house, my own children, some more dogs. I dream and . . . I have to let em die gone . . . cause I know it never will be for me. But God, it hurts somebody. Sometime I hate my legs, but they can't help it. It just me . . . and ain't no use in dreamin. I got to learn to stop dreamin. I'm gonna die just like I am now. I wisht I had died and my brother and mother had lived."

Lovey fell back in the bed, pulling her useless legs up on it. Tears slid down her young, pretty cheeks, wetting her pillow and her hair. She closed her eyes to try to sleep. "Give me somethin, Lord, give me somethin. I'll do somethin with it, I betcha that! Bye, Lord, see you tomorrow." She raised her head one last time. "And give my brother Luke and my sister Lettie somethin for them, too." She lay her head slowly down. The moon moved on and darkness filled the little room as Lovey, heart and tears with her, thankfully sank softly into sleep, ending her day.

Outside on the road, at last, everything was so quiet to Hosanna. She could hear the crickets and a bird call now and then cutting through the night. She listened hungrily to every sound as she pulled her little red wagon. Home. She felt like crying she was so full of the desire to be home and she was almost there—sweat pouring down her body, tired as she could be. She began to recognize some of the landmarks. Some rich person's big house sat far back from the road, closed now, until some season when they would return. A huge, beautiful tree, things like that remembered from her last looks as she turned back with huge eyes when she was taken away by her aunt. These things seem to give her new strength.

Hosanna finally saw the house. Her house. She walked slowly into the yard and stood there a moment feeling the silence and the thrill of being home. "The house kinda looks the same," she thought. "Small. But it's neat, looks clean. Not painted, just clean. Look at that large porch. I don't remember that too much. Three chairs. One of them sure is cut low. Well, they gonna need one more." She walked around the house. "Plenty big garden all round the house. That's good. I sure hope they cook some of them turnip greens for dinner! I don't remember them animal pens. But I could'a forgot. They must be doin alright! Lord, don't let me commence to cryin."

She did commence to crying. Didn't mean to, just couldn't help it. She started running. She held tightly to her wagon handle and began to shout "Mama!" but did not know it. A lamp light came on. The door opened. Hosanna screamed, "Mama!" Someone ran out, then somebody else came out behind them. That red wagon was just bumping and rolling behind her. She screamed again, "Mama! It's me. Hosanna!" The wagon ended up running into the porch as Hosanna stumbled, falling up the steps and into the open arms of her sister Lettie, her brother Luke. She felt someone, Lovey, wrapping her arms around her hips. She looked down. "My sister Lovey." With a gasp, Hosanna stopped crying suddenly. She just held onto those holding her. She was home. That's what she said, "I'm home. You all, I'm home."

It was a happy time and a sad time when Hosanna came home. They were happy to see their sister, their mother and father's flesh and blood. Home! But as poor people have to do, they also thought in terms of her help. Her making things lighter for all in the house.

The house was clean though you could tell it was kept up by someone who could not do things so well. Lovey. It was bare except for essentials. There was an old wood-burning cookstove. It worked, but it was inadequate. Used also for heat for the whole house. An unmatched set of table and chairs. Three beds, old, one held up by bricks underneath. Mattresses were filled with cornshucks and cotton. They had to be aired and fluffed up every two weeks or so. Some places in the house you could see through to the outside and the floor beneath. The wood drying, shrinking. The holes were filled with newspaper and rags. Not too many holes, but they were there. And even light rain showed signs of coming through the roof. Hosanna thought of her three hundred dollars and sighed, though she told no one she had it.

Hosanna, Luke, Lettie and Lovey sat around the stove in the darkened kitchen. Glowing flames from the fire lighting their faces with flashes of warm gold. She told them about the big city. The jobs and the schools. She told them about her day getting to them. About Aunt Ellen, Yin and the baby. Lettie asked, "Did she pay you?"

Hosanna smiled, slightly, "I'm gonna take care of that."

Lettie didn't smile. "You must have money then."

"Well, I wouldn't say that." Hosanna didn't know why she made those answers, but she was not ready yet to bare herself. It was also something about the tone of Lettie's voice. Hosanna wanted to know more about her family and the house she was to live in.

Every once in a while, Lovey reached out and patted Hosanna's knee or arm. Hosanna turned to her with a bright, loving smile when she did that. At last Lovey burst into tears and no one knew exactly why. Hosanna hugged her tightly.

Luke spoke as man of the house, a role he had taken on as a child. He was a man now. "You all betta get some sleep. Daylight be here fore you know it." Lovey had the largest room and the largest bed and wanted Hosanna to share her room. "You sleep with me!" she said. "I'll share my room with you!" Hosanna agreed. Lettie didn't say anything. They loved each other, these sisters, but between Lettie and Lovey there were quarrels because Lettie was tired and Lovey couldn't do more. Lettie's bed was smaller, but she still felt something of an outsider with Hosanna in Lovey's room. Them alone. Together. The mattress was uncomfortable and, being used to sleeping alone, the bed felt crowded to Hosanna. "I'm gonna have to do something about this." Hosanna thought on her first night home. "A few days will be alright though." And so it was.

The next night Luke said to Hosanna, "I get up early and sometime I don't even come home cause I got to be there so early. I work over at the Befoes as garden man and horse helper, like daddy did."

Lovey laughed as she pulled and tucked the rags around her knees. "Oh, he in love with that ole, slow white woman, Richlene!"

"I ain't! You betta quit sayin that on me, Lovey. You gonna get me into some trouble!"

"You can't get in no trouble if you don't do nothin wrong!" They all laughed but Lettie. On this the second night, she rose and stretched, saying, "You all hush now, cause I got a long day head of me tomorrow."

Hosanna turned to her. "You work at the Befoes, too?"

"Naw, I does housework for two other families round here. They ain't rich as the Befoes, but they near it. I work for some other rich folks when they here in the summers and things. I worked for Mrs. Befoe once, but she talk too mean to people!" Lettie yawned and stretched again, preparing to leave the room.

Hosanna caught the tail of her dress. "You all talk strange. Don't you all go to school round here?"

They looked at her like she was crazy. Luke spoke first, "Ain't nobody got no time for no school round here. I went sometime when Mama was alive . . . and we had a teacher here for a quick minute. Didn't no teacher want to teach in that ole, leandown barn Mrs. Befoe gave em. Anyway, the man of the house ain't got no time to be sittin up in no school wit no book. Lovey got a girl come by here sometime to teach her. Indian girl, name of Little Wisdom. We all learns somethin. I read some, write some. Miz Richlene help me some. I makes out."

Lovey got out of her chair, asking, "You been to school?"

Hosanna watched her walk on her knees to the bedroom. "Enough. I had help." She thought of Butler.

Lovey spoke over her shoulder, she sounded tired. "I'll clean up tomorrow." She pushed herself up on the low bed Luke had made for her. She took off her dress and turned her body to lay down.

Hosanna called to her, "Don't you take those dirty rags off your legs fore you get in bed?" She had been too tired to notice before.

Lovey answered softy, "No. Ain't nobody here, wasn't nobody here but me. I just have to get up and put em on again in the mornin." She lay down, then asked, "You want me to take em off? For you?" She sounded about to cry.

Hosanna sighed, "No. No, that's alright this time. You gonna get some clean rags to put on in the morning?" She moved into the bedroom.

Lovey sighed, "I wash these out every Sat'day." She looked at her knees like they were strange to her.

Hosanna stretched out on the bed. "You ever exercise your legs?"

Lovey laughed, "I get plenty exercise."

"I mean the parts you don't use much."

"No. I don't use em cause I can't, so how I'm gonna exercise em?"

Hosanna patted her sister, "Go to sleep. We'll talk about it another day." Lovey patted her back. "Hosanna, I'm so glad you here. I thought about you all them years when you sendin us some money sometime. And I knew you loved us and didn't forget us. I loved you, too. I'm glad my sister is home."

Hosanna put her arm around Lovey and held her until she went to sleep, thinking, "What kind of life would Lovey have if she had no learning at all?" Hosanna thought of the few books she had brought. She thought of the red wagon. She determined she would do SOMETHING about Lovey getting around. "I know I better look for some way to bring some money in and get this here house fixed, but first, I'm gonna make it run better!" Then she fell asleep. A deep, deep, good home sleep.

chapter
3 3

hosanna spent her first few days just getting used to being home. Lovey seemed so happy to be sharing her room with her, she decided to stay there. She gave it a good cleaning, the both of them sharing the work. Lovey's body was strong, but it took double the time and a lot of effort to get back down on your knees from one place and trudge to the next place, where with legs you just made a few steps. Hosanna began to appreciate her own body more. They were both pretty girls. Hosanna had a browner tone to her skin, where Lovey had a golden tone. Both had long hair. Hosanna had one braid down just below her shoulders; Lovey had two braids, one on each side of her head. Both had skin that was smooth and soft. Both had hard hands and chipped nails from their hard work. Hosanna's eyes were round, clear and almost black. Lovey's were almond shaped and a lighter brown, like the gold had slipped from her golden eyelids to run to her eyes. Lovey's breasts were just beginning to bud; Hosanna had a moderate but full sized bust. Their parents would have been proud they had made such lovely, healthy children. Except for Lovey's legs.

In the middle of something, Hosanna would look up and Lovey would just be staring at her, eyes full of joy and love. Lovey loved to hear about the city. After a few days of this, Hosanna would just sigh, smile and tell her again, leaving out the sad parts. She would then change the subject.

"When are you going to start doing something about your legs, Lovey?"

"Naw, ain't nothin I can do. They just . . . hang there."

"You been using them whether you know it or not. You ought to try some real exercise with em."

"They ain't gonna be no good."

"Lovey, you given up before you try."

"Tell me bout the city again. Tell me bout Washington, D.C."

"Oh, Lovey, a city isn't anything but a whole lot more people than there is in the country all together in one place. It's a lot of brains, all working in their own way. Thinking up things to do to survive. All kinds of brains think of all kinds of things. Some think how to survive on their own, some think of how to get somebody else to help them survive. Some think of how to go into business, somehow to get rich. But lots think of how to steal, how to lie, even how to kill. The whole thing is all wrapped around money, even the churches, seem like to me. Some of them city people even come to you, want you to sell your body."

Lovey shook her head. "Wouldn't nobody come to me to sell my body."

Hosanna nodded her head back. "They probably love you to death, 'cause some of them brains are twisted and broken."

Lovey put her hand out, reaching out to Hosanna. "You mean ain't nobody gonna want me less their brain is twisted and broke?"

Hosanna reached out for Lovey. "Oh, no, Lovey. I just mean you thinking about love. Their twisted brain ain't thinking bout no love. They thinking about another kind of satisfaction, what ain't really no satisfaction for nobody but them."

Lovey turned back to her work. "Maybe I don't really want to go to no city. Maybe I just want to be in love and have a man someday."

Hosanna turned to her own work. "Well, I ain't . . . haven't been here long, but I just know the country got a little bit of everything the city got. Cause that's where most all people in the city come from . . . the country! Wasn't no cities when everybody first came here! You all got some of the same kinda minds here in the country! Sick! And you have plenty time to think about love, child, you haven't even grown up yet!"

Lovey's voice was so low, Hosanna almost didn't hear it when she said, "Ain't nobody gonna love me like I am noway. I just be dreamin."

Then they worked in silence until Lovey found another question and Hosanna tried to answer all her questions the best way Lovey's youth could understand.

hosanna helped Luke when he worked in their own garden for the food for the family. He wanted to know about the city, too. He would rise from digging around a cabbage or some such thing and ask, "What kinda men they in them cities? I bet you got them men what makes money and take care they famly and everybody be happy. Goin to school . . . and then colleges. And workin in them offices and even ownin they own business."

Hosanna bent over, digging, too. "I saw some was going to college. Small college. Big college. I heard of some was taking care the family, planning for their own children. Not too many. White or colored. I know a man named Butler, was a good man, and he liked other men."

Luke's head shot up. Hosanna kept talking, "He didn't have no family to take care of but that man of his, but he was a kind man. He was good to me. I ain't met everybody, but I never met none like you are a man. Staying here, taking care your daddy and mama's land and your sisters. Hadn't been for you, I wouldn't have no place to come home to. That's what you done for me . . . for them. I remember it was you who wouldn't let Uncle sell this land. You decided to stay here and try to make it work! You stood up for that and you wasn't grown then. Look what you have done. You have done it!"

Luke grinned, his body moved in the pleasure of her words and thoughts. She made him proud. "Awww, I ain't done nothin. We all done done it!"

Hosanna knew his pleasure. It gave her pleasure. "Yeah, but you stayed. You are the man of the place. The only one. You could'a done . . . You could have left here already and sent some money home. That money might not'a meant what it means to have you here. Leading em.

Being a rock or something they can count on. I can count on. You have helped my sisters use the strength they have."

Luke was silent then. Thinking. After a little while of plucking, raking and digging, he spoke, "I know what you sayin . . . and I'm glad, proud I been here . . . but they ain't doin so good. They ain't happy, ain't satisfied. Course, ain't nothin here to be satisfied bout! Lettie, she in love and can't go get married up with him even if he would marry her, which I don't know bout. But he a fast young man, nothin don't seem to grow under his feet. Lovey . . . well . . . Lovey probly goin be here all our life . . . all her life. Hosanna, I don't want you thinkin hard of me, but . . . do I want to . . . I can't go nowhere. I ain't got no freedom. I can't afford my sisters right . . . less alone a wife."

Hosanna leaned on her hoe, looking at him. She spoke softly, "You love somebody? You want to get married? Bring her home here. This your home."

After a long moment, he answered, "I loves somebody." He wiped the perspiration from his brow. "I love somebody. But I ain't givin up nothin. I can't never be with her no way no more than I am. I'm a man though. My body want to . . . be a husband man. But I guess I ain't willin to give up what I got to do here. Cept for my famly, my sisters, I ain't got nothin to give . . . to share."

Still softly, Hosanna spoke to him, "Luke, I have looked in many a face and I ain't seen such love. I seen fear, greed . . . and a lusting after the flesh. But I ain . . . haven't seen such love. In the city you see all kinds of people who know how to make it LOOK like love or something good. But the backbone to it ain't there. They only got what looks like love. If you got that . . . real love . . . don't give it up. For nothing else. You are a good man, a kind man with real love in your heart. I know you loved me and I was a long, long way away for a long time." Hosanna thew her hoe down, ran to her brother and hugged him. "But you gotta be happy, too. You're a man. Been a man since you were a child. I love you. You my dear brother. Mine."

Luke held her, then let go quickly because he wasn't used to holding women in his hungry arms. "I feel better, sister. I feel . . . better."

"I do too, brother. I do, too. I'm home with my family. And we gonna try to do something bout this here satisfaction business. For all of us!"

. . .

Lettie stayed a bit distant from Hosanna, and quiet. Not knowing what to say to Hosanna. Thinking Hosanna above herself. Thinking she could have stayed gone and had a different life . . . a good life. On the third day home, Hosanna followed Lettie out the door on her way to work. "I'm going to walk you to your job, sis. Pretty soon I'm going to have to get out here and find something for myself to do." She caught up with Lettie.

Lettie looked at her and kept walking. "Ain't no sense you goin over here with me. They ain't got no jobs to give nobody but me."

"Oh, I'm not goin just for a job. I just want to be with you a little bit, Lettie. I ain't been with you in all these years and you my sister. Let's just talk."

"What you come back here for? Ain't nothin here!"

"My family is here."

"We gonna be your family whether you come back or not!"

"I want to feel my heart . . . so I came back cause I want to . . . for me. Wasn't nothing where I was."

Lettie kicked the dirt in the road as she walked, "Well . . . it ain't nothin here neither."

They walked a moment in silence, then Hosanna said, "I hear you in love. You must'a found something here."

In spite of herself, Lettie smiled. "He ain't nothin."

"What's his name?"

"Boyd."

"What does he do?"

"Nothin. Work like all of us. He do yard work and a little carpenter work, and a little . . . I don't know. He don't do much."

"You want to marry him?"

Lettie sighed, "Yeaaaaaah."

"How is he going to take care of you, if he don't do too much?"

"I can work. Been workin all my life."

Hosanna stopped walking, Lettie didn't. "You are going to get married thinking how you can take care of your family?" She caught up with Lettie again.

"You don't unnerstand. We goin to work together."

"He asked you . . . to marry him?"

"No! Cause he know I couldn't leave Lovey and Luke."

"He could join you and help, too."

Lettie stopped and turned to Hosanna. "Why should he?"

Hosanna answered softly, "Cause he love you."

Lettie jerked herself around and started walking again. "Oh, you don't know what you talkin bout! That man ain't got to worry bout my problems!"

"Well, you do! And if he loves you, then he do, too!"

Lettie was almost in tears, but she was getting angry. "I don't think it's none of your bi'ness. You my sister and all, but you ain't been here and you don't know nothin bout roun here! Specially nothin bout me!" Her walk picked up speed.

Hosanna didn't let up. "Love is love. No different here than any place else in the world."

"Well, we diffrent here."

"You say you different here. But you all don't change life. Life is the same all over the world, and if he loves you, he takes what you got."

Lettie laughed, "I want to give him what I got, alright."

"And he give you what he got."

"Sho will." Lettie smiled.

"Which is nothing."

Lettie got angry again. "Oh, you don't know everything! Just cause you been to a big city!"

"Do you know how to read, Lettie?"

"A little."

"Do you know how to write?"

"A little."

"Then that's just how you are always gonna live . . . a little."

Lettie turned to her again. "How you livin? Who you?"

"I'm not through learning."

Lettie turned, walking faster. "Well, you done learned your way. I'm gonna live my way."

Hosanna put her hand on Lettie's arm, they were walking so fast. "I love you, Lettie."

"Well, I guess I love you, too, but I KNOW I love Boyd!"

Hosanna just wouldn't give up. "Why? What are you going to give your babies? Don't you remember Mama and Daddy?"

Lettie spun around. "Do I remember? You gotdamned right I do! I remember you left. WE stayed here. WE worked, while you laid on your ass somewhere in the city of Washington, D.C. WE kept everything goin here and now you home, callin it your home cause you sent a few dollars once a year or somethin. You ain't done nothin for us! We done somethin for you! Now you want to come tell me what's gonna make me happy! Who are you? You ain't done nothin for me!"

Hosanna's voice was tiny, coming from the tears in her throat, "I will try to. I am tryin to."

"You so smart, Miss Lady! You don't know nothin bout my heart or what's in my head. You so smart, why ain't you satisfied? Work on your own life!" Then Lettie ran away from her sister's outstretched arm. She ran the rest of the way to her job. Hosanna watched her as she dissapeared.

hosanna went back home, sat down, cried a little and did a lot of thinking about her money she still had pinned to the brassiere she had not taken off except to bathe and then put right back on. "Butler said put it in a bank till I know what I'm gonna do. Save it, add to it or need to spend it." She divided the money in her mind. "Some for a cow, we need milk. A roof repair. An extra bed, small. And if I'm gonna be in my own business, like he said, I need a better cookstove. That ought to leave about a hundred dollars to go to the bank."

Hosanna walked to the bank, had never been to one before. She stood looking through the big window at the man sitting at a desk way in the back of the bank under a sign that said "Bank Officer." She frowned, "Lord, what am I doing here?" The man looked up now and again, smiled at her and went back to his papers. At last she went in. He stood, holding his hand out to shake her hand.

"Good morning. I'm Russell Moore.

Nervous, Hosanna answered, "I'm Hosanna Jones."

"And what may we do for you?"

"I want to talk about a bank saving account."

"Fine. I'll be glad to help." Russell was good, kind and helpful. He gave her all the information, took her hundred dollar bill, wondering where she had gotten it, and opened a savings account for her, repeating again and again, "Yes, you can take it out whenever you want it." Satisfied, with her savings book in her brassiere, she started home and decided to stop by Yin's house.

Ellen and Yin were doing fine and little Joseph Richard Befoe Krupt was a well taken care of baby. Yin was preparing herself for a guest. "The baby's father," she whispered to Hosanna. Her bed was fresh, her gown fluffy, ruffled and lacy. The baby was prepared in a like manner. His skin tone had darkened ever so slightly, his hair curled smoothly around his head. He smiled at Hosanna, but then she did not know he smiled at everything. He was a happy baby. Ellen looked happy, too. One thing, she was full and she was smiling.

Yin was working on her hair when Hosanna came. She smiled over her shoulder at Hosanna. "Well, Miss Doctor, how are you doing? Was your family glad to see you? I know they were! Listen, why don't you need a job? You got money hidden somewhere?" Yin laughed, but she was thinking of that empty shack she had gone to, way back on her land. There had been no gold there, nor a diamond ring.

Hosanna sat down on one of the little satin seats. "Not a lot. I saved some up on my jobs in Washington, but I can see it ain't going far here!"

Yin turned to her. "You know, I paid you too much money the other night, just because I was in extreme pain. You took advantage of me." She was not smiling, so Hosanna did not know if she was serious or not, but she treated it seriously.

Yin continued, "You know, I could have done it alone, after all. Aunt Ellen says I didn't have the same kind of trouble some women do."

Hosanna found something to stare at on her knee. "But you didn't do it alone. I helped."

"Your help wouldn't have cost a hundred dollars!"

"My help . . . would cost whatever I think my time is worth."

"You should give some of it back to me."

"Give me my time back."

Yin turned away from the mirror to Hosanna. "Well, what are you thinking of talking to me like that?!"

Hosanna looked at her. "I'm trying to think of how much more you owe me. I thought of Aunt Ellen. You couldn't think of anyone. I went to get Aunt Ellen for you, too. You owe me. Friend forever." The last two words were spoken with irony.

Yin made a little gasp, but smiled. "Why, you're just a child. What would you need all that money for?"

"I'm colored. I'm a woman. And everybody needs some money in this world."

The mood was past and Hosanna had Yin's respect. Yin turned back to the mirror, primping. "Then why don't you want a job? I know where I can get one for you. At the Befoes. Can you cook? Sew?"

"I can cook most anything. I learned under somebody that loved French food, some Italian food and German food. I can do it all, especially desserts. I specially learned how to care for lingerie. That's about all what I expect to do right now."

Yin stared at Hosanna with appreciation. "Lordy, girl, your future is made. Any of these ladies around here would take you on in a minute!"

Hosanna smiled. "Well, I have a plan. I don't want to work for anyone. I want to work for myself. I know I do what I do, good. Very good. I will cook and direct service for any special time, be paid and go home. People can send their lingerie to me or I can pick it up for a small charge, and I will charge them by the number of things they send. But not like they pay these other people round here. I know good lingerie costs good money and they need special care. I can do that. But I am going to work for myself. I don't want to belong to nobody again."

Yin looked at Hosanna very thoughtfully. "I wish I had thought like you when I was your age. I'd be . . . way better off now."

Aunt Ellen spoke, "I wish I'd a had that much sense myself. But I really didn't know how to do all them things she talkin bout!"

Yin got up, smoothing over her nightgown. "Alright. Now I know. I still think I can do you some good. I'll speak to a few people I know. We'll get you some money."

Hosanna smiled, gratefully. "Thank you."

"I need to go in business with you. You're smart. But you're going at getting rich the hard way." Yin leaned back on the freshened bed.

Hosanna rose to leave. "Yea, but there ain't no trouble in it."

Yin raised up. "What do you mean?"

"I mean I can't get in no trouble cooking food and washing clothes. Friend forever." She started out the bedroom door. "I'll let myself out, Aunt Ellen."

Yin called after her, "Hosanna? Do you know someone round here named Ruth?"

"There must be lotsa Ruths. My mama was named Ruth."

"Your mama?"

"Why?"

"Nothing. Nothing right now. Alright. Does Aunt Ellen know where to find you if I need you?"

"Ask anybody for the Jones residence." Hosanna called back.

"Good-bye, Hosanna. Friend forever." Yin laughed, but was satisfied. She did like Hosanna, very much.

Luke and Hosanna bought a cow. Mr. Creed was paid to repair the roof, Luke helped him so to save money. Hosanna borrowed Yin's carriage to go to Mythville to get a real stove. Wood-burning, but ever so much more modern than the one they had. She bought two mattresses on sale. Gave Luke the one Lovey had had. "Well, at least I can sleep good," she thought to herself as she counted the money she had left to spend. She thought of Lovey making a living someday, so she bought a second-hand sewing machine. "We'll learn together."

She bought Lettie some pretty combs for her hair and a small bottle of dime-store perfume, all she could afford. When she gave them to Lettie, Lettie was silent as she looked down at the pretty thoughts. She cried. Hosanna hugged her tightly, saying softly, "I love you, Lettie." Lettie sniffed, "I love you, too." Feeling relief, Hosanna thought, "Maybe I think she is silly about that man, but it is her business. God help me with my family."

Everything being taken care of at home, Hosanna decided to see Yin again. She sure enough needed some work now.

Yin had indeed revived from her ordeal. She nursed the golden baby happily. Ellen, given the money, had walked to town to get three dresses for herself—one for Sunday, two for wear and wash during the week—and some aprons. She cleaned, cooked and took loving care of the baby, getting along well with Yin.

The last time Hosanna had visited Yin, the guest Yin expected was Richard Befoe. He had sent word he wanted to see the baby. He was excited to have a son, illegitimate or not. He had thought of the child through the past nine months and had checked up on Yin to see if she had been seeing anyone else in the area. He did not think of the fact she may have been pregnant when she arrived there. Yin had kept company with no one, so he believed the child was his. He had even, on his last trip to his attorney, added a codicil to his will. He wasn't always feeling well and thought he had better not wait, knowing Carlene would do nothing to alleviate any problem the child might ever have.

When he arrived at Yin's, his excitement showing all over his face, Yin was fluffed up, perfumed, combed and sitting in bed holding little Joseph Richard Befoe. She hadn't told Richard the last name, Krupt.

Before he even saw the child, his first words were, "I brought you a present." He handed her a jeweler's box and placed an envelope on her dresser. She squealed with delight and opened the box as he took the baby from her. He leaned over and stuck his finger in the lacy cover, pulling it away from the baby's face. He saw the glow of gold. He blinked his eyes rapidly and blanched. Knowing the child did not, could not have a sun tan. He lifted his eyes to Yin who tentatively smiled as the gift, a new diamond ring, twinkled on her finger. He drew a haggard breath and tried to stand. He clasped his chest and his eyes rolled back in his head. He pointed a finger at her as he fell helplessly to the floor. He was having a stroke.

Yin grabbed the baby, shoved it across the bed and jumped up, screaming, "Richard, Richard!" She felt for his pulse not knowing what to do with it and screamed for Ellen. When Ellen came, Yin screamed at her, "Go get Luke! Get Sally, get Creed! Get somebody! I don't want him to die here!" Richard could not speak, but he could hear and, sometimes, he could see.

When Ellen was gone, Yin spun around and put the jeweler's box away. She removed the envelope from the top of the dresser, checking its contents first—it was money—then put it in a drawer. She then returned to Richard who was trying to get up from the floor. He could not make it. He struggled futilely.

"Oh! Why is she so slow?!" She got a towel, a diaper really, and tried to wipe his face and mouth where the saliva was oozing out. "Oh, Richard! I'm sorry, I'm so sorry. I never meant to hurt you! Never! I just wanted to live."

His lips moved with great effort. "Not . . . my . . . baby. Neg . . . negro baby." His eyes were wild and filled, not with hatred but pain.

Yin stopped crying. "Oh, Richard! It is your child! I am half Negro. That's me you see in him!" She jumped up, remembering the baby when he began to cry. She held him to her breast, wrapping his blanket close. She spoke to the baby in soft tones, "I will put you away in your room. I'm not ready for all of them to know about you yet." This done, she heard the carriage and voices as Luke was coming to get Richard.

They took Richard to his huge, rich house and lay him in his huge, rich bed. Luke went for the doctor. Later, the doctor shook his head slowly as the family gathered, waiting outside the bedroom door. "You better say your farewells."

Richlene cried, little Emily cried; both had loved this man. Sally cried and was distraught. Richlene was heartbroken, uncontrollable. The doctor gave her a sedative and they took her to her room. Emily would not leave her mother's side. Carlene remained in her room where she said her grief prohibited her from coming out. It was decided to send for all the family. The doctor said Richard might go at any time, but he held on for several days more. When you could understand him, he was saying, "My son, my son." Sally knew who he was talking about because she knew Richard was raising his son Phillip. She sent a message to Phillip that his grandfather was dying. She and Richard had agreed long ago that the best thing to tell young Phillip was that Richard was his grandfather, Richlene his mother. That his father had been divorced and was gone. And so the boy had believed. Why not?

Satan lingered around watching Richard, watching Carlene. He had never really cared for Richard. He thought Richard was in an excellent position to do so many things for him, Satan, and had not done them all, by far. He did not like that Richard did not have enough rapaciousness to be predatory, did not hate, was not a destroyer of souls by design. He despised Richard because Richard wanted love. Not more money and power. Satan was laughing at him now softly.

But Richard was holding on for something. Even he did not know why. "Let me die, let me die, God." In his mind he marveled at himself. "Why do I say, 'God'? I have never prayed to him. Sometimes I have talked to him in that little chapel I built. And sometimes, in the nights of misery I have had, I have thought of Him. But I knew He did not know me. Yes, I prayed when my . . . father died. I prayed when my mother died. Did I believe in Him? Who is He? No one ever talked to me about Him. Oh, why didn't I seek Him out? I knew His commandments, and I have tried to live by them. Not because of Him, but because they were true and just . . . and good. But, I have no sons by a wife. Each time there was a child given to me, there was adultery. A lie. And this one is not even mine at all. Is that why He warns you, tries to guard you from adultery? Because of the pain it brings? But how many times I did it and there was no issue. Or was there and I do not know? He is right. It has never made me happy. Nor has my wife. She committed adultery, too, and helped ruin my life. I have nothing to give and have given nothing but money." He thought of his son by Richlene. "I gave love, also. I have loved. Phillip, my son, I hope I have done right with my will. But it is too late, I can do nothing else. I wish I had given you God."

Tears rolled down his face as he struggled to raise his right arm. He wanted to write something. The arm would not move. The tears rolled on. "And now . . . I believe God is alive, He IS there. And He does not know me at all." But Richard was wrong. God knows about everybody. I don't think He thought Richard was evil, but I do think He might think Richard was a kind fool. A sad fool, but a fool, at least in his private life. He would have been able to live in a kind world, though. God knew that.

It was after all of this that Hosanna decided to go back by Yin's house to see about jobs. Yin was distraught, wearing a large diamond ring which she kept looking at with pleasure, then turning to her anxiety again. "I know they will need you to work at the Befoes if anything happens to Richard. They all seem to think he will die. Poor Richard. I will send for you when things are . . . clear." Hosanna left to go home to her own business where she found Luke was indeed very sad at the thought of Richard dying. He and Creed talked many hours about Richard. They had sincerely liked him.

At last they knew his death was imminent. All his family went in to say their last words. Richlene sat beside his bed and lay her head on his shoulder, sobbing out her love for him. They had to take her away. Richard was sorry for her but glad to know he had been loved, sincerely.

Carlene had asked to be called last. She closed the door behind her as she went in to Richard. She sat and stared at him a long time, smiling at the last. He looked back at her, his face a little twisted, tears in his eyes. Finally, he spoke first, "I . . . have never . . . never been happy . . . since you came."

Carlene leaned closer to him to answer, her voice was soft and low as if she were enjoying the moment. "And I have never been happy with you . . . or your daughter."

Two great tears came to his eyes and rolled slowly down his face. He tried to smile, however. "I . . . love . . . Richlene . . . but she . . . is . . . not . . . my . . . child. She . . . is . . . my . . . sister." It was such an effort for him to speak, perspiration was forming on his brow.

Carlene, startled, blinked her eyes rapidly and sat up and back. Her voice changed, she hissed, "What do you mean, 'not yours'? She is the child . . ."

"You . . . gave to my . . . father."

Carlene gasped, "You have gone insane! I won't listen to this. I don't have to, you are dying."

Richard spoke through his twisted smile, "No . . . and . . . I don't . . . have to . . . think of . . . it . . . again." He sighed deeply as if the breath hurt.

"You are dying."

"I . . . know. I . . . am . . . glad."

"How fortunate for you, you are glad."

"I did . . . love . . . you . . . once . . . Carlene."

That threw her a little, she had expected hate. "You . . . loved me?"

"I . . . loved . . . you many . . . years. Even left out . . . I . . . loved . . . you." He grimaced with the effort. "Pro . . . bably . . . the . . . only . . . one who . . . has."

Carlene laughed softly in ridicule. "My father loved me. Your father loved me. Deeply. As a woman."

Richard was now more exhausted. He could only shake his head slowly no . . . no . . . no. Then he said it once, "No."

This infuriated Carlene. Anger and hate pulsed through her heart. She stood, leaning close to Richard. She screamed a whisper, softly as possible. "Don't you tell me no! I have been loved!"

With his last efforts, he continued to slowly shake his head no. It infuriated her. Slowly Carlene raised her hand and struck him across his face as hard as she could. The shaking stopped. Carlene took a deep breath that shook her body, and she stood up straight. She almost smiled because she had stopped that shaking head from telling her no. The smile slowly faded as she leaned closer to hear his breathing, see some sign of life. There was nothing. He was dead.

Satan laughed and laughed. Now Carlene could even be called a murderer. Carlene's smile never returned. She stood a short moment, then hastened to the bedroom door. As she passed those standing in the hall, she said, "He is dead. Burn him. We will burn him." She saw the look of horror on their faces. "We will cremate him. He is gone." She looked at Richlene. "Your dear father is gone." Then she walked sedately back to her rooms with all eyes on her back.

Sally sighed. "The poor man." The doctor nodded yes, but he did not know what Sally meant.

When all was said and done, Richlene did not want her father cremated. She wanted to be able to bury him under beautiful trees and the sky, with birds and other wild life around him. "He would prefer that." She smiled firmly through her tears. She fought her mother firmly. He was not cremated.

c h a p t e r
3 4

m any grand people came for the funeral from all over the world. Richard Befoe the second had been a very rich and powerful man even though he had avoided most of the traps set by Satan for those who are so powerful. He had not hated the poor or color not his own. He had simply done nothing for them. He had sympathized with widows and orphans and the hurt in life. He increased the fortune left to him, but thought there was no blood on his increase that he directly knew of. He knew that munitions killed, but he had felt some distance from it. He had kept the munitions plant because Carlene insisted he would be the greatest fool she knew if he let it go.

Many powerful people came because they knew this money and power was going to be handed over to someone. Someone who would surely be at this funeral. Many from Wall Street were there. Senators and congressmen and their wives came for the day, returning to their homes that evening. The riverboat made many trips that day. Even the president of the United States sent a telegram.

Arabella Befoe came. It seemed Richard had been a friendly visitor to her over the years. She respected him. He had respected her. She even knew his son Phillip, who had visited her frequently and knew her own children. She brought with her the present, at last, for Sally from her father, Carl Befoe. The present Carlene had never mentioned to Sally.

Phillip Befoe came, but he stayed with Mr. Creed, by choice. He brought Mana with him but asked her to stay away from the funeral, for if they saw her, they might remember she had disappeared when the baby did and Carlene might surmise he was there. "It is not time," he told her. So Mana stayed with her one remaining relative. A childless woman, her life had been so wound up in the Befoes, she had no other life now, no other loves except Richlene and Phillip.

Phillip and his father Richard had spent many, many long times together. Richard had wanted to prepare Phillip for his future. Among the things he had told Phillip was that in Yoville, Creed would be a true friend and would tell him whatever he wanted to know and would help him do whatever he wanted to do if he could. Phillip went to see Creed from the riverboat. Later, he had walked the streets of the little town of Yoville. He had stood looking at the Befoe mansion for the first time. He had been on vacations and to special events at the other mansion that had belonged to his great-grandmother, but this house he had not known. He had been told that his grandmother Carlene did not want to be reminded of the unplesantness of his birth. He awaited the day of the funeral to go see his "grandfather" for the last time. He was grieving.

When Arabella arrived, Sally told Carlene, the grieving widow. Her quick response was, "That bitch cannot stay in my house! Richard had nothing to do with her! Just because she married my father does not mean she is part of my family! She won't climb up in society on me! She is tainted forever!"

Sally sent word to Yin, who was upset because she might not be well enough after the birth of her son, to attend the funeral and she knew, just knew! that many rich men would be there. Yin sent word back, "Of course, Arabella Befoe is welcome in my house. Please extend my invitation to her and I will prepare a room immediately."

Before Arabella left for Yin's, she gave Sally her father's present. It was a diamond locket that had belonged to her mother, Victoria Befoe. Sally was overcome when she opened the small package. "Oh! Oh, he did love me, didn't he? He thought of me?!"

Arabella laughed gently, "Of course he thought of you. He loved you. You are his daughter! I would even say his favorite daughter, in the end."

Sally shook her mature and still pretty head. "Oh, no. I cannot believe that. He left all he had to Carlene. He left me nothing to say good-bye, farewell."

Arabella frowned. "Are you sure? I'm positive he left you half of his estate, after he took care of me and our children. It was a huge estate. He left trusts for Richlene. I KNOW he left you half of his estate."

Sally, bewildered, said, "I have a letter from his attorneys telling me there was nothing for me. That he thought my husband's family would take care of me." Arabella looked confused and distressed until she heard Sally continue, "They told me not to contact them, they would contact me if something was to come up for me."

Arabella narrowed her eyes. "Who gave you the letter?"

"It was in the mail."

"Anyone can mail a letter. Did you never contact them?"

"Oh, no. They said not to."

"Sally, you are your father's daughter, are you not?"

"I am."

"Then how could you be such a foolish woman? Any fool would look into their business! For God's sake!"

Sally was confused and too overwhelmed to think. Servants were seeking her out constantly for some information or other. She turned Arabella over to Luke who would take her to YinYang's house. "I will bring the letter to you. I would like you to read it and tell me what you think. And . . ." She touched the locket fondly. "Thank you, so much, so much." Then she was off to her sister's business and her dear friend's funeral arrangements. Carlene had sent word she was unable to do anything.

before the funeral began, Carlene cried openly, emotionally, as though she had lost the love of her life. Her gown, specially ordered, flowed full to the floor in black silk bombazine, with many tucks to hide the lumps that were now part of her body. The dressmaker had done quite well; Carlene looked rich and lovely. The veils covered her face in stark light were pushed back when the lights were more flattering to her.

Clutching the arms of the rich and, some, handsome men who extended a hand to her with sympathy or other plans, Carlene looked at them all. And they all looked at her. Some with schemes, some with ambitions, some wondering how much she knew of her husband's business, his very private financial business. Of course, there were some there who were as well off as Richard had been or better. They came because others like themselves would be there and it was going on 1916 and there were things to be addressed in private. Like the coming wars. Or other devious plans. The labor business. The international business. Of course Satan was there, he saw many friends of his own in one place that day.

This was a rich woman indeed! She controlled millions and millions. A woman with no new husband to advise her. Everyone milled around her. Wives of ambitious men fluttered near her offering condolences and friendship. A proper squeeze of the hand may mean an invitation to one who looked to get ahead in life and only lacked a bit of power. No one looked at her with love or true sympathy.

Richlene sat in the garden that she knew her father had loved, where he had sat so often talking with Luke or Creed. She had chosen to wear white. It was a full-length, quiet dress. She would sometimes go into the little chapel Richard had built and there she would think of him and cry a little. Her tears were almost all shed, she had cried so much. "He was my friend as well as my father. He loved me. Really loved me," she thought to herself. "Now, there is only Sally and Luke. And no, I do not like my son, Carl, God. He is like my mother. He does not love anyone. Oh, he tries to fool her, but I know him." Then she would cry again quietly. "Oh, Daddy. Why did you leave me here in this house alone?"

In another proper room, Richard Befoe lay upon a bier. And there was no one in there with him except Phillip his son by his half-sister. The flags on Wall Street and other places in the financial world were at half-mast for Richard and here he lay, a man who had no real children by those from whom he would have wanted children. Children he could have raised, loved and shown to the world from their birth. A man, he was, who had cried himself to sleep sometimes. Whose wife had helped to kill him. A man who had been lied to by some of those nearest and dearest to him. A man who had wanted love. Love. Who had love to give. Would now miss giving it to the son who would want it in his adult years and would have given him love in return. Had Phillip not done so already? A man whose legal wife, in name only, had slapped him even as he lay dying. A man who never rested comfortably in the arms of love, carnal or married. But then . . . but then, he was loved. Richlene and his son, Phillip, truly loved him. That is far more than some have.

Satan lay his head in his hand and laughed and laughed and laughed. He looked among those at the funeral and said, though of course, they could not hear, "Look, see, what many of you will have . . . or not have. What you too will come to." He laughed at them, but he did not leave. There was too much capacity for evil at this assembly for him to leave. Some of these very men were controllers of great parts of the world, of wars, of poverty, of pain. Many friends of his. He could not leave. He had many suggestions to make to many there who might join forces, businesses. He looked at Carlton standing near his grandmother, solicitously listening for and doing her simplest request. "Ahh, there is such duplicity, such ambition, greed. Not too much backbone, but a good liar nevertheless. Such potential for evil. There was hate there also. Good! The one weakness was that the boy, way in the back of his mind, wanted love. Well. When the time comes, we will see what we will see."

Satan looked at Richlene. "She will have so much money of her own now. That should make her interesting. But . . . she does not know evil from the inside of herself. She does not really hate anyone, not even her mother. She just does not want to be around her. But I can reach her through her love. Ahhhh, that is such a weakness humans have."

Satan looked at Emily, sitting close to her mother. He smiled, "That one is going to be someone to deal with! She knows love, though. She has learned through her mother. Well, never mind, she loves money and the power it will bring. Let's see what happens to the love then!" He turned his ravaging eyes to more positive people with more possibilities.

Carlene had urged the minister to be quick because "no one really feels like standing around the dead for too long. And I am too sad and full of grief to take too much, so . . . . if you will hurry through your text. That is what you call it, isn't it?"

Soon the funeral was over and Richard had been laid to rest. Carlene noticed Richard's attorney standing over the gravesite, shaking his head sadly. "Hmmmm, I didn't know he cared. Or that he was such a good actor!" Then she was lifted into her carriage and taken to her house.

Carlene was still being courted or honored by all the rich men of opportunity. Everyone planned to stay for the supper. They had heard, somehow, of the cook. The cook was Hosanna and the food was going to be marvelous. The smells wafted even to the outside of the Befoe house. Hosanna had several helpers and had even brought her sister Lovey in the wagon to help and make some small money for herself, and to learn, of course.

Arabella was there now; many gentlemen admired her and showed it. Carlene said nothing. When Sally came near to offer a drink to the gentlemen surrounding Carlene, she was wearing the locket that had belonged to her mother. Carlene saw it at once and spoke sharply to Sally, "Where did you get that, my necklace, Sally?" Hearing the sharpness in her own voice, Carlene softened it. "That is our dear mother's locket. She gave it to me, she loved me so. I had it put away. Where did you find it, dear Sally?"

"Why, it is my necklace, Carlene."

Carlene stiffened, she did not expect to be opposed by Sally. "I know what belongs to me and what does not, Sally dear. You may wear it today, of course, but return it to me tonight. It is very dear to me."

Arabella spoke from almost across the room, "You must be mistaken, Carlene. Your dear father gave it to me to give to Sally from her mother. Sally was too young when your dear mother died. He kept it for her, for love. I brought it just yesterday. Dear."

Flustered, Carlene answered, "Well then, I must be mistaken. Oh, yes . . . I see now, it is not the one she gave to me herself. Forgive me, dear Sally."

Arabella smiled. "How can she not?"

Carlene leaned back in her chair, whispering, "My smelling salts, please."

Creed's son, Lincoln, came with his father. He stood back from the general crowd. He could see Lovey who had been carried out of the kitchen in the red wagon where she finished her work. She was forced to remain outside now in the garden and on the sidelines of everything so she would not be in anyone's way. She did not want to be too noticed. However, she had seen the tall, handsome colored man who was dressed so nice. She caught his eye, she stared at him so, he stepped to the side of the red wagon. He thought she was a very pretty child. "Too bad about her legs," he thought. "She would have been a real heartbreaker. May still be one, for some fellow like her."

He spoke to Lovey, "Hello! Enjoying yourself? These are lovely gardens, aren't they?"

Lovey smiled, shyly, "Yes, sir, they sho are." Her face lit up and her pretty, clean teeth showed in her smile. "My brother, Luke, he do the gardening here. Sometime I help him and Miz Richlene work in it."

Lincoln smiled back larger, "You do? You are very smart!" He knelt down beside her. "Is this your little automobile?"

Lovey laughed softly, shyly. "No, sir. My sister Hosanna, she just came here carrying her things in it." Her eyes widened. "From Washington D.C." Lincoln laughed. She continued, "It just a easy way to bring me here so I wouldn't have to stay home alone again." She thought a moment. "But I wouldn't want to miss this. All the ladies in them pretty clothes. I would'a trudged over here on my knees like I usual do if I'd a had to!"

Hosanna had come up to them and heard the last few things Lovey had said. "Here my sister, Hosanna, now! She the cook here! Don't that food smell sure nuff good!"

Lincoln turned to Hosanna. "That food sure does smell sure nuff good." He smiled at her.

Hosanna smiled back politely. "Are you Mr. Creed's son, Lincoln?"

"Yes, I am his son."

"I have heard of you. You are the one who is away in college?"

"For now. If there is a war, I may be away in the army."

"What army? I haven't heard of any new war."

"After they settle it in Washington, you will hear of it."

"You study all those big important things in college, don't you?"

"Well, they're important to me. I'm studying law."

"Do you learn how to fix things? You know about cars?"

"I only know the principle behind them. I haven't built one." He laughed, amused.

Hosanna was now serious. "Well, Mr. Lincoln, I would like you to see what you can do to this wagon for my sister. It would be a good way to make her more independent if she could get around in the street without being on her knees." She leaned down to the wagon where Lovey was sitting looking up at them. "See, this handle could be made so she can work it better from the inside of the wagon. You know what I mean? Then if she had a stick or something like an oar they use on boats? Well, she could push herself where she want to go, mostly."

Lincoln knelt down. "Yes, I do see what you mean. It's not really something I know, exactly. But I sure can think about it. I think I can come up with something that will help a little bit."

Hosanna smiled her brightest smile to him, even though she was tired as she could be. She and Lovey had been there cooking and preparing since before daylight. "Lovey, Miz Sally say I can lay down on her bed a little minute. I've got to rest my back, chile. You want to go with me or you want to stay out here?"

The answer came quickly, "Oh, I wanna stay out here and watch all the people! You go 'head, I'll be right here."

"Okay." Hosanna was gone with a "bye, Mr. Lincoln, thank you" over her shoulder.

Lovey looked up at Lincoln, waiting for him to move away, but he didn't. Her little young, twelve-year-old heart was so proud, so pleased that this tall, handsome brown city man had even stopped to talk to her. Strangely, tears came to her throat, but she would not have cried for all the world. He looked down at her, noticing the misty eyes. "Are you alright? What's your name?"

"Lovey."

"Hey! What a beautiful name. You've got to grow up and live up to that lovely name!"

Lovey laughed, pleased again, even thrilled. They talked a while longer, then he went away to join Luke and Mr. Creed. She looked after him, wanting to follow him to where her brother Luke was. But she would have had to be pulled there in the wagon and she did not want Lincoln to be reminded that she could not walk. She sat there in the hot sunlight, for the shadows of shade had moved with the sun, and thought of when she would be grown up, a woman. She watched him, rubbed her knees, wishing she could walk in beautiful dresses like the other ladies. To him.

hosanna went to Sally's room to throw herself across the bed for a short while. Sally had taken the letter from her father's attorneys out so

Arabella could see it later. She had left it on the bed. Hosanna moved it so she could lay down, and then she read it lazily, without intending to be nosy. "Well, no wonder Miz Sally live up here like a servant. This ain't right. Something is wrong here." She put the letter down and started to think about it but fell fast asleep. When she was awakened and called downstairs, she had almost forgotten about the letter, until she saw Sally again. Then when she ran into Russell, the lawyer-banker, she thought of it. She had seen Sally and Russell walking together in the gardens several times, talking softly and laughing. He seemed to care for Sally quite a bit.

Hosanna decided to speak to him. When she pulled lightly on his jacket, he looked around expectantly. When he saw it was only Hosanna, he frowned. "What is it, Hosanna?" Hosanna said in a loud whisper, "One time, when you have time, I want to talk to you about somebody we both like a lot." Russell was slightly annoyed but good-natured. He thought, "What can this be? I don't want to be involved and considered a personal friend here." But he said to her, "Alright. Come to the bank when you can. We will be open after the weekend." Hosanna smiled and nodded her head yes and was gone.

Phillip Befoe casually walked around observing everything. He had placed himself in front at the funeral gravesite in the private Befoe cemetary, not bothering to look at anyone to see whether they liked it or not. This was his grandfather! They had noticed him surely, but after the coffin was lowered, he had disappeared and been almost forgotten.

The supper was plentiful, hot food served buffet style, except those Carlene thought were the most important to entertain and these were served seated in a private dining room. Naturally, Phillip was not invited among these important men.

During the buffet supper, Phillip had been quiet, answering when spoken to but preferring silence. Better for observing Carlene, Sally and mostly Richlene, whom he tried to stay close to. He wanted to hold and comfort his mother, but it was not time yet. "In time," he thought, "in time I will give you all the love I can see you need, that I have been unable to give you until now." His heart ached for her. He loved her without knowing her except for all the wonderful things his grandfather had spoken to him about when he talked of Richlene. Her kindness and gentleness were on her face. "She may be slow, but she is definitely not retarded," Phillip thought. He watched his sister Emily closely, and she watched him, also, as soon as she kept noticing him everywhere she turned. Always around Richlene. She was very protective of Richlene. Phillip noticed she looked at Carlene with something resembling scorn. "Surely the child is too young to feel so strong an emotion for her own grandmother," he mused. Carlene had long noticed it but chose to ignore Emily, "that child!" It was clear, her favorite was Emily's older brother, Carlton.

The men noticed Phillip never entered into any conversation, though he listened carefully whether invited to or not. At first they thought, "Must be some of the help." But his clothes were too good, too well cut, the material was too rich, expensive. "Well," they mused, "could be hand-me-downs from Richard. There is a resemblance to Richard and the family though. A servant's child? Some misstep of Richard's? Ahhh, a distant relative, perhaps?" A few handed him their glasses to test the young man. "Get this filled for me, will you?" Phillip always stepped back with a smile, signaled for some of the real help and indicated the waiting man who still held his glass out.

He wandered around until he saw his mother Richlene going outside looking for someone she called Luke. Phillip followed. The fresh air was clean and clear and felt good to him after the rooms full of smoke, various perfumes and smells of food. Richlene walked over to a colored man and took his arm and waved her arm indicating the gardens; she was smiling. The colored man stepped back from her clutch. "That must be Luke," thought Phillip. "Ahhh, there's Lincoln, right in there with them." He casually rushed over to where his mother was talking to his friend Lincoln and the man Luke.

Phillip smiled, happy to be so near to Richlene and even speaking to her. "Hi, Lincoln. Hello, Mrs. Befoe."

Richlene looked at the young man. She had noticed him before, the way he looked at her. "Hello, how do . . . you do?" She smiled. "You know, I . . . think . . . I know you . . . but . . . I can't . . . remember why. You . . . look so . . . familiar."

Phillip did not want to chance her reaction to him there, among all the people. He held out his hand to her, holding back the love from his smile. "My name is Phillip. How are you, Mrs. Befoe?"

Richlene reached out to shake his hand, but her thoughts made her hand hesitant. Her mind was telling her something, but it was not clear yet. Their hands finally touched and clasped, but they did not shake hands; they held hands as Richlene looked wonderingly into his face that no longer smiled. Lincoln coughed meaningfully. Phillip smiled again and gently let her hand go.

Much later, as the guests were leaving, Richard Befoe's private attorney, Mr. Ways, went to bid good evening to Carlene and express his regrets again. Carlene, tired of her huge performance, glanced at him with a wary eye. "Well. Do you think everything was to my husband's satisfaction?"

"You handled everything beautifully, Carlene. I'm sure Richard would be satisfied with the services."

Carlene sighed. "Good."

Mr. Ways took a deep breath. "However . . ."

"Yes?"

"I didn't want to disturb you earlier . . . because things were so far along. You know, it really would be good if you were to have one of these telephones way out here. I could have reached you in time."

Carlene turned to look up at him. "Yes? In time for what?"

"Richard, expressly, in writing, wished to be buried on his mother's estate where he was born."

"He is already in the ground, Ways. Besides, I am his wife and he belongs here, where I am to be buried."

"Yes, but . . . however that may be, he expressly demanded . . . to be buried in his birth place."

"Damn! Man! Shall I dig him up? Absurd!"

Mr. Ways placed his hand on his chin, his voice gentle. "If I do not follow his demands regarding his funeral requests and arrangements, there will be a great problem . . . for you."

"And just what, may I ask, would that problem be, Mr. Ways?"

"The will cannot be opened. Nor any of his financial business touched. All funds accruing interest, etcetera, will be going to charities."

Carlene stood without help. "What?"

"Those are his demands . . . not requests. He specifically said you were to have nothing to do with his final arrangements . . . and that I will not be . . . remunerated, at all, from the estate, if I let you have your way. Unfortunately."

Anger exploded from the bereaved widow. "I'll see about . . ."

Mr. Ways held his hands up for peace. "Carlene. Just dig him up when everyone is gone. Send him to his mother's estate. I will take care of the rest. The tombstone is to be chosen by Richlene and . . . another."

"I am not even to be allowed to choose my own husband's tombstone?!"

"I am only following instructions. It is very nice, and not irregular at all, for the children of the deceased to choose the tombstone for their loved one."

Carlene chose to have a near fainting spell. She swooned, calling, "Sally! Minna! Help me to my rooms." Carlton came running.

Richard was dug up the next day and shipped to his mother's estate, accompanied by Richlene and Emily. They were met at their destination by Phillip Befoe. Richard's wishes were carried out to the letter. Mother and son were reunited. Richlene was shocked, of course. All the different lies her mother had told her about what had happened to the baby. But the fact that she was reunited with the son she KNEW she had given birth to overwhelmed her, and the flood of love she had held in abeyance for so many years broke through her heart. Tears and love flowed. Emily was hesitant but soon knew Phillip truly loved their mother. Then she relaxed and found her brother Phillip easy to love, too. So different from Carlton.

chapter
3 5

The black widow spider had now been living and settled for many months in the fine plants in Carlene's room. The spider had learned the room, knew where the window was that led to the tunnel leading to her escape to the outdoors. She had eaten her first set of children because she had grown hungry before she learned all about her living space. She had to eat them. Now she went down the tunnel when she felt the need to find a mate to become impregnated, then she returned to the room. What kept her coming back was there were no predators to fear there. She hated fear. Yes, she preferred the dark, damp earth outside, but in the potted plants she had some darkness and dampness. And privacy. She wove webs, occasionally catching some unwary fly. Food lasted a long time, she did not need to eat every day. Now she was pregnant again, awaiting birth, as she curled her legs around close to her body and watched Carlene.

On this morning after the funeral, after her toiletries were taken care of and while she was having her coffee, Carlene asked for Hosanna to be sent to her. Carlene had slapped Minna a few times in the past week for some small mishap. Minna was sullen. She planned to leave as soon as she could find a new job. But she still became a little alarmed when she was told to fetch Hosanna for Carlene. She did so grudgingly. "Yes, mam."

"Minna, do you know the girl well? I don't know of her, her family. That was not any regular food menu from around here. I want her here."

Minna felt only a little better. "Yes, mam."

"And, Minna, stop looking so absurd. My nerves are gone. I have been through a great tribulation these last few weeks."

"Yes, mam."

"GO!"

When Hosanna was informed, she was watching Little Wisdom with the children she was teaching, putting in a few words here and there because she knew so much more than Little Wisdom, whom she liked a lot. But she went right away to Mrs. Befoe's summons.

She entered Carlene's rooms and waited for Carlene to invite her to sit. Carlene didn't.

"I understand you did the cooking for the funeral supper."

"Yes mam, I did."

"It was very . . . passable. I want you to work for me. It's been years since I've had some of the things you prepared. I must say, usually only in New York or Europe. Now, your salary. I will pay ten, no . . . eight dollars a week. You will live in, so you will be here when I want you. And we will find some other things you can do to fill in the empty time." She watched to see the pleasure in Hosanna's face. There was none.

Hosanna was looking down at the floor and thinking. Then she looked up, smiling. "Miz Befoe, I have my own business. I do special jobs. I do special cooking for special events. I even do lingerie, special lingerie. For special prices. But I work at home, alone. And I get paid that way. Every time. I charge ten dollars for cooking, depending on the job. I charge by the garment. Here is my card." She reached out to hand Carlene the homemade card she had printed and Lovey had drawn flowery designs on.

Carlene looked at Hosanna like she was out of her mind. "Girl, you are refusing? Me? Steady employment? A home? The city has made you stupid!"

Hosanna smiled. "I am working for myself."

Carlene sat up. "If I don't want you to work for anyone else, you will be out of business for yourself! Now! Enough. You will work for me . . . for ten dollars a week. Girl, do you realize what year this is and what people are making who do what you do?"

Hosanna's smile faded. "No mam, I will not take your job that way. And I think I will make it. I do professional work. And I'm good at it. You said so yourself."

Carlene sat back. "Not here, you won't. What I say goes in Yoville. You had better reconsider my offer before I change my mind."

Hosanna turned to leave, opening the door. "Miz Befoe . . . ? I lost my mother when I was very, very young. I have lived and done without my mother. I can sure live and do without you."

Carlene was livid! After Hosanna was gone, Carlene thought, "Well, I'll see about you when I return from the reading of the will. I'll get rid of the Indians from my school and stop that little Indian girl from coming on this side of the river. Teaching Negroes. When they learn too much, they think too much of themselves. Anyway, it's the blind leading the blind. Where did I hear that? Never mind. I'll stop the school and everything else that makes them so independent. I'll take that land back I sold them! Imagine a snippet, a nigger, talking to me like that! Minna! Minna!"

after leaving Carlene, Hosanna decided to stop at the Befoe bank and see Russell Moore. He saw her looking in the window and beckoned her to come in. When she entered, he said, "Good morning, Hosanna. It's good you caught me. I'm about to leave for Philadelphia. They are going to read Mr. Befoe's will in a few days. Have a seat. Now what may I do for you? More money to save from that good job you did yesterday?" He smiled.

Hosanna sat in her little cotton dress, looking intently at Russell. "Mr. Russell, when a lawyer . . . writes you a . . . writes a letter to

somebody . . . don't they usually say, 'Call us if you have any questions' . . . or something like that? Least, the ones I have . . . seen
did."

"Yes, yes, I believe that is true most of the time. I always do, anyway."

Hosanna stirred, uncomfortable. "Well, I saw . . . I accidently saw
a letter when Miz Sally sent me to lay down in her room for a while. It
was to her from a lawyer . . . telling her her daddy didn't leave her
nothing and not to contact them. Now . . . does that sound right . . .
or does it sound kinda funny?"

Russell became serious. "I see what you mean. Well, Hosanna, Miz
Sally and I are . . . friends. Close friends. And she has never mentioned it to me."

Hosanna leaned toward him. "It was an old, old letter. Maybe she's
'shamed. I don't blive that letter. Specially since I have met and had
business with Miz Carlene. Scuse me for saying that, but . . ."

Russell almost smiled, but this was serious. "What do you want me
to do about it? What can I do about it?"

Hosanna stared at him. "Well, you all are friends ain't you? What is
a friend for? That lady is not happy in there like she is living now. Can't
you ask somebody something?"

"Yes, yes, I guess I might."

Hosanna stood to go, she was a little upset. "Mr. Russell, I came to
you because you are sposed to be her friend. Ain't no friend going to
stand by and see a friend cheated. I think something is wrong in that
house. You don't have to report nothing to me! Just see, for her! I like
Miz Sally, and I bet her daddy loved her, too." She turned toward the
door. "Oh, Mr. Russell, I have a friend, Ellen, I think somebody is
stealing her house from her." She searched her pockets and found the
slip of paper. "Here, I wrote it all down, her name and the number of
her house. Can you see who the house really blongs to? She say she paid
for it, somebody else said she didn't. She's an old lady and she need that
house her husband and her paid for."

Russell smiled and nodded as he took the paper.

She got to the door, leaving, but turned to say her last words, "Mr.
Russell, you white folks are strange sometimes. Too many words and no
action to try to make things right."

After Hosanna was gone, Russell sat a long time with his fingers tapping his chin, thinking. He finally took out a pad and made a few notes on it, putting it away with a firm, final gesture.

On her way home from the bank, Hosanna met Aunt Ellen driving Yin's buggy into town to do some shopping for the household. Hosanna rode with her, Aunt Ellen glad to have the company. While Ellen shopped, Hosanna bought two good, smooth irons and ordered some business cards with the words:

HOSANNA S. JONES

PROFESSIONAL CATERING COOK

EXPERT LINGERIE CARE

They would be ready in a week. Hosanna really was in business. She went home to worry about it. But she felt good inside.

chapter

3 6

russell left Yoville quickly and returned quickly on the day before the will was to be read. Sally had, of course, not planned to go to the reading. Russell told her it was very important that she accompany him to New York. She declined, thinking it was some ruse regarding his marriage proposal to her. He told her it involved money. Her money. In need as she was, Sally decided to go and began her preparations. Carlene didn't notice because she kept all eyes on her own self as she prepared to go to New York for the reading of the will of her dearly departed husband.

Carl Befoe Senior and Richard Befoe II had used many law offices in different locations in the international world of business. In New York, the main law offices that both men used were separate but in the same building. While the will was being read in one office on the eighth floor, Russell was taking care of Sally's business in another office on the tenth floor.

Carlene, Richlene, Emily, Carlton and the still unknown Phillip were seated in the boardroom of the attorney, Mr. Ways, for the reading of Richard Befoe's will. Seeing Phillip, Carlene noted to Mr. Ways, "You are certainly training them young these days, Mr. Ways."

"Who do you mean, Carlene?" He knew who she meant.

"That young man seated over there." She pointed with her black handkerchief to Phillip. It was odd she never had noticed the resemblance to her husband and the man she had loved, his father.

Mr. Ways smiled. "Oh, that one. He is not being trained by me, though I wish he were."

"Then," Carlene continued, "what is he doing here?"

"We shall see. He was asked and designated to be here by the deceased."

Something in Carlene's mind twitched, it moved to her stomach. She became wary, looking at the young Phillip more closely. All heads had turned to him briefly. Richlene smiled, looking at him a long time, finally saying "hello." He smiled back. His look of love stunned Carlene. Emily was looking at all of them, smiling an elfin puck smile at her grandmother Carlene. Carlene was caught by the smile, there were so few of them for her on Emily's face. But still she was Carlene, she didn't smile back. She spoke to Richlene. "Do not speak so to strangers, Richlene."

Richlene turned to her, her face clear and bright. "I do . . . not think he . . . is a . . . stranger."

Carlene was about to speak a disparaging word when the attorney, Mr. Ways, called the meeting to order and the reading began.

all the smaller gifts were efficiently listed—servants, Baily, Creed and many others Richard had known from his affairs and offices everywhere. Then Richlene was given ten million dollars of her own. Carlene smiled inwardly, "That may well be in my hands anyway. I will be the executrix." Mr. Ways kept on speaking, however, noting that a demand was made by Richard that Richlene, being of adult age and good mind, was to handle her money any way she wished or the money was to go to charity.

Emily was given two million dollars in a trust fund until she would be of certain age deemed capable of handling her business, then she would receive eight million dollars more.

Carlton was given a lesser consideration because, Richard had noted, he would eventually inherit all of his grandmother Carlene's wealth.

Then Carlene was startled by the next words, that "any issue of Richard's body" was to be given one million dollars in trust when he or she was twenty-five years of age. The child was to be well educated for the trust to be completed. The as of then unborn child of Yinyang Krupt was indicated.

Carlene hated Yin even more now. "When had he done this?" She waited silently for the end of the will. There were still many more millions and the huge estate Richard had inherited from his mother. She sat back, expectant and relaxed. "I will change most of his wishes later," she thought. "A little talk with Mr. Ways and he had better do what I wish." She was a little concerned Richard had left even Sally something of sufficient size to free her. If this was so, Carlene would lose the best housekeeper she had ever had. But "we will see." She smiled at Mr. Ways.

The lawyer's voice, going on and on in the list of Richard's vast holdings, received Carlene's total attention. "To my grandson, Phillip Richard Befoe, I bequeath and give the entire balance of my estate except for one hundred thousand dollars to go to Mrs. Carlene Befoe, my wife in name only.

"If Carlene Befoe or anyone tries to break the will that I have herewith made in sound mind and body, all cash and valuables will be immediately given to my favorite charities without recourse, my faithful lawyer, Mr. Hardy Ways, shall not, SHALL NOT be paid for his services, and a suit, which I have prepared for, shall be instituted against him, and her, immediately. Be it so noted."

Carlene knew there would be no breaking of the will. All eyes turned to Phillip Richard Befoe, who stood and shook the attorney's hand and said, "I hope you will continue in my service, Mr. Ways." Then he turned to Richlene. "Mother, we can go now. I have waited many, sad and lonely years to be able to hold your hand and love you as I can from today on."

They left the lawyer's office separately. Richlene crying, Emily crying and holding on to her brother Phillip.

Carlton was not pleased about his bequest. It was not enough. "Perhaps," he thought, "I did not work this out right. It's a start though. It's a start. And I am Grandmother's favorite." He looked at Phillip with

hate sparkling from his eyes. He jumped up, reaching for his grandmother Carlene and the many millions of dollars she still controlled of
her own. Carlene stopped near Phillip, saying, "I don't know what you
did to my husband, but I shall find out and I will see that you get what
you deserve. I will break you."

Phillip turned from his mother to Carlene. "I will tell you what I did.
I loved him."

Carlene turned back to Carlton, her voice almost wailing, and they
continued on their way. Carlton did not know exactly what to do. It was
just too much money to glare at, should the young man really get the
money. His brother? So he nodded his head with a faint smile over
Carlene's shoulder as they left and thereafter kept his eyes on the floor as
he helped his grandmother out.

Carlene cancelled the reservations at the rich hotel where she had
anticipated and ordered a five-day stay with rich lunches and dinners,
theaters and shows. They returned immediately to Yoville, much to Carlton's chagrin. He wanted to be where his mother and Phillip were, to
hear their plans. But Grandmother was still a very rich woman. So he
went back with her to Yoville . . . for the moment. He had to get back
to school anyway. He consoled her as the train rushed over the tracks
under the darkened sky. She cried and kept asking for her smelling salts.
Carlton was a bit annoyed with her. "Such a greedy old lady! She is not
satisfied with all she has already!" But to her he said, "Don't cry, Grandmother, I will think of something. They can't do you like this!" She
answered through tears, "Oh, my boy, my boy, you are the only one who
loves me."

All during the train ride from New York, Carlton asked questions
urgently. "Who is this Phillip? How is Grandfather his grandfather?
Where did he come from? Why didn't we know him if Grandfather is
his grandfather? Who? Where is his mother? My mother?"

Carlene, in her wrath, wanted to tell him the truth, but Richlene was
his mother and . . . then . . . she did not want the name Befoe to be
tainted, it must remain beyond any foulness. "He is your . . . brother.
Oh! Do not ask me now!"

"Really my brother? Richlene is his mother?"

"Yes!"

"But, how, Grandmother?

"She was married, you know!"

"Yes, to my father. Is he my father's son? Whose son is he?"

"Ask me no more. I am faint. I am ill with anger . . . and pain. I have been betrayed. That young man has befouled us all."

Later, when she had gotten rid of Carlton and all his questions, Carlene tried to think of some way to pay Mr. Ways back, as if he was responsible for all that had happened and the way it had turned out. "He could have stopped this . . . in some way! He could have told me about the will long ago and we could have changed it right after Richard died! Before everyone knew what was in it! That damn man shall pay!" Her mind raced, trying to think of some way, some way.

Satan almost rubbed his hands together in anticipation. He felt no sympathy for Carlene. He liked her only when she was busy doing his work. He smiled down at Carlton as he sat in his room, pondering, scheming. "It will be interesting in any event." Satan laughed as he flew away.

c h a p t e r
3 7

Upon entering the house in Yoville, Carlene screamed for Sally. Minna had come to help her to her rooms and so Carlene momentarily forgot Sally in the midst of all her other thoughts and turmoil. Now Carlene screamed for Sally again. Minna came, again. "Where is that damn woman?! I have been calling her for hours!"

Minna stepped back from Carlene's arm's reach. "She ain't here, Miz Befoe. She been gone all night and all today."

"Well! I will see about that. She can get out of my house if she is not here when I need her!"

"Yes, mam."

"Send her to me as soon as she dares show her face." Carlene thought a moment. "Have you seen Russell Moore? Has he been here looking for Sally since she disappeared?"

"No, mam."

"They must be together then." She opened her mouth to say something else, then the thought occurred to her, "That handsome man surely has not married Sally! I am sure he wouldn't. She is such a mouse." Then, thoughtfully, "But what are they doing?" Carlene looked up at Minna. "Send Baily to Mr. Moore's house. See what they are doing there . . . alone . . . all day and all night."

"Baily don't work here no more since Mr. Richard died. Mam."

"Who told him to go? Well, send someone! Or go yourself!"

"Yes, mam." Hastily, Minna was gone.

The black spider woke from its musing at the sounds of the loud voice. It stared at Carlene a long time, then its full stomach lulled it back to its dreams.

Sally did not arrive that day or the next. Carlene was livid with rage. Richlene and Emily returned, bright with smiles, further adding to Carlene's rage. But they were rich now in their own right. What could she do?

She sat seething, waiting for Sally to return. She didn't really need her, she just could not stand being ignored. And she wanted Sally to write letters to lawyers. While she thought of how she would work things out with the lawyers, she thought of Yinyang. "Now then. I will get Yin to pay Mr. Ways back. Yin just might be able to marry the old widower and take all his money from him. I will help her to do it. What do I care if she has money? It won't be as much as I have, by far." Carlene smiled to herself. "Now . . . what does Yin want . . . besides money. Yes! The yacht trip! Done! We will go."

Carlene sent Yin a message to begin preparing for the yacht trip. Yin was overjoyed. She had been bored. Tired even of the fat, cute baby she loved. Tired of never being able to wear her beautiful clothes. She had missed the funeral where all those rich men had been! And she could have been so beautiful in her new finery. Arabella had told her about everyone there. They were the crème de la crème! Yin was well over giving birth to her son now though, so she could go. Her body had returned to its lovely shape. "Only," she mused, "I want Hosanna to go with us. To watch my back from that tricky bitch. And she can take care of our clothes. That way, Hosanna can make some money, which I know she needs." She sent the message back to Carlene, "I would be delighted to accompany you on the trip. I shall bring my maid." Carlene received the written message and laughed aloud for the first time in a long while.

When Sally returned to Yoville, the first place she went was to Hosanna's house. She spoke to Hosanna.

"Hosanna, it is not good to read other people's mail. But I am so grateful you did. I want to do something for you. I know you are poor and trying to work. I will help you with your work, but what else would you want? Would you like me to have a shop built for you here on your own land, where you can do your lingerie as a specialty? Or have a small bakery? I will build it for you and buy all your first supplies." Sally was smiling, hugely.

Hosanna thought a moment to herself. "Now I can be very dumb or very smart. What will it be? For myself? Or something for these poor people round here?"

She said, "Miz Sally. I'm going to call you Miz Sally because I am younger than you are. But, nobody ever calls me Miz Hosanna, and I don't know whether I like that or not. I think I don't. But, I'll get older someday." She smiled. "Now, if I was to build something for my business, I would want to do it myself. I would rather have the money to do that, for myself. Not have it built for me like I am a child. If I had it built, it would really be mine."

Sally made a tiny gasp, "Oh! I . . ."

"Wait a minute, Miz Sally. I know what I want. I would rather do something everybody can get some benefit from. I would like you to build a school around here somewhere, where these children can get some kind of education that will let them know the world is bigger than Yoville. Cause there ain't nothing here for them to do besides domestic work. And people like my sisters Lettie and Lovey and people like Lil Wisdom don't have to be shamed by that white school. If you do that and make it a GOOD school, I'll be satisfied. Oh, and something else, they're gonna need good teachers, too."

Sally was tired, exhausted from all that had happened in the last few days. Her whole life had been changed. But she smiled at Hosanna.

"Miz Hosanna, I should have thought of that myself. That would be something I would like to do."

Hosanna leaned toward Sally, tilting her head. "One thing I would like to ask you, Miz Sally, if I can."

"Well . . . certainly."

"How can it be . . . How could you live all those years over there and not do something, find out something about your own money? All those years?"

Sally looked down at her hands, a very serious look on her face. "In all the years of my life . . . I simply cannot imagine anyone doing what Carlene did to me. I would not do it to anyone. I couldn't. Not, and watch them suffer, help them suffer, so long."

Hosanna nodded her head slowly. "But Miz Sally, now I am very young, and I haven't had all that much experience in the world, but I know, that I am the way I am. Other people are the way they are. This lets me know that I have to see and understand the way another person is for themself! Don't you know that? Just because you are a kind person and cannot imagine yourself cheating somebody else, does not mean that Carlene or anyone else will be that way."

"Miz Hosanna, as a man thinks so is he. I did not think of such lies being perpetrated on another. Especially a sister. Well, I have learned. I will never forget."

Hosanna laughed softly. "Sally, you don't have to call me Miz Hosanna. Just call me Hosanna and I will call you Sally, and we will be friends."

"Friends call each other Miss or Mrs., Miz Hosanna, and, if it pleases you, I will be delighted! Done!" She stood up to leave. "I have some very important things I must get done, so I am going to go now. We will talk again soon. Good-bye for now, Hosan . . . Oh! I forgot! Miz Hosanna!"

Hosanna laughed. "Miz Sally, I don't mind what you call me. Your heart is alright. Good-bye for now."

When Sally had gone, Hosanna sat on her bed, thinking. "You sure are a big fool, Hosanna girl. No, you ain't. You did right. A real school. A real school for everybody." From that day, Sally called her Miz Hosanna, Hosanna called her Miz Sally, and they were more than good friends.

.   .   .

Carlene was alone in her room preparing drafts of letters to the lawyer when Minna came in to tell her Sally had returned. The spider had been watching her, its legs curled around itself. It thought Carlene was a strange spider, indeed.

Carlene decided quickly to put on a black dress to emphasize the burden that had been left upon her in her grief.

Sally pushed open the door to Carlene's room and stood there. Carlene looked up and the sisters stared at each other for a long moment. Finally Sally walked in, holding an envelope in her hand which she held out to Carlene. Neither spoke. As Carlene took the envelope, she searched Sally's face for some sign of apology or even fear. There was only anger and resignation there. Carlene spoke first. "Where have you been?! I have needed you! Here. We've looked everywhere! Were you off sneaking with that devil Russell? I shall fire him immediately! Sit down, you make me nervous."

Sally continued to stand. "I have been off, yes, about my business. Read the letter . . . please."

Carlene held the letter up. "What is this letter?

"Read it, Carlene. It's from Father's attorneys."

The letter was opened and read, explaining that Sally Befoe Gentle had been given her inheritance, that the account was therewith clear since it had been removed from their hands, and that there would be no need in the future to inquire as to interest, etc. The attorneys thanked Carlene for her patronage in the matter and hoped that any other business they had in her own personal matters would continue, etc. etc.

Carlene slowly folded the letter and laid it on her desk. "So . . ." Her voice was as clear as though she had had nothing to do with Sally's problem. "Father left you something . . . after all."

Sally spoke softly, "After all."

Carlene continued as though she had not heard and understood the last few words. "How wonderful for you!" She tried to recover her former stance. "However, that does not mean you can leave me here, uninformed of your whereabouts."

Sally still spoke softly but firmly, "I need never tell you, inform you, of anything I am doing . . . again."

Carlene smiled sardonically. "Oh, I see . . '. the money has changed you. I've always heard it changes some people." She turned to the mirror over the desk, patting her hair. Sally was silent, watching her.

Carlene continued, "Or is it that dreadful man, Russell Moore? You should be more on guard against your possible enemies, you know, dear. I am your sister . . . and your friend." She turned to look at Sally.

Sally's voice was soft but held years of anger in it. "You have cheated me out of years and years of my life. The quality of that life." Her voice rose, "My life!"

Carlene looked away from her. "You have lived . . . very comfortably."

Sally's voice was again under control. "Years and years of my own money!"

"Oh! Did you need money, dear?" Sally's voice filled Carlene with rage.

Sally looked into her sister's face, thinking, "An old face, well kept. An old body, well kept. But it is all just a shell. There is nothing . . . nothing inside. No care given, at all, to the heart, the mind."

Satan almost shouted with glee, "Hate, at last!" But his glee was too soon.

Sally spoke outloud, "I am enraged. I thought to hate you. I should hate you. But you have even less than I have had. You don't even have sense enough to feel sad for yourself, your life."

Carlene laughed at her, desperate people can take nourishment from anything. "I have had everything. I still have. Your money meant nothing to me. I have never used it."

"You couldn't, legally."

Carlene looked down at the floor. "I did it for you." She looked up into Sally's eyes. "I did it for you. So you would not waste it while you were young. You would have it now, when you are old, as you are and as you need it now. I have been a sister to you. Our father would want me to be."

"Then why didn't he leave it all to you?"

Carlene laughed again, weak laughter. "Oh, I thought he had, dear. That old fool." Her laughter was stronger now, as she looked in Sally's eyes. "I didn't plan all this. I thought he had. I regretted it, but I thought, if those were his wishes . . . what else could I do?" Noisy sounds filtered through Carlene's wall. "What is that noise?!"

Sally spoke firmly, "They are cleaning out Richard's rooms."

Carlene looked up, gratefully, at her sister. "You had them do that? Oh, thank you, Sally. I need you so much! I knew we would be alright, that you would not stop . . . helping me. Loving me."

Sally shook her head slowly. "I do not love you. I am not helping you, at last. I am helping myself. I am cleaning his rooms because I am moving from that . . . that room in the servants' quarters. I have purchased furniture and everything else I will need to make my new rooms into my apartment. I own half of this house and everything in or around it. I shall now live as my father and mother would intend."

Carlene stood, started to speak, but Sally interrupted her.

"Further, I am buying my own house. I have plans. I intend to open a school for all the children around here and those across the river."

"Even Negro children? And Indian children?" Carlene was aghast. "I will not allow it!"

"You cannot stop me. Or my money."

"Oh, yes I can! And will!"

"I am buying the Bilk house. They have gone into bankruptcy."

Carlene almost shouted, "But I planned for Carlton to take that house after he is married someday!"

"Oh, is that why the Bilks went bankrupt?"

"No, I . . ."

Sally almost smiled. "Never mind. It will soon be mine. I will be leaving this house, but my rooms will remain." She moved closer to Carlene, her smile gone. "There is an evil in this house. It fills every corner, almost every room. It reaches out to the servants. To your children and their children. No one who lives here, or has lived here, since you were born, has ever been happy here. I will never allow you into my new home. You will never visit me . . . unless it is upon a bier . . . for your funeral . . . and that had best be here in this house, also. This house you have made a grave of."

Carlene, standing, raising her voice, "Where is that young man, Phillip?"

Sally moved to the door, preparing to leave. "You wish to attempt to corrupt him? I don't believe you can. He is richer than even you and he was raised apart from you. His father had excellent sense on that matter."

"I asked, where is he?"

"He has gone to his own home. His father's mansion, greater than this one. Gone about his business."

"We shall see. He IS my daughter's child."

"He is a man now. His father did a fine job with his mind. I don't believe you can defile him."

"Since you insist on misjudging me, get out of my house!"

"I am leaving your rooms."

"Get out!"

"Your words are late. I have been leaving all the time."

Carlene followed Sally to the door. "No one likes you! I have all the friends! You are weak! And a despicable fool!"

Sally turned to her, one hand on the door. "But . . . better than that, I am not a liar. I am not a thief. You be careful of the world's parades. They usually betray and grieve their promises. I was foolish because I believed in you. You are a fool because you believe in yourself."

Carlene almost shouted, "Get out! Go away! You will get no help here!"

"Help?" Sally began laughing, she laughed and laughed all down the hall on her way to her new apartment.

Later, Russell looked into Aunt Ellen's house and land and found it was hers. She was being cheated. He cleared the papers and demanded a sum of money from the guilty person. They refused. Russell told them, "She has a very important friend in these parts, you had better not create more problems for yourself." Fear being so potent, the guilty party paid the money. The money was used for Creed and Ellen to repair the house to good living condition. Then Aunt Ellen wrote her niece in Philadelphia that she had a place for her if she needed it. Aunt Ellen smiled at Hosanna, "How wonderful it feels to be able to help somebody!"

Hosanna smiled back. "I know."

c h a p t e r
3 8

When Yin received Carlene's summons, she had already heard of Sally's good fortune and about the stranger, Phillip Befoe, inheriting all the money and power. But she knew Carlene was a long way from having an empty purse. She thought of her own son's good fortune, but that would not come for a long, long time. "It's a good thing Richard didn't live long enough to change that will after he saw Joseph! Poor Richard. I truly liked him. I am sorry he is gone."

Yin was smiling when she entered Carlene's apartment. She laughed lightly when Carlene said, "Well, motherhood seems to agree with you. You look very well. I guess the fact that your son received all that money for his education and life has helped some? And why haven't you brought him to see me?"

Yin flounced down into a soft, satin chair. "Oh, he is so young . . . and you know, he is not well. It may be a long time before he is able to go about visiting. But, about the money, that is not much and it is in trust!" she pouted.

Carlene laughed at this woman she hated, "Certainly it is in trust. It's for . . . the baby, not for you. You can live with a million dollars within your reach, I'm sure."

"I will have to." Yin did not mention anything else she had heard.

Carlene waved her hand casually. "Well, since I've decided to go on the yacht trip, we must be ready soon. We leave in four weeks' time. We will meet the others at New York harbor, we'll be picked up there."

Yin, excited, said, "Where are we going?"

"It's to be a beautiful surprise."

"How will I know what to pack . . . to buy?"

"Buy as you travel."

Yin leaned back in her chair. "Will . . . I . . . have enough money to do that?"

"We shall see what we shall see. We will have a little talk, and then whatever happens with the money will be up to you."

Yin sat forward again. "I would like to take Hosanna with us."

At Carlene's suprised expression, Yin explained, "She can take care of our clothes and even cook, if need be. Like a ladies' maid."

Carlene frowned, "She is a good cook, but she is too arrogant."

"I would like her to go."

"There is something I would like you to do, also, Yin."

"Again?"

"Yes." Carlene adopted a very casual attitude. "Have you met Phillip? My grandson. Richlene's first son?"

"No . . . But I hear he is very good-looking." Her voice lowered. "And very, very rich . . . now."

Carlene did not laugh. "He is. And he is the right age to marry."

Yin laughed lightly, "Carlene, I am too . . . old for him. He is in college."

"People marry in college."

"Why would you want him to marry me? Have you thought about what that would mean? And how do you know I don't want to marry for love?"

"You are right, Yin. Perhaps having you that close to me would not be a wise thing at all. Well, either him or the attorney Ways. Because . . . you and I . . . are . . . friends in some way . . . and I want to help you achieve your goals."

Yin thought, "That will be the day." Aloud, she said, "Poor little me?"

Carlene ignored her, "Besides, it is what I want you to do . . . in exchange for this trip."

Yin stopped laughing, "My life? In exchange for a trip!?"

Carlene looked at her seriously, "You have a child now. You should be more . . . settled."

Yin laughed again. "Your concern . . . touches me, Carlene."

They parted amiably, but Yin was committed only to the yacht trip and . . . maybe . . . the attorney.

chapter
3 9

When Phillip and Richlene spoke together after the reading of the will, there was no difficulty in the meeting of their minds. Richlene had always loved and missed her first son, her first child. Her consolation over the years had been that Mana was with him as Mana had been with her. As Richard had wished, Mana also met them at the mansion when they carried Richard there to bury him properly.

Phillip often held his mother tightly and tenderly for long moments. They sat and talked many times as she held his hand and stroked it, smiling often through tears of joy. Phillip was elated, happy, ecstatic to have his mother, a family, at last. He belonged somewhere WITH them, at last. He adored his little sister Emily, who adored him in return. At first he thought to have a baby-type little sister, but Emily had fooled him.

Though she was quite young, Emily was very interested in her mother's fortune and her own. She studied money. She saw that boys had much more opportunity to attend colleges and learn about stocks and bonds and investments. She was not interested in learning how to be a good housewife right then. She was interested in everything her grandfather had owned, and her great-grandfather before him. She had no illusions about her brother Carlton. She never wanted to be treated as her Aunt Sally had been by Carlene.

Emily also knew she would never inherit Carlene's money, so she decided she would make her mother's money grow. Phillip respected that and admired his little sister's determination and no-nonsense mind. He determined to help her, though he told her she would never have to worry about Richlene nor herself as long as he was able to do anything. Emily was serious when she answered, "I don't want to depend on anyone. I have seen Aunt Sally's misery."

Emily loved her mother dearly. The only thing that worried her, and Phillip as well, was when Richlene said she loved Luke, the gardener, and wanted to spend her last years with him.

Phillip pleaded with her, "Can't you go on, as you have done for years, being friends?"

Richlene smiled at her son, happiness glowing in her face. "Oh we . . . are. We are. But . . . Emily wants . . . to . . . go away . . . to school. Then . . . to university. And . . . you . . . you are . . . gone already. I want to be with . . . Luke."

Phillip frowned. "Has he . . . Have you ever . . ."

Richlene still smiled. "Luke . . . would never . . . do anything . . . to me. I have . . . not even . . . told him . . . yet . . . that I . . . am . . . going to be with him!" She laughed. "Except . . . I have . . . told . . . him . . . for a long time . . . in many ways." Her voice softened. "I love him. He . . . won't touch . . . me. He won't . . . take . . . any . . . money . . . to fix . . . his house for . . . his sisters. I know . . . I am . . . older . . . than he is, but I . . . am . . . not . . . real . . . old. My hair . . . is not . . . gray. But . . . I know he loves me . . . I know . . . it."

Phillip sighed. "Perhaps time will work it all out. It will pass."

Richlene laughed happily. "Yes . . . yes. Time . . . will work it . . . out."

But they did not mean the same things. She knew that. She took Phillip's hand and held it to her breast. "Son . . . you know . . . I have . . . always . . . wanted a . . . real family. I have . . . always . . . always . . . wanted to be . . . really . . . loved. I have . . . been . . . touched . . . by . . . people, my . . . father, and in a . . . different . . . way, my husband. But . . . son, I . . . have never

. . . really . . . been touched . . . inside. I have . . . never . . .
never . . . felt any . . . thing . . . with . . . anybody. But, Luke
. . . Luke touches me . . . inside . . . on my soul, . . . my heart
. . . no matter . . . how far away . . . he is. I . . . am . . . not an
. . . emp . . . ty . . . shell . . . with Luke. I . . . am . . . a full
. . . woman." She smiled shyly at her son. "What does . . . color . . .
matter . . . compared with . . . happiness? Because I . . . love him
. . . and . . . he loves . . . me."

Later, alone, Richlene lay in her bed and thought about when she
and Luke worked in the gardens together. Lately, his mind seemed to be
taken up with the problems his Indian friends were having. It seemed it
was possible they would have to move on, far away from their homes.
No one, Indian or not, seemed to be able to get through to the government. The government talked legal gibberish when they did get to speak
to their Indian representatives in Washington, D.C. They were not Indian representatives after all, they were simply the ones chosen to be the
middlemen for the government.

Richlene had asked Luke, "But . . . won't they . . . send them to
another . . . place . . . just as nice?"

Luke had answered, "This is already a nice place. It is their home
now, for many years. Why should they have to move? This is their own
country! And it's in a treaty, too!"

They had talked for hours, many times, until one day Luke
mentioned that Little Wisdom wanted to marry him so she could
stay near her friends and, maybe, even keep some of her family
there.

Richlene said, "Oh . . . she . . . does, does she?!"

"That's what that chile says."

"Well, what . . . about me?" Richlene looked into his face and was
not smiling as usual.

Luke had sighed, weary. "Well, Miz Richlene, I done told you, I love
you, too. But I am a poor man and ain't none of that gonna change.
What would you do with a man like me? I am a Negro man, too. You
would have to bury all your family, if you was with me!"

"Well, I . . . done told you, Luke, I . . . love you. I want to love
. . . you and . . . work in . . . our garden. We'd . . . have . . . a
beauti . . . ful garden, Luke."

Luke smiled. "We can still have that, little lady."

"But . . . I . . . don't want . . . to . . . stay here . . . with
. . . Carlene. I . . . never . . . would be . . . happy."

Luke wiped his brow of perspiration. "Well, Miz Richlene, I don't
know what I can do. I can't even help my Indian friends. I ain't free, but
I don't think nobody can make me move. They ain't free and somebody
is making them move. If I could do anything, I would help them to be
free. First. See, I love you, but I love freedom. For everybody."

Richlene stretched in her bed, uncomfortable now, thinking of the
fact that Little Wisdom wanted to marry Luke. Suddenly she sat up and
spoke to herself, "I have . . . an idea . . . now!" In the morning, she
told Phillip her idea. He didn't try to change her mind. "Hell, she can
never spend all that money anyway. She deserves whatever she wants,"
he thought. He smiled and promised to look into it right away.

during the time Carlene, Yin and Hosanna were off on their trip,
Phillip had investigated, requested and received help with the Indian
Affairs offices. He purchased for Richlene, with her money, 100,000
acres of hills and land across the river in Yoville, with frontage on the
river. The cost was very little compared to what the government had told
the Indians. Because he was who he was, he paid about ten cents an
acre.

When he told his mother the land was hers, she had him prepare
papers to sign it over to the Indians, with a little land reserved for her, if
she should ever want to build over there. She already knew she would.

Then she told Luke. He looked at her in wonder and, for the first
time, when she threw her arms around his neck, he hugged her back.
Both were happy for themselves . . . and others, too.

Richlene leaned her head back, she would not let go of Luke. "Will

. . . you . . . build a house . . . for me, Luke?" She was still thinking of Little Wisdom.

Luke laughed and hugged her. "I'll build you a castle!"

Richlene hugged him tighter. "I know."

Luke leaned back from her. "With a beautiful garden."

Richlene smiled back at him. "Inside . . . and . . . out!"

c h a p t e r
40

When Carlene, Yin and Hosanna returned several weeks later, Carlene and Yin were hardly speaking to each other, except through Hosanna. The yacht had been beautiful, Yin and Hosanna had learned a great deal. Hosanna had learned a few more tasty recipes and she had visited a castle or two. In fact, she was the only one of the three who had enjoyed herself.

Yin huffed off the riverboat almost before it docked. She was still complaining about tired, old men and watchful, jealous wives. Carlene laughed at her, glad at Yin's discomfort. Carlene had known what the trip would be like, but she had plans for Yin and Phillip or Mr. Ways. She hadn't intended for Yin to meet anyone she would want.

Yin rushed home to find a fat, healthy baby and a smiling Aunt Ellen standing on the porch waiting for her. She reached for her baby. "Joseph! Mama has missed you! She missed you in her bed every morning!" She also had a letter from Arabella Befoe, inviting her to come visit for some festivities. Yin screamed with joy. Here was a woman, a friend, who know what she was after!

Hosanna went home loaded with packages for her family. Happy. She was hugged and kissed, even by Lettie and especially by Lovey.

While Hosanna was gone Lovey had received a beautiful wagon made of highly polished wood and metal with a sterling shaft just right for her and even a strong, rubber-tipped stick to push herself along with. It was from Lincoln, with a note saying, "You thought I forgot, didn't you?" Lovey would sit in it with stars in her eyes, thinking more of Lincoln than the wagon which now made her more mobile.

Carlene went home to find the house empty except for the cook and Minna, who had really enjoyed Carlene being away. Sally had moved into her new home. It had been entirely redone and furnished.

Carlene sighed, "Good. We shall see what we shall see." As Minna helped her undress, Carlene sighed. "I'm tired. I'm too old for these trips. That's my last one."

While Richlene was still living with Carlene, Phillip came to see her as often as college and business would allow, and they were falling more in love as can be said of a mother and son just reunited to each other.

While Phillip and Lincoln finished law school, Phillip asked Lincoln to work for him, to live on his grand estate, make himself at home and check every paper written in the last year in each of Phillip's inherited businesses. All was going well. Lincoln was exceptionally smart and understood the legal terminology enough to catch and correct, to Phillip's advantage, many things usually left to attorneys with no real interest in Phillip Befoe or Richard Befoe before him. Lincoln was well paid for his time and effort. They had grown quite close. Lincoln Creed was, indeed, trustworthy.

On one such visit to his mother's home, Carlene sent for Phillip. She was wondering how much he knew, how much she should tell him about his real father. She decided she would hold it as an ace. She still did not want the name Befoe tainted. Unless, of course, it was necessary to gain some control. Richlene had been told so many times Phillip was her husband's child, she had become confused. "But . . . I . . . remember . . . something," Richlene said to herself sometimes. It had not all come back to her, so she could not tell Phillip who his father really was. It would never come up again, unless Carlene decided to tell. Carlene considered telling Phillip but couldn't decide what control that would give her over him.

Carlene did not know about Richlene's new ventures, the Indian land, or Luke. She had not long returned from her yacht trip and Minna no longer gossiped with her. She only knew the house was often empty. Emily was begging to be sent away to school to prepare for university. Carlene often thought Richlene was working in some garden somewhere.

On the day she heard Phillip was coming, she left word for him to come to her. It was early afternoon when he arrived. The spider, older now but not really old because spiders can live up to twenty years or so, sat wrapped in its legs, watching Carlene, as usual. Waiting, as Carlene waited.

At the knock on the door, firm but gentle, Carlene called, "Come in, come in." Phillip entered. Carlene spoke in her friendly voice, "Well, what a fine, handsome gentleman it is. My grandson. How is it you never come up to see me when you visit?" She smiled at him.

Phillip tilted his head and slightly smiled back to her. "I waited until you were ready, Grandmother."

Carlene laughed softly. "Well, I've been ready. Waiting. How are you? And how do you like our home, your home here? Your other home is much grander, of course. Older."

Phillip smiled again lightly. "I like them both. I particularly like this house because my mother is here."

Carlene nodded approval, "Yes, yes. Well, I hope you understand that it was all for the best, the things that . . . happened. Your mother was so young . . ."

"And I was so young, also." Phillip looked into her eyes.

Carlene looked away toward the windows. "Yes, well . . . we can see it has done you no harm."

"You can not always 'see' harm, Grandmother."

Carlene looked back at him. "Well, everything seems to have turned out for the best."

Phillip still smiled. "What is best, Grandmother? Who's best?"

"Surely, Phillip, you do not hold me responsible? I had nothing to do with what happened. Your . . . grandfather was responsible for any decision about you."

"Well, I am here, safe and sound."

"Yes, well, what are your plans now, my boy?"

"Nothing has changed, except I have more work to do. I will finish law school and then get to work."

"I understood you had already 'gotten to work'."

Phillip smiled down at his hands. "Everyone should know their business. First hand."

"Where will you be living when you finish college, Phillip?"

"Grandmother, I haven't decided."

Carlene gave him her best, most charming smile. "Then I insist you live here. With us, your family." She was watching his reaction. "I know a great deal about our business, your business." She laughed good naturedly. "I can be a great help to you. As a matter of fact, if you give me power of attorney, I can take care of everything for you and you can finish college at ease, knowing everything will be taken care of. Then, my boy, I suggest a year or two of travel, Europe, the Far East. See the world. You have business everywhere!"

Phillip smiled brightly at her. "Thank you, Grandmother, very much. But I have already taken care of everything so I can continue my studies at ease. But I am young, I am not looking for ease. I am quite anxious to get into the middle of everything that is in my hands. I have hired . . . the proper people to see to my interest. I would not dream of bothering you. You are old, now. You deserve your rest."

Carlene's smile dimmed. "My mind is not old, it does not need rest."

Phillip's smile brightened. "My mind is not crowded or tired. I am fresh. I will be capable. Don't worry about me, Grandmother. Perhaps . . . there is something I can look after for you?"

Narrowing her eyes, lowering her head slightly, Carlene answered, "No, no. I am quite capable myself. Thank you."

She was silent for a moment, as Phillip waited. Then, "Phillip, do you ever think of getting married? Are you in love? Is there a lucky girl? . . . Somewhere?"

Phillip laughed softly. "No, Grandmother, no, there is not. I like them all, but nothing special. I have time, I hope. Because I know what I want and I will wait for it, I hope."

Phillip stood up. "Well, Grandmother, I promised my mother we would go for a short trip across the river . . ."

"How nice. I don't know what Richlene is always going over there for. If she likes being outdoors, she should go into the gardens right here!"

"Say, Grandmother . . . would you mind terribly, if I called you Carlene or Granny? 'Grandmother' just seems so long a word."

"But it sounds so like a family, Phillip. 'Carlene' sounds so distant. And not 'granny' ever! If you don't like 'grandmother,' how about 'Grand'?"

"Well, Grand, if there is nothing else, I will say good-bye for now. Perhaps we will see you at dinner."

"I seldom come downstairs, Phillip, but perhaps . . . my boy."

"Do me a favor, Grand? Don't call me your 'boy.' I am a man."

"Well . . ." Carlene started to speak.

"Good-bye, Grand." Phillip smiled and was gone, gently closing the door.

Carlene had noted two things. "He is like my husband, Richard. He did not ask to take care of my business so he could discover what my business and finances are and, perhaps, take advantage of me. And," she closed her eyes, "he is like my lover, Richard, my uncle. When he turned back and smiled, I saw my lover in his face, his body, and my body was stirred as it has not been for years and years and years." Carlene stared at the door after he was gone, for a long, long time. The spider stared at Carlene all the while.

Emily had been begging her mother for several months to let her go away to a good school. "I am young. I need to know so many things, Mother. I have to get prepared for a university. I am going to need the best knowledge money can buy."

Richlene's voice was sad. "But . . . why? Why . . . do you . . . want to leave . . . me? We have . . . money . . . enough money."

Emily wanted to put her arms around her little mother, but she could not weaken. "Mother, I have explained to you. As I get older, I may have to battle for my rights. Any money you leave me is going to be schemed on, especially by my brother, Carlton. And others. I have to know what I am doing. I do not intend to lose anything to anyone just because I am a girl and they will not allow me to understand what they are doing with my money! I have to get an education, the same education they get, so I will know what they are doing! All the time! A tutor at home is no longer enough! If the tutor really knew anything, he would not be here teaching one child!"

"Ohhhh, Emily. I . . . can . . . not . . . bear to . . . lose you."

"Oh, Mama, Mama, you will not lose me. I am your daughter. I will fight for us. And you have Phillip. He loves you. He loves us. He is the only one I trust in this house, in this world, besides you, and you are not a match for anyone. You are too kind sometimes. I will be the one who makes your fortune grow. Our fortune. Grandmother is not going to leave me anything and I already know it. I have to count on myself. So I am begging you, let me choose where I want to go, then let me go."

"Oh, my baby . . . my baby girl. I don't care . . . about . . . a fortune."

"That is because you have one. Look at me, Mother, I am not a child any longer. I will soon be fifteen years old. And I am dumb. Phillip is only nineteen or so and he is almost a lawyer. I want to study the law and economics." She put her arms around her mother and held her tightly. "Oh, Mama, Mama. I have to work on my future, too."

"Alright . . . Emily . . . Choose . . . and go. But . . . you come back . . . to me. You hear . . . me?"

"I will never really leave you, Mama."

Luke was building the house for Richlene across the river on the river's edge. Richlene often went to see it and even helped stack bricks and carry nails, any small thing she could do. She was happy. And so was Luke. Only Little Wisdom was not. She was happy about the land and a home that was stable. But she did love Luke. She did not dislike Richlene, but, she envied her.

Satan wondered how far Little Wisdom would go to get Luke for herself. "One is dumb, one is black, one is young. There ought to be something interesting there." But he couldn't wait around, there were some large, grand things going on all over the world. Something called television was in the making. "I can get into every home at the same time!" Satan gloated. The new America was going into debt for wars and the new war was due any minute. The old world needed help thinking of new ways to get people to go to war. To still be willing to die. "No rest for the wicked!" he laughed as he flew away.

chapter

41

Sally's new school was open. She was still working on it in small details, but it was comfortable. Many children were hesitant to come, but as time passed, they came, clean and smiling. Negro, white and Indian. The dirty ones, the lame, all were welcomed. She also had a small schoolhouse built on the Indian land for those who were adult and didn't want to attend the children's school, and she spent a few days a week over there.

Russell had proposed again and again. Sally liked him, might even love him, she mused. He was very kind and sweet. He even liked what she was doing. Never called her a fool, wasting money. But . . . she was an older woman now, and free! With money! Really free.

Her own children, Reginald and Lenore, had begun writing her lately. They had heard about her inheritance. They declared their love, separately, in letters and apologized for not writing sooner or more, but they said, "Life has been so busy and we knew you were well."

Sally waited before she answered them. She wanted to think about them and life a bit more. In her heart she longed to see them and her grandchildren. Perhaps, she thought, she would go and visit the grandchildren. She would see. There was time. But right now, she was busy living, thinking and teaching.

Before she made up her mind to go visit them, she received a letter from Lenore about one of Lenore's children, Ann. It seemed Ann was a problem child and kept the family from being the peaceful, happy family it would be without her. "So I am wondering if her very good grandmother would like a visit from her granddaughter. I am sure she will love you. Reginald and I agree, she reminds us of you, Mother. I can put her on a train, she is very grown up and capable. She just does not get along with her sister and cousins. May I say in a month or so? We think of you often, Mother, dear." Lenore was really thinking of the inheritance she might miss because of her actions when she thought her mother was destitute. "Mother will grow to love Ann and that will take care of that. Mother was always soft." Reginald began to think of which of his children he might send to accomplish the same thing.

Sally didn't know whether to become excited or not. What could a child do to upset a household? But she remembered growing up with Carlene, and her heart beat faster for the child. Then she wondered if Ann was like Carlene or herself. "I will wait and see. What can it hurt?"

On the appointed day, Sally rode to Mythville, her thoughts rather excited. Her own flesh and blood! A blessed grandchild. The train had come and gone! She had to look all over the station, inside and out. She went back in to sit and think about whether the child had stayed on the train and what to do to get her back to Mythville. She leaned back on the wooden bench and her eyes fell on a thin, tight little being, about fourteen years of age, huddled in the corner of a bench way in the back of the station. "How did I miss her! If that is her." Sally went directly to the little girl.

"Ann?"

The little girl straightened up, looking into the eyes of this woman who must be her grandmother, she looked like she, herself, did. The voice was timid, but clear. "You are my grandmother?"

Sally wanted to reach out and grab the child, to smother her with kisses and the love she had been holding in her heart while separated for so many years from her own children, but something held her back. "Yes. If your name is Ann?"

The young girl stood. Her clothes were fairly good, not the best that Sally knew Lenore could afford. The colors were dark and somber. She had one small bag with her. "My name is Angela. I don't like 'Angela.' Please call me Ann."

"Well, Ann, if we are the ones we are looking for, let's go home."

Ann was a thoughtful child, quiet, taking time to think before she spoke. She was not a Carlene. She was not really a Sally. She was an Ann. In time, Sally's warmth drew her out. In time she began to laugh. In a month, she was going to the schools, helping Sally, which the child seemed to enjoy. She loved going on the Indian side of the river. She worked with Luke on the land. Luke was kind and patient. She soon loved Luke. She followed him around when she was not in school.

Ann was a giver. She gave away almost everything Sally bought her. She liked to see the pleasure on the faces of those who had never had anything before. Sally started to fuss about it, but decided the child was right.

Ann played at last. Not vigorously, but she played. Her spirit had been stunted by empty demands and values, which somehow the child understood to be empty. She had questioned them, embarrassing her parents and the sister who did not like her. So she had been sent away, gotten rid of, to a grandmother who could not have been more pleased.

Sally relaxed about the child one night when they were lying in Sally's bed reading. Sally had turned to Ann to emphasize the last words of the story, when she realized the child was looking at her intently, very seriously. "What is it, Ann? What is the matter?"

"I love you, Grandmother."

Sally drew the young girl closer. "Why, I love you too, Ann."

"I have never felt this way before, Grandmother."

Sally looked into the child's eyes, understanding her completely. "Grandmother is such a long word, Ann, how about you calling me Grandma?"

Ann laughed, her face lost that tight look and softened, was full of open joy. "Okay, Grandma!" Then they both laughed, and were happy.

The sun, wind, earth, the loving and giving turned Ann into a beautiful, young girl who would soon be a woman. Phillip saw that in her. He watched her growing and spent much time with her when he was in Yoville visiting his mother. His love grew in a different way. He decided she would one day, maybe, be his wife, if he could watch her closely so that no one else would take her. After a time, Sally saw all these things. She did not mind. She even laughed, thinking of Lenore and even Reginald, how they would learn one day that the child they had not wanted in their families had married one of the richest men in the world. "And he is not only rich, he is kind. Which is like finding a needle in a haystack!"

All the years of loneliness and grieving for his mother, a family, had made Phillip very introspective. Had broadened and deepened his values. He understood a great deal about true life, true values. There were very, very few wealthy men who were like him. But Ann never thought of him or these things at all. She was learning about other things like the earth and people, animals and rivers and trees and Grandma. Those kinds of loves.

Yin visited Arabella. Arabella, knowing what life was about and what Yin was about, had given many dinners and musicales in Yin's honor. "You must dress more like a lady than a passionate woman! The kind of man you need goes to whorehouses for his passionate women. He shows the world a lady when he presents his wife."

"But I am not a whore! I have a son, a house, some money!"

"So do some whores. It is not a case of you looking like a whore or being one. You want the type of man who is respected as well as rich! He decides what he wants from you when he sees you. You must show him you are what he wants!"

They argued, but not long. Yin knew Arabella was right, but she thought her clothes were beautiful. They went shopping. Arabella helped Yin spend loads of money on dresses that looked so simple Yin could have cried. "I shall be a nun!"

Arabella laughed. "You shall be a rich man's wife!"

On Yin's body the simple dresses took on another dimension. They were gorgeous. They brought out all her beauty and subdued it so that it would be inviting as well as reserved and special.

Yin found her rich man. After a proper time during which he learned about her property and how, as Arabella told him, Yin was a fine lady from an old fine family, he proposed. As instructed, Yin had shyly refused. But he was swept off his feet; he proposed again. Yin coyly accepted, much like her mother years ago. He was an older man, much older than she was.

Yin took her time. Aunt Ellen was still taking care of Joseph back in Yoville. Yin had to take her time. She wanted her son, but she wanted this rich man, too, and he would, surely, never accept a Negro son. "This color stuff has ever and always caused me problems!" she thought to herself. "Why can't people just be people!?"

Yin married the man, Mr. Monigold, and stayed in the East. She came home as frequently as possible to see her son and Aunt Ellen. He never suffered for anything but a mother. She had another child by her new husband. It was a girl. A white girl-child. When Yin looked at the child, she would think, "Joseph's sister. I will teach her love for all races. I will teach her what God has said, that we are brothers and sisters, all of us."

Yin really thought she had stayed long enough in the marriage. She had given Mr. Monigold a child. He was not so concerned about having a new child, he had other older children by his former wife. He was not easy to get along with unless she was in bed doing some of the perversions he so enjoyed and demanded more and more the longer they were married. One day Yin said "enough!" to Arabella. Arabella said, "Well, get a good attorney if you wish to continue being a lady. Divorces are taboo!"

"To hell with being a lady! I want money enough to pay me for all I have gone through with this, this . . . man! I want to be with someone I love!"

"I have no doubt you will have all the money you will need. I don't know about love." Arabella's satisfaction was in being a respected lady, with money of course. She was not sure she wanted love again. Love, before Carl, has cost her a great deal. But Yin's satisfaction was in having money, a family and being loved. Her dissatisfaction drove her on.

That night when Monigold reached for her, Yin insisted on un-perverted lovemaking with her surprised husband or no lovemaking at all. The next day, she found the lawyer Arabella had recommended and filed for divorce. She had compromising pictures of her husband she had found among his private things. "There is no date on a picture so they can't prove it was before our marriage. It'll work! Rich sure ain't what it's cracked up to be."

Then . . . she returned to Yoville, taking her daughter Kay with her.

chapter
4 2

now, all these things were going on and on. Hosanna had given out her cards during the time when many people had returned to Yoville for the season. Sally had helped her. Hosanna stayed busy catering and very busy washing and ironing fine lingerie. She hired Lovey and Little Wisdom when they were not in school. Sometimes, Lettie. A few years passed.

Lettie had married Boyd and had two children, Ruth and Boyda. Hosanna loaned Lettie, not Boyd, the money to purchase a small, inexpensive house. The family moved into it so Hosanna could do her business in peace. She had to continually check to make sure Lettie sent the children to school. She loved to see her two little nieces, the older one pulling the smaller one, as they walked down the road on their way to school in their little, cotton dresses.

Lettie and Boyd argued most of the time now. Boyd did not like to work. Could not keep a job, no matter how many jobs Hosanna found for him. Boyd did not like Hosanna. "She try to be too damn independant! She need a man to whip her ass!" He sometimes whipped Lettie's. Lettie was thin, unhappy and evil most of the time. Her satisfaction was love, and she didn't have a man who loved her. She sometimes envied Hosanna, but refused to work much for her.

Men came to court Hosanna. She was very attractive. Some of them thought she must have some money because she worked all the time. A few really cared for her for herself. One in particular, Homer. Homer always tried to help Hosanna in some little way. A better fireplace for her soaking tubs. A better platform for all her tools. He would make things at his house where he lived with his mother and bring them to her completed. Always afraid she might not accept them. He would bring her a bunch of wild flowers, even a box of candy sometimes. He helped Hosanna in her garden sometimes, so they could talk.

Luke was living with Richlene now, they had been married the Indian way. All his garden time was at his new home now, though he did help Hosanna when he was on that side of the river or she sent for him for something special. He was proud of Hosanna. He liked Homer and was glad Homer was around to help his sisters.

Homer kept Hosanna's kindling pile full, putting wood there even while she slept at night. She would just wake, go out, and there it was. Hosanna liked Homer, respected him. "He ain't always over there at Choker's juke joint, lappin up that liquor and the ladies hanging round there!" she would say. But she did not love him. In fact, he bored her. She thought his mind was too country, too slow. She treated him nice, joked and teased with him, because when he came around where she was working, he could make her laugh and she wouldn't be so tired anymore. But she never let him touch her or get too close. Lovey watched them, longingly.

Lovey had heard that Lincoln had gone to fight in the war and had lost a leg. He still worked with Phillip, made a great deal of money, invested it. But when he came to Yoville to visit his father, he always stole into town and left the same way, quietly. He did not want anyone to see him with his one leg. Lovey always "just missed Lincoln," old Mr. Creed would say when he passed on his way to visit Aunt Ellen. Older now, grown more beautiful, body filled out and luscious, Lovey had no boyfriend, no man. Lovey still loved Lincoln.

. . .

lovey and Hosanna were alone in the little house now. Luke gone cross the river, Lettie in her own house. They had more space and they had fixed it up very nicely. Each would lay in her bed in their own rooms after a full day, thinking. Lovey of love and Hosanna of whether anyone would ever come along in Yoville who would be right for her.

Hosanna would toss and think, "I don't want none, none of these no account men around here. They are too satisfied with makin do. I want some nice things. Yin is a woman and she has some nice things. Sally is a single woman, she has some nice things. Course they have plenty money now. I'm not going to have that much, don't need that much, but I want SOME! Ain't gonna be poor no more. Poor killed my daddy and my mother. I'm gonna have children some day, Lord willin, and I don't want nothing to happen to them like it happened to us!" Hosanna had begun to pray more lately. She would say her prayers, have a long talk with God and slip into sleep before she was through.

Lovey would lay in her bed, thinking and praying at the same time. "I'm just layin here lookin at the rest of my life. Nobody ain't ever gonna really love me. All this schoolin ain't gonna do me nothin. I ain't never goin to go nowhere away from Yoville and workin this little job for Hosanna. I'm savin money, but what am I going to buy?" She gave God a mean look at the ceiling. "Shoes?! WHO? Who gonna hire me any-where else? I don't even care about that either! Who gonna LOVE me?" Lovey's pretty, little young body was awakening to its own music and life. Well fed now and exercised, it was a healthy body. Though its legs were lame, everything else worked really well!

don't misunderstand, Hosanna loved her life now. Getting up in the mornings, fresh beautiful mornings, rain or shine. All the trees, their own trees and those off in the distance, green and tall and beautiful. Filled with birds of all colors, flying off and flying back to their nests with the sky, clear of clouds, still beautiful beyond everything. The sun coming up casting that golden glow over everything. The very color of the morning, even without the sun, was a mellow, blue-gray fresh feeling of beauty. And their garden, green, gold and dewy, growing and healthy.

Little by little Hosanna was improving the house. It stood small, bright and proud. Yes, it was a good feeling to get up and begin a new day, every day. But . . . it was lonely sometimes. She turned to the Bible more, reading it alone or with Lovey.

Luke had Richlene and the work he was doing and he had Little Wisdom who loved him. Luke's satisfaction was love, peace and no worry. Richlene's satisfaction was family, love and peace. They were happy. When Richlene's hair started graying, she wanted to dye it, but Luke stopped her. "If it yours, I like it just like it is." Sometimes he would look off into space and say, "Richlene, you got all that money! It's a plenty poor people you could help. We got to think of somethin to do to help make other people as happy as we are."

Richlene was, after all, Carlene's daughter. "Aren't . . . these Indi-ans . . . happy? I did . . . that already."

Luke would smile at her. "You broke?"

"No."

"Well, let's think of somethin else we can do."

"Well . . . let's do . . . something . . . for us."

"We don't need nothin else, Richlene."

Then Richlene would speak of something else to distract his mind.

Little Wisdom had begun allowing other men to court her after Luke and Richlene's marriage. She saw and respected the love in Richlene and Luke's eyes. She really thought Richlene was too old, "At least ten years older than Luke!" but she knew from experience, "What does the heart care about time?" Little Wisdom's satisfaction was love, respect and family. It was there, just around the corner, if she could just get Luke out of her eyes.

Sally had Russell whom she might marry. Her mind went back and forth. And she had Ann. And it was possible another grandchild, Wil-liam, would be coming. Another "problem" Reginald had said, but he really did not want his sister's child, Ann, to inherit all of Sally's wealth, so he chose the child of his own he did not like, William. By now Sally knew what Reginald and Lenore called "problems," and she was more than ready to welcome her grandson. Sally's satisfaction was peace, giving and love. She was happy.

Yin had had her rich husband, now divorced. She had her two children and Aunt Ellen, and all seemed to get along well. The baby girl was still quite young, and Monigold was trying to take her away from Yin. He knew Yin left for long weeks, leaving the children with Aunt Ellen. No one knew just where Yin went, except perhaps Arabella. Yin was an excellent mother when she was home. Her satisfaction was love, money and family. She seemed to have it all.

Old Mr. Creed had been lonely, too. But there was a worn path from his house to Yin's to visit Aunt Ellen where he had dinner quite often and stayed to putter around for many hours. They were almost like a family. Creed's satisfaction was an independant son, a little loving and doing what he felt like doing, which wasn't much more than fishing sometimes.

Old Mrs. Befoe had an almost empty house. Minna had moved in after Richlene and Sally had gone. She still threatened, under her breath, to leave, but so far she had stayed. The spider still lived, going back and forth outside as it needed. Mrs. Befoe had seen it once and it had frightened her greatly, but she could never find it again. She asked Minna to look for it. "I don't want to see no black widow spider!" The spider still watched Carlene through curled legs.

Sally never came to see her, but sometimes left fresh vegetables that grew profusely in the garden that she, Russell, Ann and now William tended. She left them on the back steps of the huge, almost empty house.

Lettie was usually silent when she came to visit Hosanna and Lovey. She seldom smiled. She would sit holding her smallest baby, listening to Hosanna tell a helper, "No, don't rub that, just squeeze, see? Squeeze. These are delicate things!" Hosanna would ask Lettie how she was doing, Lettie would usually answer, "Just holdin a baby, holdin a baby! All my life just a holdin a baby, mine or my mama's! Cookin and washin clothes! From Luke to Lovey to my own! Never nothin in my life! Just holdin a baby, holdin a baby! No! I ain't gonna help you wash no clothes! Ain't never nothin in my life but work!"

. . .

So the days went. So the years went. Two or three more.

One day Lovey raised her head up over the washtub from squeezing some lingerie, looked at Hosanna and asked, "This all we ever goin to do all our life? You ain't married and I ain't never goin to be married!" Lovey broke into crying and ran on her knees into the house, not even using the ramp. Pap, the dog, quite old now, followed Lovey into the house.

Hosanna stood there a minute, arms covered with soap suds, staring after Lovey. Then she sighed and turned her face to the horizon. "Everybody wants somebody. I still got Homer. None of the women I send him off to can get him to marry them. I'm kinda half satisfied because I don't want no problems. But . . . I am twenty-four years old now. I must be the oldest virgin in the world, God.

"And God, Lovey, Lovey is a virgin, too. I'm sure of it. God, you have given us all these tools on our bodies to work with. Why can't you send somebody to use these tools? With love, I mean. Lovey is a young lady. A young woman now. God, who is she going to have? She got to have somebody. A life! Legs or not!" Hosanna dried her hands and went in to find Lovey crying, sprawled across her bed with the lovely chenille bedspread on it and all the little love pillows strewn across the head. Pap lay on the floor beside the bed, looking up at Hosanna as if he were imploring her to please help Lovey.

Hosanna looked at the stack of magazines on the table next to the bed. Love stories, romance, all the same kind. Hosanna pointed at the magazines and looked up to God meaningfully. "Help," she thought to herself. She patted Pap's head as she sat on the side of the bed.

She put her hand gently on Lovey's shoulder and asked, "Want to go out and buy a new dress? Let's go get Homer to take us to Mythville and get us some new clothes. We deserve it! I'll pay. You keep your money."

Lovey's voice was muffled in the spread, "I don't have no money noway."

Hosanna eye's opened wide, "Why? I pay you. Good."

"I give it to them poor kids over to the school."

"Poor kids!? You are poor, too!"

"I know, Hosanna." Lovey raised her head and sniffled, "But I got more than they do. Sides, where I'm going to wear a new dress? Church? I'm sick of that ole lyin preacher. Always tryin to feel on people. Don't nobody care what I have on noway."

"It's the only church we got round here, Lovey. We don't go for the preacher, we go because . . . because . . . I don't know why we go to that church. Cause God is sposed to be there. Sometimes it seems more like Satan's church though." She thought a moment. "You care what you have on whether anyone else does or not, don't you?"

"I ain't nobody."

Hosanna leaned over her sister, stroking Lovey on her soft, feminine back. "Honey, Lovey, someday somebody is going to love you. Going to come and love you and marry you and take you away."

"Where? To the shit house? Ain't nobody around here got no place to take me. Probly want to come live here and have our home! That's the only reason somebody would marry me. Don't nobody else want them either!"

Hosanna persisted, softly, "I don't think that's true. I think you are beautiful. Your legs may not be like everybody else's, but you work, you are independant. You can do whatever you want to."

Lovey raised her head to wipe at her eyes. "I can't run to no husband. I got a heart with no legs."

Hosanna searched for the right words to say to this sister she loved so much. "Wellll . . . there's more ways to get a husband besides walking and running to him." They were quiet a long moment. Finally, Hosanna went back outside and Lovey lay there thinking about what she had said. Lovey was sad, sad, sad, lonely and alone. She had a grieving spirit and body. She felt her empty heart would ache forever.

Hosanna commenced to squeeze and rinse the lovely lingerie roughly, thinking. "I think I will get Homer to take us over to Choke's juke joint next time they have some live music. Ain't nobody worth nothing in Choke's, but maybe Lovey will feel good just getting out. And we will go get some new dresses, too!" She began to squeeze and dip the lovely garments so hard, she had to remind herself, "These are delicate things." She looked toward the house Lovey was hurting in. "The heart is a delicate thing, God. You made em. You must'a made one to match. If You visiting anywhere Lord, come by here, please."

Hosanna looked in the direction of the chicken house where she kept her money buried until she could get it to the bank. With the war, taxes had increased, so she kept more buried in the chicken house than she took to the bank nowadays. "I'm a'get those dresses."

So . . . the day came when Homer drove them over to Mythville in an old secondhand Ford. A real car! They shopped and shopped until Hosanna finally put a sad, little smile on Lovey's pretty face. Hosanna picked out a dress for Lettie, too. Then they planned when they would go to Choke's juke joint.

Lettie smiled when Hosanna gave her the dress, but shook her head sadly, "Boyd won't let nobody keep the kids but me. He say a mother should be home with her children."

"Well, what about the father? I hear he is out all the time. Dancing and drinking at Choke's and even out of town."

"Well," Lettie picked up her smallest child, too big to be held too long now, "he says he a man. That's why."

Hosanna put her hand on her hip. "Well, I say you are a woman! Aunt Ellen will keep these beautiful children as good as a grandmother would. You going with me!"

Lettie sat down, starting to cry softly, "Oh, Hosanna. I'm so unhappy and sorrowful. Boyd don't love me. I got him to marry me and now he ain't never home. He have other women. They come by here to pick him up. He laugh, say, friend! and run out to em. We don't never make love no more. Not since this third baby and he goin on three years old now. Boyd say, 'I didn't want that one and I don't want no more!' He make me do things to him so he can come and then he leave me unsatisfied. And alone."

Hosanna got angry. She knew something had been wrong, but Lettie didn't usually like to talk her private business, so Hosanna hadn't asked her, being so involved in her own business, too. She put her arm around Lettie now. "Listen, Lettie, honey, you fought till you got that man. Got mad at everybody because you didn't have him. Now just like you fought then, fight now. For your own happiness. You can't stay with him if he is goin to wrinkle your forehead and put tears in your eyes. He put those marks on you that you have been hiding?"

Lettie nodded her head. "But it was my fault, I nagged him. He was tired."

Hosanna nodded her head, "Yes, tired from being out doing what he wants to do. Please, put this dress on and go with us tomorrow night. He can't fuss at you about being with your own sisters!"

"Yes, he can."

"Well, let him. He ain't God. This ain't his world and you ain't his child! Now! Have you got enough gumption to do something YOU want to do? For a change?"

Lettie's tears dried, she nodded and took the first new dress she had had in years with a smile on her drawn face.

The evening of the going-out party, everyone was cleaning, combing, curling, pulling, smoothing, looking in mirrors, patting perfume and powders, bathing, painting and polishing. Getting ready for a night out. Hosanna laughed happily to herself. "Going to Choke's!"

chapter
4 3

Lettie dressed at home with Hosanna and Lovey. Lovey laughed out loud happily, "Goin out to a nightclub!" The old, tin tub had been emptied and refilled two or three times already and was a'splashing and a'sudsing, cleaning the happy bodies. Ladies going out to have a good time. "Living, chile!"

When all was ready, Lovey made Homer put her wagon in his car. "I'm not gonna be carried in no nightclub. I'm going in on my own!" Everybody laughed happily. Homer looked nice in a pressed, clean suit and some two-toned shoes he usually wore to church.

At the entrance, Homer stopped to let the ladies off. He looked at them with pride. "Three beautiful ladies! All to myself!" There was happy laughter as he drove away to park. They could hear the band even outside on the street. The procession was a sad, happy one. Two beautiful stand up ladies and one beautiful one in a wagon . . . sashaying and wheeling into the club.

Inside, the bass drum shook the building. The music was blasting, but it sounded good. Through the smoke you could see the glinting, golden horn. "Listen to that man play that thing!" And the guitar man! "My Lord, my Lord!!" somebody hollered. Nobody noticed the smoke, nobody cared. There was a crowd. Painted women in red, yellows, gold and green dresses, some with slits up to their knees! Men—cleaned, polished, oiled and slick—stood around at the bar. Some men were in coveralls, clean, poor but ready to laugh and party.

Homer had arranged for a table in advance, thinking of Lovey. Her eyes were huge, taking in the whole room of people, men and women, having FUN! Her ears were opened wide, she loved music. She moved into her seat by herself. Just lifted and plopped herself right over. Her heart was filled with such joy . . . to be out! At night! With regular people! And all dressed up! She was beautiful. And . . . she was happy!

Lettie was less secure but held her head up and kept walking, sitting prettily in her pretty dress with her hair done so nice by Hosanna. Lettie felt pretty for the first time since her second week of marriage. She was happy, but she kept looking for Boyd who had been angry when she had taken the children over to Aunt Ellen, telling her, "You betta have your ass home when I get back!" She knew he might be there, in Choke's somewhere. Still . . . her legs kept carrying her on, through the evening and into Choke's to her seat.

Hosanna felt as though all this was beneath her. "All these Negroes in here pretending they're somebody! Well, the music sounds good so . . . let's have a ball!" She felt beautiful, too, and her eyes sparkled as she felt the people looking at her and her sisters. They sure looked good!

Homer was thinking, "It's gonna cost me some money, but ain't that what I work for? To make my lady happy? Someday my lady, I hope!"

After they were seated, the smiling waitress struggled through dancing people to get to them. Hosanna and Lettie each had a Tom Collins "with a cherry please." Homer had a beer. The ladies smiled. Lovey ordered a Singapore Sling which she had read about in her magazines (and which the waitress went back two or three times to find out how to make.) Lovey finally settled for a shot of bourbon, one of rum, one of gin and ginger ale mixed. They all laughed.

Hosanna told Lovey, "You aren't having but one of those!"

Lovey sipped her drink, grinned and said, "I got money. I'll buy what I want!" Then they all laughed again as she sipped her "Singapore shit," as they called it.

When the band took a break, Hosanna sipped her drink, looking around the room which held less people now, most having gone outside for . . . ? The kitchen was frying chicken and fish. It sure did smell good! She saw the ladies and men, slapping each others' shoulders as they playfully flirted and talked. She saw some others in corners, holding hands, looking into each other's eyes. She saw men standing around, looking over the different ladies before they decided who they might try to win for the night.

Lovey was looking, also. She saw women looking from under their lashes at the different men who looked handsome, away from their plows, in the bright colorful lights of the nightclub. Lovey and Hosanna would look at each other, sharing unspoken thoughts, smiling because they were out and everything looked and sounded so good. They looked at Lettie who was looking for Boyd. She was having a good time, but she was afraid of Boyd.

Then, the band came back on and started to play. Their drinks were low, so Homer ordered another round for everybody. They laughed when it came to the Singapore Sling, but Lovey said, "I'm grown. Give me another one!" laughing, because she was already high.

The music shot through the air. All eyes turned to the stage. They played a low-down-dirty blues. All of them, everybody, felt the music. They snapped their fingers and rolled their eyes, smiling, laughing. OH! The drummer was mellow now! The horn player was low and sweeeeeeet. The base player was deep and sweeeeeeeet. But the guitar player . . . he closed his eyes, he plucked the strings like he was making love to his guitar. Good, mellow, slow, down-deep-inside love! Hosanna closed her eyes, put her head back and smiled, snapping her fingers to the beat, shaking her head. They were all doing it, enjoying the music in their own way, it's meaning all their own. Even Lettie closed her eyes, forgetting to watch for Boyd.

The guitar man played so sweet, so low and so blue and loving that Hosanna opened her eyes, leaned forward and looked at him good. Studied him from the top of his head to his shoe soles. His hair was slick like a city man. His jacket hung over his shoulders and back casually. Looked good. His waist was slim, as were his hips. His pants draped on his body, just so, just right. Her eyes moved back down to his feet, she was entranced by them. He patted his foot, not with up and down pats, but by throwing his foot out to the side at each beat. And . . . he had on green suede shoes! Hosanna's eyes moved slowly back up to his face.

Glory be! His eyes were open and he was looking at her, moving his head to the music and smiling . . . at her. Her heart leaped right in her breast. When he sang out the words, "Baby, I'll do what you want me to!" Hosanna's heart flew right out of every opening in her body, straight to him. His guitar talked to her all night.

Lettie had never seen or known so many men were in these parts around Yoville. She looked around at all of them. "My Lord, look at ALL them men! Where were they? Why, Hosanna was right, I hadn't seen nothin! My goodness, my goodness." And Boyd fell right out of her heart. Just like that. Well, he had been mean and he was not loving. She was not smart enough yet to know almost all the men in the club were Boyds.

Noticing the other women, Lovey asked for a cigarette, got one and coughed and drank and flirted from her seat. Every once in a while she would think of Lincoln, but the thought soon disappeared in the crowd of good-looking men in the lights. A few asked her to dance, her wagon was beside her chair. Lovey frowned, she felt like crying. Then Homer picked her up on a slow playing piece of music and carried her around in the dance. Her face was so rapturous and lovely, two other men did the same thing. The words to one song played were "You know what I need." Lovey threw her head back and said, "I'll never get fat! I want to dance forever!"

When the jukebox played again, Greenshoes came down from the bandstand to ask Hosanna to dance. She glided into his arms and then they hardly moved from one spot. She looked up at him and he smiled down at her, moving slowly. He told her his name was Billy, but they called him Bowlegs, Billy Bowlegs.

"My name is Hosanna."

"That's what I thought when I first looked at you. HOSANNA!"

Homer was laughing with Lovey until he happened to look and see what was happening in Hosanna's face. Then he was quiet for the rest of the night, because the look never left her face. They stayed until the end. Hosanna was all eyes for Billy Bowlegs when he was playing and was in his arms when he was not.

When they left the club, Billy had Hosanna's address. A new man knew how to reach Lettie. Lovey had a few, nice memories. All of them were smiling and laughing as they walked to the little old car. But it was quiet in the car, all the way home. Hosanna was thinking of the last thing Billy had said to her, "Think of me till I see you again. Good thoughts."

Homer seemed to have nothing to say. He was sad. When he let the ladies out at their home, he stood watching them until they were in the house safely, then he got into his car and drove slowly away. He had helped make everyone happy, but himself.

billy Bowlegs found Hosanna and, in the following weeks, he slowly but surely wrapped her heart in his cocoon of soft, blue love and music. She was no longer a virgin and had not demanded marriage as she always said she would. She talked about it but didn't demand it. Her body just would not stop, could not stop answering Bowleg's call. She was in love. Her body was not satisfied fully but eagerly anticipated the next time when it would finally feel to her as good as it felt to him. But she loved him so much that just being with him, by him, under him, was all she thought of as she squeezed, hung, stirred, served and did her work.

Hosanna was too full of her own life to notice that Lettie was either very happy or very sad. More marks and bruises appeared on her body, more tears were shed. On other days, Lettie would be laughing and so happy her face shone. Lettie had a secret new man. Boyd knew it and beat her lightly because he didn't want no truck with Hosanna and Luke. Lettie took her beatings and kept running back out to the new man.

Lovey sat on her bed in the now often empty house, looking into her mirror. Several of the men had told her she was beautiful. Now she painted her face, posed, combed and posed. Dreamed again, but only of Lincoln, again.

One day Lettie come running over to the house. One of her eyes was black, her arm was broken, hanging down from her shoulder. She carried one child in her good arm, the others stumbling behind, holding on to the hem of her dress. "I'm not going back there!" she screamed through her snot and tears.

Hosanna was enraged. She wanted to go have it out with Boyd. Lettie stopped her, "No use in that, cause I ain't going back. I can work.

I can work for Miz Sally, she always askin me. And I can work for you."
Her broken arm hurt, her tears started again. "I ain't goin back to that
man!"

Hosanna said, "Well, he can't keep that house and live in it! It
belongs to you! He gonna have to get his cheating ass out of there!" She
turned to Lovey, "Send for Luke! Tell him his family needs him, now!"
Then she took Lettie to a doctor to see about that arm.

When Luke came, leaving his peace behind, they went to Lettie's
house. Boyd was gone. There was a note to Hosanna, saying, "This here
is my wife and my biznes, you stay out of it!" To Lettie, "You betta have
your behind back here when I come home. And cok me som dinner."
They threw the notes out with his clothes, changed the locks and left
him a note pinned to his clothes: "Boyd, don't come in my house again.
Get your own or stay with your women! Stay anywhere you want to, but
you can't stay here." Signed by Hosanna and Luke and Lettie. Then
Hosanna went home, taking Lettie and the children with her. Luke left
saying he would check on them in the morning. Lettie was smiling. She
had a family who looked out for her!

Hosanna didn't really want Lettie working for her. Lettie was sometimes lazy and slow. She helped her get the job with Sally. Lettie was
anxious to return to her own home, so Hosanna moved her back into
her own house.

Things worked out for Lettie, for a little while.

But Hosanna was miserable. Billy Bowlegs was a traveling man. He
liked other women. He fought against marriage though he loved Hosanna. He knew she was not like his other women. She had been a virgin
and she did not fool around. He knew that. But he couldn't help himself. "This is just me, Hosanna. Me! I ain't never promised you nothin!
Just a good time."

Billy lied to her about most everything. Promised to come to her
after his work many times, but didn't. At two or three o'clock in the
morning, she would get up and go out in the dark, cold, scary nights,
trying to find him. Sometimes she found him, sometimes she didn't. It
was always another woman, and the woman always smirked, thinking
herself the better woman, until he did the same thing to her.

Hosanna, more than once, went to the house where he roomed. His
landlady, an old, toothless woman, laughed and said, "He ain't not

home, honey. Which one is you?" Later, Hosanna climbed into his window to make sure. He really was not home. She would go through all his things, read all his notes and letters from other women writing misspelled words of love. Turn his pockets out, looking for she knew not what. Then she cleaned his room up and took some of his clothes home to wash for him. It was pathetic, but she could not let go of the promise of "almost" in her thoughts, "He almost makes me feel good, have orgasms, when he makes love to me. Almost." Billy did not completely satisfy Hosanna's body sexually. But once begun, she could not stop her pathetic actions to keep him. To keep those "almost" feelings.

Hosanna bought him clothes. Gave him some of her little money. Tried to set him up giving lessons to youngsters wanting to learn music. "Your own business," she told him. He spent the money on liquor and other women. Hosanna would not let him go; she was trying to hold on to her cherry (as it is sometimes called) Bowlegs now had, because she wanted to marry the first man she had made love to, given her virginity to.

Hosanna hated herself for the things she did in regard to Bowlegs. "I don't want to be the kind of woman he is making me! Jealous. A shrew! Nagging. Sneaking. I don't want that to be me!" But she was. He didn't bring out the best in her, he brought out the worst. If he hadn't loved her, it might have been smart of him to have everything his way. But he loved her, so it was very stupid of him not to look into the future and guard his love. Satan was very pleased with the whole thing.

These things went on a long time. These things didn't work out so well at all.

Then . . . Lincoln came home to visit again. Creed saw that his son was a sad, dejected man. Creed had his own little life, visiting Aunt Ellen. He was thinking about marrying her. His thoughts were, "She is clean, a good cook, honest and—heh, heh—nice little kisses now and then." He did not want to have to sit sadly and watch his son grieve for his lost leg.

Creed thought some company, another lame person, might make Lincoln open up some and not be so sad if he could see somebody worse off. That is why he told Lovey, as he was passing on his way to see Ellen, "Lincoln's home. You ought to go by and see him in that little wagon he sent you."

Lincoln still had a place on Phillip's estate and the same important job that he handled very well. Lincoln could have bought himself a lovely home at any time with the money he earned and had saved. But he didn't. He wanted to farm on his father's land. He spent much money on farm equipment he wouldn't operate. He hired workmen to do the work. Lincoln was just too sad to be interested in anything but the job he had to do for Phillip. He was satisfied to dream of his farm and let other men run it.

Lincoln would not go out much when he was home in Yoville. He would sometimes sit at Choke's juke joint, drink and drink and drink. He seldom went with the women. He thought they laughed about his leg or felt sorry for him. He most always went alone and left alone. He knew his father was thinking of marrying Ellen. He was glad for his father. But he wanted nothing for himself. "Show a woman my leg!? My leg that is not there!? Hell, no!"

Lovey thought about Lincoln a great deal. She loved him. One day soon after Creed had told her Lincoln was home, she bought some rum and gin from the bootlegger and some ginger ale to make herself a Singapore Sling. Mixed a huge drink, sat in her wagon, looking out the open front door and drank it slowly, just thinking.

Hosanna was out for the night. She would not let Bowlegs sleep in the house she shared with Lovey. "I'm the oldest sister, I have to be an example of what's right."

Bowlegs laughed, "She know what you doin!"

Hosanna didn't laugh. "She THINK, maybe, but she don't know!" Lettie was at her own home, entertaining her new man, peeping through the windows looking for Boyd sneaking around outside.

Lovey sat in her wagon and thought and drank her liquor, thought and drank. Finally, she said to herself, "I know what I want. I'm a grown woman. And I ain't gonna stay alone this way forever. I want him. I want Lincoln." She drank some more. Then she bathed, combed and patted on powder and perfume. Dressed. Then she got in that wagon and pushed herself down the little ramp Homer had built for her with Luke's help. She pointed herself in the direction of Lincoln's house.

"Here I come! (hic!) If all you get is all you give, then I'm going to give all I got. This is my life. I want some love in it."

She rolled along in the wagon, pushing steadily. "Now, I got my own dream. Time going by. I'm getting old and I'm . . ." She laughed out loud, "I'm still a virgin. A virgin! I ain't even got no memories to hold in my heart at night. I ain't got nothin! I don't know nothin bout life. I don't care nothing bout what tomorrow brings! I'm in this here game of life and I want to play!"

She passed people on the road but paid no attention to them. They looked after her, the woman-child, talking to herself. Some of them smiling, some frowning, thinking she was going crazy maybe. She gave them no thought, just passed them by.

She kept talking to herself, "I want what's mine. It must be mine or why do I keep thinking bout that man? Nothin I do can make it no worser." She pushed and prodded her way to Creed's house. When she got there, she stopped at the door and sat looking at it for long moments, her good sense catching up with her liquor. "Will I embarrass myself? Will he be away . . . or be with some other woman?" Lovey threw that out of her mind, but, "How will he be? We was close for a minute once. He's lonely. I know how that feels. I'm goin in."

She crept out of the wagon onto the large porch. She walked on her knees to the door and pushed it open. She stood there a minute. Finally, saying a wary, "Creed? Mr. Creed? Lincoln?" She heard no answer, so she went in further. She moved softly and slowly through the house. It was a nice house, very nice and clean, even with no women there. She looked in two of the rooms, . . . nothing. Then . . . in the third room . . . was Lincoln. His face to the wall. A bottle of bourbon, hardly used, and a turned-over glass on the table beside the bed. She moved in so close she could see him breathing, smell his breath. Then, even closer. Said, "Lincoln, I'm here. Your woman, Lovey is here." He didn't answer, but she knew he was awake.

Lincoln had been lying in bed thinking of how much he wanted to be loved, thinking that he never would be loved now.

Lovey leaned closer over and against him, she felt the heat of his body. She knew her breath smelled clean so she spoke right into his ear, her head near his face. "I want to be your woman, Lincoln. I want to be loved by you. I have waited and waited and waited. For you. I want me somebody. Ain't no use of you thinkin of my legs, I don't need em. I am a full one hundred percent woman. I know it. Cause I know what's in my heart wouldn't be there if I couldn't use it." She leaned even closer and was silent a long moment, feeling the beat of her heart, feeling the heat and life of his body.

"I'm so happy to be just this much near to you, Lincoln." She sighed. "I'm here." She lay her head on the back of his shoulder and sighed again. Lincoln's heart heard the sighs, his shoulder felt the warmth, but he thought of Lovey as a child.

She spoke more, "I rode all the way over here in that wagon you made me so I could come to you." She sighed one of those low-down hurting sighs. His heart felt for her. "My love is so big for you, you got to feel it. When you look at me or I think of you touchin me, I hear music I ain't never heard before, way off in the night and deep inside me all at the same time. You make my nerves hurt."

She raised herself up on the bed, sitting and leaning over him. "I am hungry for you. Satisfy my hungriness." She was taking off her clothes, he knew it, but he did not stop her. She talked as she removed each piece.

"I can't handle my love for you anymore. I know girls ain't sposed to do things like speak up to a man, but, I can't help myself. You are everything to me, Lincoln. I can't hold up in this world if you don't hold me in your arms." Her clothes were all off now, except a little silk slip. (She had worn those types of clothes easy to remove.) When she gently pulled on his shoulder, he turned his body a little toward her, but he turned his face all the way to look at her. She smiled a sad, serious, little smile. Lovey had not been lying to him. She loved her some Lincoln. He felt her breath on his face as she spoke softly, "You got to feel it! You got to feel my love I been carrying for you all these years. My love is like a fire. It is burning me up." She helped him turn his body around to her, she caressed his face with her little, gentle, tender hand. She gently moved herself down and almost under him and pulled him even closer to her.

Lincoln pulled gently away. "Lovey, you don't understand. I am not all man anymore. I have lost a leg, my body is not a full man. I only have one leg." His voice broke as if he would sob. Lovey moved further under him and wrapped her arms around him. She was strong. She kissed his lips, softly, her first kiss in her life of twenty-three years. "I love you, Lincoln. What I care bout a leg? I don't have any. I don't need em for the most important things. And you . . . ? They might'a took one of your legs, but they didn't take the best one."

Lincoln buried his head in her full, soft breasts. She closed her eyes and barely breathed. She wrapped her thighs around him, cupping his body. Their breaths mingled, the heat of their bodies met. They lay that way for a long time, Lovey kissing any of his skin near her lips. Then Lincoln slowly raised himself up and kissed her very tenderly. "Little Lovey." Lovey whispered against his lips, "I'm a woman now . . . and I've always been your woman." He raised himself to look down at her and then, slowly, moved his body to accommodate hers, and this time, when he slowly lowered his body down, he buried himself in her body. He raised up once more to look down into her face when he discovered she was a virgin. He thought, "She has brought this precious gift to me." Then he slowly began to make love to Lovey. A long, tender, loving time. She cried, not from the pain, though it hurt. She cried from joy. During their lovemaking, he proved he was her man and she proved she was his woman. It was more than an orgasm of the body, it was an orgasm of the minds. He made love to her soul. They were both satisfied. Mentally, physically and spiritually.

Later, much later, under the starry sky of early morning, when he was walking her home, him limping on a crutch, her in the wagon, he laughed softly. "What?" asked Lovey, looking up to him with eyes as full of stars as the sky. He smiled down at her. "I am going to have to get a wooden leg so I can walk with you, and I am going to have to fix it so I can pull your wagon with you beside me."

Lovey's heart opened up and the sweetest feelings spread out through her body. She had been wondering if she had gone too far with him and if he would ever see her again. You know, the usual things. Now she knew he planned to see her, let her in his life. But he had been wondering if he had really pleased her, if she would still love him. They were silent until they reached her door. Lovey hadn't planned to ask, but it just came out of her mouth when it was time to let him go. To be alone again. "What are we goin to do, Lincoln?"

"Well, Lovey, you have always been in part of my mind. I never imagined it would be like this, together. You were a child to me. And being like you . . . are, I might never have attempted to get to know your mind . . . and heart better. But now I have. And what have legs got to do with how you feel? You have many things to love, Lovey. And I have learned, when your mind tells you something and your body agrees, you better go with it!" They laughed together. Both of them happy.

A week later, when Lincoln left to go back to his job at Phillip's mansion, Lovey went with him, as his wife. Pap, the old dog, was taken, too. Lovey was almost speaking Chinese she was so happy. They were both happy. Satisfied with life.

Hosanna saw their happiness. She knew Lovey had been a virgin for Lincoln. "I have two legs and I am still lonely and unloved. Billy Bow is going to have to go. I can't take anymore of his kind of life. I'm NOT going to take it! I deserve better and it's up to me to carry myself like I believe it!" So she decided to leave Bowlegs alone and told him. He didn't believe her so he didn't even worry. He told his friends, "I love her, I'm gonna get to her someday. Get married and all that stuff." And like the grasshopper, he kept laughing and playing his life away. He either thought he was satisfied or he thought satisfaction and opportunity would wait for him to make up his mind.

now . . . Luke and Richlene had a pleasent kind of love and life. It was slow, easygoing and, for the most part, satisfying. Their love-making was gentle and complete. But Luke had done all the building, was keeping up the vegetable and flower gardens, yet was still growing restless. He was a man used to working and did not like just doing nothing. He was young.

One day while Luke and Richlene were working in the flower garden, he said to her, "Richlene . . . I'm going to find me a job. I want a job. I think I got a few plans I want to do."

Richlene smiled indulgently, "Luke you . . . don't have to . . . work. I have . . . more than enough . . . for us."

Luke stopped digging and looked at her. "Richlene, you ever think of the fact that if I die first, you'll be alright cause your family can take care of you and you got money."

"I never . . . think of . . . that . . . but, it's . . . true."

Luke knelt close to her. "Well, if you die first, I'll have to start out all over again, and I maybe might be a old man cause I hope you live a long time."

Richlene was silent, thinking.

Luke continued as he placed a hand on her arm, "I want me somethin of my own. A business, a store, grocery or somethin. If I go to work, I can get me a piece of land and build me a store."

Richlene looked at his earnest face and laughed, "I'll . . . buy you . . . a store!"

Luke hugged her shoulder. "I reckon I betta do it all myself. Cause some people think it's your money I love."

"But . . . you never . . . ask me . . . for anything for . . . yourself."

"We know that, but everybody else don't."

Satan almost smiled, but it wasn't important enough.

So Luke found little jobs on both sides of the river and began saving his money. When he had enough to purchase a couple of acres of land across from his old home near the river, he did. He did not know that Richlene had bargained with the owner and paid most of the money while Luke was given a sale price much lower than it would have been. He thought it was just good luck.

He kept working which made Richlene very unhappy because he was home with her less. He was working now for lumber and material to build his store. Richlene bargained with the lumberyard without Luke's knowledge and he got some very good deals. "Let him . . . get . . . through . . . with this . . . thing," Richlene frowned impatiently.

Then Emily began coming home for vacations when she was not doing small work in her brother Phillip's law offices as an apprentice. She would not go to visit her mother on the Indian land, she wanted her mother to come home to "our house," she said. Emily began to explain to Richlene that she would soon be graduating and be coming often to Yoville, perhaps with a husband and she could not, WOULD not introduce Luke to anyone as her stepfather.

Satan did smile this time. "A problem in the making!"

"You have done this long enough, Mother! You have had your way. Now it is time to think of me!" She raised her eyes to the ceiling as she said the next words, "I know Luke makes you happy." She looked back at her mother, saying slowly, "But it makes me unhappy. I need you at home. Alone. Carlton will soon be moving back here. He is thinking of it right now. He plans to renew this old house. Now I must be here to protect my interest, and you must be here to help me." Emily knew the words sounded cold, so she reached her warm hand out to caress her mother's back that had sadly bent lower and lower with each word.

Richlene, head bent low, spoke softly, "I won't . . . I won't . . . leave Luke."

Emily did not give up. Each time she saw Richlene she battered her with words about the love and respect she was supposed to have for her only daughter. Phillip did not interfere. He wanted his mother to be happy, but he was more used to her now and her every wish was no longer his command. He spoke to her thus, "You can go back to Luke and your house on the Indian land whenever you wish. The only change will be that this is your real home. I would like you to even visit me on my estate in the East. I would like to take you on my travels sometime. But, Mother, dammit dear! I like Luke, very much. It is not his color. It's just . . . where would he fit in? among our friends?"

"You take Lincoln . . . with . . . you in . . . your business."

"Lincoln is different. He . . . fits in. He thinks like I do, most of the time. And really, he's always rushing off to be with his own people."

Richlene looked at the son she dearly loved. "Luke thinks . . . like I . . . do. Where . . . would . . . I fit . . . in? I . . . can . . . hard . . . ly be fascin . . . ating company."

Phillip took her in his arms, "You are my mother, that is enough."

Luke's store was full of supplies, he was busy and happy. He noticed Richlene was not smiling much anymore. She looked so thoughtful with the new lines creasing her brow. He hugged her, held her more often.

Lil Wisdom noticed the difference in Richlene when she brought some homemade bread to their house. She did not ask any questions though. She liked Richlene better now, and she did not want to interfere. But she watched Richlene's face when she said, "I am going to ask Luke to let me work for him in the store on days I am not teaching the children."

Richlene looked across the table at Lil Wisdom, seeing her youth and beauty. Her eyes filled with tears that moved slowly down her face. Lil Wisdom got up quickly, moving around to Richlene, placing her arm around her shoulders. "I will not ask him if you do not wish me to. I will not say a word."

Richlene looked gratefully at Lil Wisdom. "No . . . no . . . It is best . . . that you ask him . . . and . . . help him. I know . . . you . . . love him."

"But I love you, too. You are kind."

They held on to each other as two women will who understand a little about life.

The store was going well, bringing in enough for Luke to do little things for Richlene with his own money. He was happier. Richlene was happy for him, but she was biding her time. She cried many times after Emily talked to her about leaving Luke. But she stayed on with him. Loving the little house and gardens across the river on the Indian land.

Satan waited.

One day after a long day of work, the store was closed and Luke and Lil Wisdom had locked up and were counting money in the back room. Lil Wisdom said, "Luke? Do you know I am still a virgin?"

"Girl, all these men after you? You betta get married."

"That won't help me."

"Why?"

"Because I have saved my virginity for you, all these years."

"For me? Ahhhh, Lil Wisdom . . ."

"It belongs to you. You are the one I want to have me for the first time."

"Lil Wisdom, I'm a . . . married man."

She began to undress in the dim light of the back room. "It's a spiritual thing. If you once make love to me, I will be free to leave you for another man."

"But what will you give him if you give this to me?"

"What is left. Which is all I have to give anyone else anyway."

Her clothes off, she was now naked standing beside the little cot Luke kept in his office for himself to rest on. She looked beautiful. She glowed in the soft evening light. She reached her arms out for him. "If you do this for me now, you will set me free."

"Lil Wisdom . . . I . . . I can't."

"You don't like me at all?"

"I love you, Lil Wisdom, I love you since you was a little girl helpin my family. But . . . I can't. . . ."

She lay down on the cot. It was not vulgar, it was just giving.

Luke looked at her a long time.

"I . . . could kiss you. That ought to be alright."

"Alright," Little Wisdom breathed, "come close to me."

He went closer, he bent to kiss her, placing his hands on her warm shoulders. His hands that slid down her arms, onto her waist, over her hips. He started to rise, but she held him and drew his head down to hers. They kissed. That's how it began. All of it.

Now all Luke's lovemaking with Richlene had been sweet, gentle and loving. Like a gentle rain on flowers and leaves with a bit of sunshine now and then. It had been good. But Little Wisdom's loving was different. It was a storm, a deluge with lightning and rolling thunder. Passion held back for years, unleashed, given with her whole heart.

After, Luke said, "You were not a virgin."

Little Wisdom smiled. "Did you think I was never going to do anything?! You kept my body hungry for you and you never fed it. I had to do something! Once. But, yes I was a virgin. I have never really been touched before. My body needed you. And now I am satisfied."

"I ain't gonna do this no more, Lil Wisdom. I love Richlene too."

"We don't have to do it again, Luke. I know you love me now."

They parted, each going their separate way, satisfied, complete.

That is the way they left it for a long time.

Satan wasn't sure what to do, because he is not sure about real love. If he helped Richlene to leave, Luke and Lil Wisdom would be happy; if Luke left Lil Wisdom alone, Richlene would be happy. He didn't want anyone to be happy. So he waited.

chapter 45

It had been several years since Hosanna had seen Miz Befoe.
Though she had tried, Miz Befoe had been unable to stop Hosanna's
work; but Hosanna's work was good, and people knew what she did was
hard to find in the city, much less in Yoville. However, Carlene never
used Hosanna herself. She wasn't entertaining very much, in any event,
since she was the only one in the house now except for visits from
Carlton and, infrequently, Richlene. At rare moments, a visitor arrived to
bring her special reports or papers to sign. It had even been a couple of
years since Carlene had been to any city.

Minna was her woman of all jobs except cooking. Carlene did not
like Minna's cooking, so she brought chefs in from the city. They usually
stayed a month or two, three at the most. The salary was never enough.

One morning Minna passed by Hosanna's, on her way home, mad.
"I done quit that ole bitch for the last time. She ain't gonna haul off and
slap me one more time in her white life! And if the Bible tellin the truth,
she ain't gonna have no other life!"

Hosanna smiled. "You all still don't get along?"

Minna huffed, "Who can get along with that woman? You didn't
either! Huh!" Then she huffed on away.

Hosanna thought about Carlene later in the day and decided the old lady might need some help, so she went over there. She knocked at the back door, there was no answer, so she pushed it open and went in. The house was not filthy, but it was rather messy. Hosanna called out "Miz Befoe?" several times, but there was no answer. She kept going until she reached Carlene's rooms. The door was open a crack, Hosanna knocked and pushed it open.

A raspy but strong voice asked crossly, "Who's there?"

"It's me, Hosanna." Hosanna went in, looking at the woman in the bed. Carlene seemed to have shrunk, withered. The face was thin now, but wrinkles covered it. Evil and malignance stared out of the questioning eyes. She took off a lace cap that covered her uncombed, tangled hair. "Did you come to comb my hair, Hosanna? I don't know where that girl Minna is. She is never here when I need her and she does not answer the bell!"

Hosanna smiled, "No, I didn't come to comb your hair, but I will." She looked for the comb and brush on the dresser. They were dirty and gray. "These things need cleaning, Miz Befoe." She began to undo the long braid that hung crooked down Carlene's back. "How you been doing, Miz Befoe?"

"Horrible! You can't get any decent help. Everybody is so independent now! Sally and that school! These young ones grow up and leave town! Don't stay here anymore!"

Hosanna smiled at life. "How is your family?"

"What family? Richlene with her hackled brain is over there in a teepee with Indians and a nigger! They tell me she sleeps with a nigger!"

"Well, she's with somebody. His name is Luke. He was your gardener for years. He's not a nigger, Miz Befoe. He is my brother and a fine gentleman." Her voice held no anger, she didn't really care what Mrs. Befoe thought. "Turn your head a little this way and hold it still now."

Carlene snatched her head around. "He is stealing all her money, she'll be broke someday! She is getting older. She should be here! With me! Her mother!"

Hosanna smiled. "I don't think so," she said musingly.

Carlene growled a moment, "He will throw her out for a younger woman. Soon as she is broke! He won't get his hands on my money because I am leaving her nothing! Tell him that! Richlene tries to come over here, like she thinks of me. I know her schemes. She brings me food, but I won't eat it!" Carlene added with passion, "I wouldn't give it to my dogs! Poison!"

Hosanna, still smiling, said, "I don't think so."

Carlene continued to rail, "My sister, Sally, brings me food and leaves it on the back porch. Like I am Snow White and will eat it. It's poison also!"

"I don't think so, Miz Befoe."

Carlene laughed, "I give it to the servants. Let them die, they're not worth a damn anyway!"

Hosanna said seriously, "Sally is a very good woman. You are lucky to have such a sister. Hold your head still now."

Carlene almost shouted, "Sally is a liar! And she does not like you at all! None of you! You should hear what she says about you!"

"I don't think so."

"And she slaves those grandchildren of hers. Working them in the hot sun, burning them brown! Like the rest of all those . . . She should let servants do that work!"

"I don't think so. They work early mornings or late evenings."

Carlene ignored Hosanna. "Her grandchildren hate her, I hear."

"I don't think so. I think Richlene, Luke, Sally, Ann and William are happy."

"You would, Hosanna, what do you know?"

Hosanna, thinking of Bowlegs, answered, "Not too much, Miz Befoe, not too much. Especially about love."

"Love?! Hah! There is no love. And when there is, you are defeated by fools!"

Hosanna nodded her head, "Sometimes, the fool is you."

"I was not a fool! He was not a fool."

Years ago, this conversation between the two of them would never have been, but Hosanna understood more about life, and Carlene cared less about life.

So, Hosanna answered, "No, because you married the man you loved."

Carlene twisted her head around to look at Hosanna, "I did not marry the man I loved! I married the man he wanted me to marry!"

Hosanna gently turned Carlene's head back around. "Well, I guess we can all be fools about love. But I am changing my style, my way of loving that man. I deserve more."

Carlene spoke as though secretly, "Don't give him any money. Don't ever give anyone any money! You hold them to you if they have nothing!"

"Money isn't everything, Miz Befoe."

"Well, give me yours then, because I will never be without it."

"You never have been. Your daddy was rich when you were born. You were good looking and you married a rich man. But now, he is dead. Your daddy is dead. You are old now. We are all dying, what can money do to help you now?"

"I can pay for what I want, what I need!"

Hosanna smiled gently. "I don't think so. Anyway, who wants to have to pay money for everything?"

Carlene laughed. "I have everything I want."

"I don't think so, Miz Befoe. By the way, how is your grandson, Carlton?"

Carlene's voice was angry as if she despised him. "Carlton! He only comes here to see how close I am to dying. He wants my power of attorney so he won't have to wait for me to die. He says he is coming home to do this house over and live here sometimes. He's really coming here to give him more time to work on me! Oh, how I wish I had someone else to leave my money to!"

Hosanna frowned. "Do you ever pray, Miz Befoe?"

"To God!? No. God is for the poor. When they have problems they always return to God."

"But, you never go to God at all."

"I pray to myself."

"Do your prayers get answered?"

"Of course."

"Then, you must not pray for much, Ms. Befoe."

"I have everything."

"I don't think so." Gently.

Carlene raised a finger at Hosanna. "God is just a figment of someone's imagination."

"A figment does not last thousands of years, all over the world."

"People are stupid and it's a strong figment."

"Lies are never strong, Miz Befoe."

"Oh, certainly they are. They rule the world."

"I don't think so, but on the other hand, is that why the world is in such bad shape? Turn your head a little this way now."

Carlene mumbled a curse. "Even the poor people who say they believe in God don't really believe in Him. They only use Him when they need something, then they forget Him."

"They don't last, just like lies don't last," said Hosanna. "I don't think anything wrong or evil lasts. The Bible says the soul that sins will surely die. And I'll be damned if we haven't been dying ever since we got here. All the great scientists in the world haven't changed that."

"But the world has lasted this long."

"Miz Befoe, the world is changing."

"Hosanna, it always changes. Back and forth, back and forth."

"That's because mankind does not change. They said it would be a better world after the last two wars. But what's better? What's different? And they're always fighting wars in Europe, it seems. It don't seem to get any better over there either. Now, in America, we leave and go fight a war someplace else! Nobody is attacking us even. But our boys still die. Lincoln lost a leg, and I don't blive he can tell himself why! The only thing different is, more taxes. And the tax money must go to people who make bullets and guns cause what else do you use in a war? And what is being given to these poor people out here losing their farms and lives, even starving to death? Or to the people dying in the wars? The women and children who die or are left alone?"

"Oh, you don't know what you are talking about." But Carlene's voice was not so strong, because she knew what Hosanna was talking about. She had made a great deal of money, millions, from her armaments investments and was still making plenty of money from them.

But Hosanna persisted, "Only more people hate more people and don't even know why. Even people in this grand United States—and I love this country America—are running around lynching, hanging, killing people, sometimes for nothing but what race they are!"

"Oh, we've always had that!"

"That does not make it right. You sound like killing is normal! That's what I'm talking about. You can't change mankind! And the world cannot rise above hate if so many people are hating! You cannot hold on to what's good, when most people are vicious and stupid about fairness and love and . . ."

Carlene interrupted her, "Your Christianity has failed the world."

"Oh, Miz Befoe, don't blame it on Christianity. The people have never tried it! Who has been a Christian except Christ and a very few others—who were killed, I might add, for loving their brothers! The world has failed Christianity, far as I am concerned! And if people are not a Christian, whatever they may be, they have failed goodness and love."

Carlene searched for words, "Well . . ."

Hosanna was on a roll, she never talked much about religion, but she had opinions "Just like the Jews. Some people hate Jews because they say they killed Christ! Well, Jesus Christ was a Jew! How can you hate his people? God chose the Jews and, besides, that was two thousand years ago Jesus was killed. What these Jews today got to do with that? And I know cause I lived in Washington, D.C. Some people who hate Jews don't like God or Jesus anyway! They don't really care who killed him. They just want to kill somebody for themselves. And the devil gives them a reason they can understand, cause they love killing. When that reason runs out then they pick on the Negro people, Chinese, the Mexican, the Russians, I read the papers. The Irish, whoever. I know, cause I worked for em. I saw things. I heard the radio. We are paying taxes right now for a war already fought and the dead are gone. And ain't nothing changed for the better! It's a depression right now, all over the world, cause we paying for a war. Love does not cost anything. Use love and these wars would stop."

Carlene interrupted her again, turning to look at her, "That's a mighty long speech for a little Negra girl to say."

Hosanna smiled and frowned at the same time. "I don't think so. And I'm a woman, not a girl. And I have a brain. I am now, also, finished with your hair. It is free. No charge. You are welcome."

Carlene said, "The war was just to preserve the constitution."

Hosanna laughed. "The constitution is a beautiful thing the way it reads, but it ain't shit if you don't get to live it. I studied, Miz Befoe. It does not take a genius to know it was written for everyone in the United States, but white folks still try to think they have to decide who it's for. They don't even want some of their own kind to be free. They send them out to die, too! But, I'm not just talking about the United States, I'm talking about all over the world. Governments! Not one of them is any good for poor people and there's more poor people, of all colors, than any other kind in the world!"

"Hosanna, you should be careful of that kind of talk."

"I am careful. God, the Bible, says choose things by which you are willing to live or by which you are willing to die. If I am right, I am willing to live or die by it. You know what, Miz Befoe? I can see more and believe more in God every day. He is there!"

Carlene laughed a rusty, old laugh. "I think you have lost your mind."

Hosanna smiled as she started out the door. "I don't think so." She turned back, "Listen, it's stuffy in here, not fresh at all. Let's open that window." After the window was opened, Hosanna went to the door and turned again to say, "I am going to see that you get a good dinner this evening and try to get Minna to come on back here to work."

Carlene spoke in a sly voice, "What are you doing? Being so nice to me. You are trying to work your way into my will?!"

Over her shoulder, as she was leaving, Hosanna laughed and said, "I don't think so."

The black widow spider, old now, felt the breeze from the opened window. She hastily uncurled her legs from around her body and prepared to leave through the window. She was almost dying of hunger. She crawled over the white walls without caring, but Carlene did not see her, she was looking in her mirror. The spider made it to the rain gutter and scurried down, a little slower now from hunger and age. To find a lover and a meal. One in the same.

One day Bowlegs went home to his room, expecting it to be clean and to find clean clothes set neatly in his drawers. He was startled to find the room and drawers exactly as he had left them. Messed up. He opened the drawers, twice, to be sure. There were no clean clothes there other than the few already left there by him. He twisted his lips to the side and stood thinking, then he smiled, "What she tryin to do? Somethin must'a held her up. She be here tonight, I know!" He looked at the inexpensive, but good, watch she had given him so he could learn to be on time. Time payments. "I betta hurry and get to Choke's. I need to work tonight!" He searched and found a not too soiled shirt and a suit, hurriedly pressing it on his bed. "Damn that woman! She knows I got to have things to go to work in! I would'a had somebody get some things ready for me. When she come down here tonight, I'll have somethin to tell her! Women don't do me this way!"

He stayed up all night drinking and talking with the fellows, hoping Hosanna would come by Choke's so she could see what he was really doing—nothing. She didn't come, so he left for home about six in the morning. He had said to himself, "Well, she didn't come down to Choke's this weekend, so I know that room is clean now and I got clothes this morning!" The room was exactly as he had left it. The drawers were still empty of clean clothes. So, he hung up his own wilted, smoky suit.

As he crawled into the musty sheets to get some sleep, his last thought was, "She be here by time I get to sleep, waking me up! And that damn woman know I need my sleep!" But he woke alone. She hadn't come. She didn't wake him up. Now he was angry.

"I'll fix her. I ain't goin over there either! I'll get Juney Bug to do my clothes. Wait till she see that! That'll teach her!" He did what he planned, but Hosanna didn't come the next few days either.

He finally dressed in his best, clean clothes (that Juney Bug had cleaned for him). "You got to look good when you go see a woman you fussin with!" he told himself. "So they can see what they gonna be losin if they don't be careful and ack right!" When he looked as clean, slick and fine as he thought he should and as he knew Hosanna liked, he started down the road to her house.

Now Hosanna had been fighting herself, and winning, about not going to Bowlegs' place. Not because she loved him so much anymore, but because loneliness can be a terrible thing. Her heart felt way down low, but she was holding her head up. She had made up her mind and talked to God about it, asking for His help. "I deserve more."

She was in her yard doing lingerie when she saw him stepping highly and lightly down the dusty road to her house. A handkerchief in his hand, nails cleaned, filed and polished, he dusted dust off his shoes, folded his handkerchief and wiped a light perspiration off his brow. He looked around for the kids, didn't see them, but kept his voice low. "Why you ain't been by the house, girl? Where you been?"

Hosanna took a long look at him, then went on about her work, "I've been here. Doing my work."

He looked around for a seat, Hosanna usually ran to get him one. She just kept working this time. "Ahhh, girl, Hosanna, where you been? I ain't seen you."

"Did you want to?"

He smiled, "I always want to, baby."

"Well, I've been here."

Bowlegs wanted to make her do something for him, the man. "Say, get me a glass of water. I'm thirsty. It's hot standin out here in the sun."

"That's right, you're used to the dark. Bow," she pointed at a pitcher of water, "reach that dipper over there. I just got that for myself. It's nice and cool."

"Hand it to me. What's wrong with you?"

Hosanna kept her voice neutral and low, "I'm working. Do I ask you to come down off your stage and get me a drink?"

"Cause you know I can't do that!"

"Well, give me some consideration. I shouldn't have to stop work either."

Bow took his handkerchief out again, dusted his jacket sleeve. "I am your man. A woman gets her man what he needs."

Hosanna stopped squeezing the lingerie and looked up at him quizzically. "Were you thirsty yesterday? Or the day before?"

"What that sposed to mean?"

Hosanna went back to her work. "It means whoever, wherever you got your water from, you got it. You didn't need me to get it for you. You know how to take care of yourself."

"Oh, you want to talk that ole shit! You mad cause I wasn't home!"

Hosanna laughed. "Weren't home? When?"

"When you came by."

"I haven't been by." She stepped aside to hang up a gown.

Bowlegs raised his voice a little. "You haven't been to my house since I saw you a week ago?"

Hosanna looked puzzled. "Has it been a week since I saw you? No, no I haven't been by. I've been busy."

Bowlegs stepped into her view, touched her shoulder, raising her up as she bent over a tub. "Doing what?"

"Working, Bowlegs. Using my time for me."

"What's that sposed to mean, Hosanna?"

Hosanna stopped working, straightened her back. "Bow, it means I am tired of you. I deserve better than you. You have to respect the person you are with. They have to respect you. I don't respect you anymore. I haven't for a long time, just didn't realize it. I'm not trying to be smart, but I think you are a fool . . . or I am a fool."

Bowlegs turned his body in a circle so she could see all of him and like it. "Ohhhh, Lord. I don't want to hear that shit!"

Hosanna was looking at a garment. "You don't have to. You asked me. You are at my house."

Bowlegs changed his tactic as though what she was saying was unimportant. "Go get dressed, let's go for a walk down by the river. It's too hot out here."

Hosanna was hanging up another garment. "I already had my walk. I went alone. I'm working now."

Bowlegs couldn't believe it. "You don't want to walk with me?!"

"I already walked."

"I want you to walk with me."

Hosanna laughed softly. "Then you should have been here when I walked without you. I'm used to walking without you again. Now, I like it."

"What you mean, what you said 'a fool'?"

"Bow, darlin, nobody should have to beg anyone else to be happy for their own self. I worried about your food, your clothes, your sleep, your rest, your progress, your life! You don't! You don't worry about yourself and your progress and you don't worry about me or mine. So . . ." She stopped to inspect something on a garment. "So why should I take my life and worry about your life when you don't? Now, I'm taking my time back. I want to be happy. So I'm going to concentrate on making me happy! Not you!" She smiled at him. "But I wish you well. I sure do."

"You always actin!"

"You think what you want to."

"You can't quit me, woman!"

"Why? Never had you. In all those two years and more, I've never had you. You are playing hide and seek with life, Bow. Well, life ain't no game." She was getting angry in spite of herself. "One of these days life is going to hide and you will be the one seeking and won't find it."

"I'm a young man!"

"You are a day older today."

"Girl, you know I love you."

Hosanna stopped her work and looked at him again, her anger under control because he really was a pitiful fool. "Bow, I'm a woman. You're a boy, that's why you only want to be a 'boyfriend.' What a grown woman needs is a grown man. I love you, in your way." He smiled. "But," she continued, "I don't want you anymore. You are not my type any more. Not what I'm looking for. I deserve better."

He had been leaning on the porch and he straightened up. "Better!? You can't get you no better!"

Hosanna laughed. "Oh, Bow. Is your world really that small? Mine isn't. I've been reading my Bible, I read something I like, 'Choose the thing by which you will live, or choose the thing by which you will die.' I choose to live. Life with you ain't living. Life with you is a misery. You lie. Oh, all that's not important. It's over. I don't want no more."

Bowlegs could not believe what was happening to him, he looked around to see if there was anyone who could possibly hear Hosanna. He said to her, as he looked, "You betta be careful what you say, cause I might not come back again. I ain't got to beg no woman!"

Hosanna shook her head. "Don't come back again. It won't do any good, anyway. My mistake with you was, I wasn't sure how much I believed in God, but I'm sure now. If I had done you His way, the way he suggested a man and a woman be together? Saved myself for my husband? A man who would love me enough to make me his wife? I would never have gone through the pain and misery I have gone through with you. Next time . . . I'm doing it His way. So . . . Bowlegs . . . don't come back. Cause ain't nothing here for you."

Bowlegs knew Hosanna was a good woman, he did not want to lose her. He forgot to wipe the perspiration dripping now from his face. "Okay, Hosanna, I'll marry you, if that's what you want so bad."

Hosanna looked at him with wonder. "Oh, Bow, honey, I don't want just a man. Any man. I want a good husband who loves me and I love him."

"I love you."

"You may love me, Bow, but, you love you so much more. Now you go on and love yourself. I'm not asking for your love anymore. I love me now." She was finished with the load of garments. She walked to the porch, climbing the steps. Bowlegs stood watching her, disbelieving what was happening. Hosanna raised a hand to wave good-bye. "See you later, Bow." She went in and closed the door behind her. Her heart was hurting, hurting. Beating fast. But she knew she was right! She told herself, "I may hurt my own heart, but he won't hurt it no more!"

Hosanna sat on her bed and, out of nowhere, she began to cry softly. "What is it I need? What is it everybody needs? To be loved and made love to. God, I'm not wrong. I need to be loved. You made it, it can't be wrong. I just have to be sure it's the right love. One that will truly satisfy. All my needs. And I'm sick and tired of waiting for it! I'm gettin old!"

Life was quiet after that day with Bowlegs. Hosanna took walks, cooked special things for herself, read, did a lot of thinking and was getting to be all right. Life was beginning to feel good again. She sat on the porch of her house one day eating a pomegranate, looking at the garden, thinking of her work, her savings and just feeling complete and good. She looked up and saw Lettie walking slowly down the dirt road to the house. She watched her approach. Smiling.

Lettie finally got there and slowly set her three children down by Hosanna, on each side. Hosanna spoke to the children, "Hey, Aunt Hosanna's babies! Want some? Here." Then she looked at Lettie. "You got to go somewhere, Lettie?"

Lettie didn't smile, just said, "It's your turn."

"My turn what? Want one?" She held a pomegranate out.

"Your turn to take care of things. Raise somebody."

"What you talking about, Lettie?"

"I'm leaving. I'm leaving. I can't stay here. Ain't nothin here for me. I can't find no satisfaction here. I took care of everything when you left. Now I'm leaving these babies for you to take care of. Cause I'm goin."

Hosanna set the fruit aside. "I didn't leave. I was taken. Sent."

"You wasn't here."

"Lettie, can you go off and leave your children after what you went through when Mama and Daddy died?"

"They left me."

"Lettie, they died."

"I ain't gonna stay here till it kills me, too. You take em, I got to go."

"How do you know I will take them, Lettie?"

"Take em or I'll leave em in the road."

"You got a home."

"I ain't made no payments."

"Why, Lettie?"

"Got no money."

"You drank and partied it up."

"That's my bizness, my way. Nothin else satisfies me."

"That satisfied you?"

"No, but I could forget I wasn't satisfied."

"Oh, Lettie, Lettie."

Lettie turned to go back up the road. Hosanna called after her. "You're not gonna kiss your children good-bye?" The children started to cry. The little boy tried to get down off the porch to follow his mother. Lettie hesitated. Hosanna reached out her hand to her. "Come on in the house. Let me give them something to take their mind off you a minute. Don't leave them no memory of you leaving them like this."

Lettie sounded tired. "I went through it. Didn't nobody wait and leave me right. Didn't nobody help me." She walked away.

Hosanna hugged the children. The little boy was crying so hard for his mother. The older girl didn't cry, she just looked down the road at the speck her mother had become. Tears were in her head, but she didn't let them come out of her eyes. She was hurt and felt very, very alone. Hosanna called to her, "Come on in the house now, baby. Aunt Hosanna got some milk and cake. You hungry?" The middle girl shook her head no, then yes. The oldest girl wiped her damp eyes with the back of her hand, took a deep breath, then went in the house, saying to Hosanna, "I'll feed him. He won't eat less I feed him." And that's how that part of Hosanna's new life began.

Luke and Richlene were still together though Emily took Richlene off with her to her apartment in the city. She thought the distance would help her mother prepare for a separation from Luke when it finally happened. Emily smiled to herself, "And it will come."

Luke kept his word. He did not let Little Wisdom be alone with him when the store closed. It was hard because his memory was good and thinking of her did things to his body he hadn't known it would do. He was always standing behind some waist-high boxes or something to keep her from seeing any evidence of his private thoughts. He knew Richlene was growing away from him, "but she been faithful," he said to himself, "so that's what I'm gonna be if it kills me." He shook his head. "Which is what it seems like it is gonna do!" Little Wisdom watched, worked hard every day and went on home to wait.

chapter
4 6

Hosanna took life one day at a time. She loved and cared for Lettie's children, worked and saved. But she was young, a healthy woman, and nights got long and lonely, even as full as her life was.

Satan had heard her declaration to live according to God's way and had sent in many snares. Men. Thoughts of making love. He even sent Bow back a few times. After long months when her body's passion had gathered strength and enveloped her mind, she had stumbled once. She made an attempt to get to know a gentleman who came to court her favor. It had failed because in her judgement he was not made up of things she thought were necessary in a marriage, would not be a lasting satisfaction for her. He was a good man, he was just not for her. She pulled her dress back down and pinned it, this time, to her heart.

But her life was full. Hosanna had plenty to do. Lovey had written that Lincoln was going to handle Phillip's tax department and that they would be moving back to Yoville except for three months out of the year when Lincoln must inventory all the accounts of Phillip's empire, with his own staff, of course. Lincoln would be on call, but he could do the thing he most wanted to do: work the land.

They had purchased one of the houses in Yoville which had gone into foreclosure after the market crash. It was a very rich house, large and beautiful. "Cause we are going to have lots of children!" Lovey explained in her letter. Lovey was happy, but "I want to live in my own home since I'm bout to become a mother! Lincoln is thrilled to be a father!" Lovey's letters came typed now. She wrote, "I learned to type so I could help Lincoln sometimes and we could be alone without his secretary all the time. When I get home, I am going to buy fifty typewriters for Sally's school so those students can learn to type. Jobs, honey, jobs. And Lincoln says we have to think of taking some of this money he is making and set up scholarships for some of the smart, poor children there." At the end of the letter, Lovey had written, "Chile, we miss our colored folks. These white folks, some of em is nice, but some of them? Chile they confused as they say we are. We want to be home with our own families."

Hosanna was happy for her and happy they were coming home. Luke was doing fine in his store. He and Richlene were happy, but somehow changed. She didn't have time to think of all that right now. With her nieces and nephew living with her, all her time was consumed. But how, and where, was Lettie? She never wrote home. That worried Hosanna.

Sometimes Hosanna saw Homer in the distance, he always seemed to be running, busy. She remembered him with pleasure. "He was such a kind man." Sometimes she wondered if she had been wrong in how she had thought of him . . . then.

Time passes anyway and things mellow out. But loneliness does not go away unless it has a good reason, so she was still very lonely. Many nights, tossing and turning in her bed, sleepless. Thinking of "Who?" Wondering, "Who?" If ever he came, "Who will he be? What will he be?" to make her life complete.

One day Hosanna went to gather kindling to fill her kindling box and found it full. The next morning when she went out to prepare water for the wash, the leg on her tool table that had been weak and broken was fixed good as new. She had planned to get Luke to fix it for her. Flowers began to appear on the porch outside her door in the mornings when she came out. In time, a pair of pretty earrings or some small precious thing would be in among her tools, easily found.

Her heart became gladdened. She began to look for these things, these surprises. She almost thought it was Homer, but since she never saw him close enough and they never had occasion to speak, she thought it might not be. But so many things were done to make her job easier. No one ever said anything to her about these things.

Somehow, even alone, the nights became more romantic. Dreams do that. And loneliness. She would think, "Someone . . . he, is out there doing things for me. Why won't he say something?" She longed to see him. Her dreams had gone so far as to long to feel his arms around her. She had made his arms good, kind, safe and full of satisfaction. "Why is he taking all this time to show himself?"

Hosanna took to putting the children to bed early to leave the night free. She would sit in the dark and peep out through the clean, starched curtains. Trying to see, wanting to know. Him.

On the morning Hosanna found a little brown radio at her door, she was thrilled and excited. And a little frustrated and angry, impatient. She stared into the space of trees, garden, thickets around her house. "He is spending big money, now. He has to really care about me. What's wrong with him!"

She hollered, not harshly, out into the quiet morning space, "You better come on now, so you can listen to this radio with me." There was no answer. All was quiet except for the soft whispering of the leaves and branches of the trees in the morning breeze. Hosanna went back in the house, plugged the radio in her new electric wall plugs and turned it on. The children got up, sleepy-eyed, to listen to the marvel of radio.

That very night when Hosanna answered the gentle knock at the door, she opened it and there was Homer, his hat in one hand, some flowers in the other. Surprising to Hosanna, her heart patted out of rhythm. She was happy to see him. All her memories of him were good ones.

Homer smiled, held out the flowers and said, "Ahh, would you like to go for a walk, Miz Hosanna?"

Hosanna stepped back from the door and with a sweep of her arm, waved him in. "Good evening, Homer. I'd love to, but I have the children here."

"Well," he smiled, "Most children like to walk. Let's all walk over by the river. If you like. It'll make em sleep better."

Hosanna was pleased, no one had ever included the children before. "Why, I sure would like to take that walk then, Mr. Homer."

They walked and they talked. Homer brought her up to date on all he had done and was doing. His mother had passed and he lived alone now. One of the things he was doing was working Creed's land. "Lincoln wants to settle in Yoville, farming. He done bought the best and latest tools and taught me how to use them when he come down here to see his dad. I'm running the farm and I'm learning. I included a whole field of flowers. That's why you get such pretty, fresh flowers! I grow em!"

Hosanna listened, her mind glowing and proud. She thought, "He is doing something! And something beautiful, too!" She said, "That's wonderful, Homer. Lovey told me they're going to have a baby. Isn't that wonderful?"

He turned to her as they walked, "Be wonderful for you, too. When you gonna think of getting married?"

Hosanna laughed. "That's all I do think of. I'm tired of being alone and lonely. But I don't want to get married just to get a man and a baby. I want it to be real . . . I want it to be love."

Homer didn't laugh, "That's why I'm still single. That's what I want. I always have loved on you, Hosanna."

Hosanna's brain smiled, her face smiled, her heart giggled happily. She thought, "Now, I been knowing Homer, why am I acting like this? Because I am lonely?" She didn't say anything, just listened to him, thought and walked.

Hosanna and Homer kept company for over two months and Homer didn't try to put a hand on her. Hosanna wouldn't have let him make love to her, but she wanted to know he wanted to. "Lord, maybe he don't know nothing bout no lovemaking! I don't want to be stuck all my life with no satisfaction at all!"

A few more weeks passed, They had kissed several times. Hosanna didn't like him less, she liked him more . . . and more. One night they spoke of marriage and Hosanna said, "I don't know, Homer, I want to be as sure as possible."

Homer only smiled, "Everybody does." He looked around the room, "It's so quiet in this house. Are the kids sleep?"

"Yes. They fell out early. Played hard all day."

Homer took her hand and held it warmly. "Well, let's take a little walk down by the river and talk a little bit. They'll be safe. All the fires out?"

"Been out."

He stood up. "Want to go?"

"Why not?"

So they walked, these two people with the sad, lonely, yearning hearts. Their lives moving along. Both good people with soft love in their souls. Easily hurt, open to love, alone and lonely.

This time as they walked, Homer took her hand and led her deep into the jungly trees to a clearing. He took his jacket off and put it on the ground for her to sit on. He seemed to try to stretch it out as far as it would go. Hosanna laughed, "I'm not gonna lie down, Homer, we're just going to sit, so that's fine."

He helped her sit down. "You don't never know. Moon coming through the trees like it is. Water sounding so cool, fresh and wet. Night birds singing to you. You don't never know. You could get sleepy and want to lie back a bit."

Hosanna laughed. "You sure can talk, Homer."

"Well, that's what I mostly do with you, Hosanna."

"What do you mean, Homer?"

Homer laughed. "Well, that's what we do! Talk!"

"Well, we talk about important things."

Homer's laugh dwindled away. "We need to DO some important things."

"Get married, you mean?"

"Get married is one of em."

Hosanna lay back on her elbows, relaxed. "What's the other?"

Homer reached for Hosanna, pulling her body close to him. He tilted her head back with his chin and kissed her. One of those long, deep, moist, warm, soft kisses. Moving, chile! He felt her relax and yearn toward him. He pressed her gently to the ground.

Hosanna spoke, her lips against his lips, "What you doing, Homer?"

Homer answered, his lips still pressed to her lips, "I want you to be comfortable."

Hosanna smiled in their kiss, "I was." But she lay back in his arms, lips still pressed close. They lay like that awhile, then he began rubbing her arm from her shoulder down to her fingertips, slowly, slowly, gently.

He smoothed her forehead and cheeks, tenderly. He kissed her again and his hand slid down, slowly, gently to her stomach, never touching her breast, never making an intrusive move.

Hosanna closed her eyes and relaxed, thinking, "Lord . . . if I'm going to marry this man and live right, I neeeeed to find out if it's gonna be alright because we are going to have to sleep together every night for the rest of our lives. I haven't done this everytime I met somebody I thought I might marry, you know that. But, I really feel I love this man. He is a good man. I think this might be it. I neeeed to know if I will have something that will complete my life or something that will worry me to death. I rather stay single and try to be good." So Hosanna pretended they were already married and watched in her mind all that he did and all that he felt like, to her, doing it. When her body was hot and moist, her loins aching for him to enter her, she became afraid and, her lips against his lips, said, "Let's stop and talk a minute."

Homer answered, never moving his lips away, but she could understand him, "I am talking to you, Hosanna baby. Can't you hear me?"

In a weak voice, Hosanna answered, "I hear you, Homer."

"Do I hear you calling me, Hosanna, talking to me?" His hand slipped under the band of her panties. Her body was wet, wet, wet and hot to his touch. "I blive I hear you calling me, Hosanna."

Well, they made love. Good love. Their love. They had waited. Now . . . they stopped speaking words with their lips. But the trees, the leaves and thickets, wild flowers and the river raised their voices in the night and sang and sang and sang to Homer and Hosanna, to the height of satisfaction.

They were married by the end of the week. Homer moved into the house with Hosanna because her work and the children were there. Homer rented his house out. Hosanna exclaimed, "Oh, Homer! I got a business, you got good work, and now, already, I got a rent house!"

Homer laughed a little. "Hosanna, I blive you're sposed to say, *we* got a rent house. Not *you* got a rent house."

Hosanna smiled at him and pulled on his arm. "What's mine is yours."

"That's why I like you so much, Hosanna." He laughed more.

"You love me."

"That, too."

"Me, too."

. . .

months later, Hosanna went out to the old chicken house where she hid her money to get some to help Homer with materials for an addition they planned to build on their house—a new baby was coming. She dug in the ground for the hidden money, but her shovel hit a different box, a different sound. She dug the small box out and opened it. It contained a ring, a large diamond ring, sparkling as though it had just been polished and set there. It also contained a note from Joel to Ruth, Hosanna's parents. It read, "Keep this for ever when I make love to you, cause I loves you. Joel."

She ran to Homer who was sitting at their table eating lunch. He looked at the ring, turning it over in his hand. "Sure is a pretty stone."

"It's a diamond, Homer! It belonged to my mother! See the note from my father?"

"Emmmm, hmmmm," Homer nodded his head. "I see what he says. You think it's somethin special to this ring?"

"They made all their babies!"

"Put it on. Let's try it out."

So they did. Later Homer said, "That there ring sure is a good ring!"

Hosanna spread her arms out in the bed. "Sure is, Homer."

Thereafter she always wore it to bed with Homer.

And they prayed together, thanking God for their blessings.

And they didn't have a bit of trouble with their life that they couldn't handle.

chapter 47

Then Lettie came home, smiling. She had been gone two years. She was not with a man, but she was happy with herself.

"I been to beauty school in that city where I was. I am a beauty operator. See, here is my license, girl! I'm sure glad I went to that school Sally has, cause I had to know how to read and study. Now, I'm gonna have my own business, like you!" Hosanna was happy for her, too. They talked and talked.

"I kept your house up for you, well, for the kids, I guess. I didn't know if you were ever coming back."

"I couldn't write. I couldn't say nothin to nobody. I was scared if I didn't keep doing what I was doin, I would stop and come back and be nothin. I knew you would love my kids. Where are they? I been waiting for them to run out of somewhere."

"They are at school. They'll be home soon, or you can go get them."

"Hosanna, can I have my babies back?"

"Lettie, they don't belong to me. They belong to you."

"But . . . you been keeping them. You been their mother."

"I have been their aunt. I have been your sister."

"Thank you."

"Ask them what they want. It's their life, too. Watch how quick they come to you!" They laughed together. Later, Lettie asked her children and they wanted to go home with her right then. Lettie was happy. She said to Hosanna, "I seen some things where I been. People travelin and doin all kinds of good things. I want my children to have a education, go to college. I want their life to be better. I'm gonna work hard and see that they do if I can."

Lettie went to see Sally to tell her about her beauty school license. Sally told her, "If I help you get your teaching credentials, you can come here and teach these girls cosmetology also. If they don't want to work at it, you can teach them how to care for themselves. I have all kinds of students now, and four teachers. White, Negro, and Indian. Lil Wisdom is talking about trying to go back to school and college. If she does, and finishes, she will be teaching. Ann is almost ready for college, if I can make her go. She hates to leave here, and she wants to teach over on the Indian land. But I want her to have a better education and to be independent. You never know what will happen in life."

"So everything is alright."

Sally smiled, "Just I'm getting old is all that's wrong, but . . . At last, everything is alright. I'm satisfied."

c h a p t e r
4 8

The old black widow spider was now fourteen or fifteen years old. She had returned from her last foray, full again, impregnated again. She burrowed down deep into her homeplant for the place to make a cocoon for the babies. But this time when the babies were born, because she didn't need as much food as when she was younger, she ate them more slowly and they had time to grow large before they could all be eaten. Finally one, a female, was left. She grew hungry as her mother slept. The daughter didn't remember their relationship. She only knew, here was food. She ate the old spider, leaving only a husk. Then she curled up to rest and digest.

Old Mrs. Carlene Befoe died not too long after the spider. She was alone in the house at the time. An old tray of food sat uneaten by the bed. She had lain there staring at the ceiling trying to think of someone she could call. She knew she was dying.

She started to cry soundlessly. Tears rolled down the expensive wrinkles on to the expensive satin and lace pillowcase. "No one knows I am dying." She thought, "No one knows I am here alone, dying." Her heart was beating irregularly, weakly. She cried a while longer until she became angry because no one was there. "I have money," she thought. She struggled to get up to get her checkbooks; slowly she reached her desk, got them and dragged herself back to her bed. "I am so tired, so tired." Her breath was ragged as she struggled to hold the checkbooks and get into her bed. "I have money." She didn't quite make it under the covers but lay on top of the slightly soiled, mussed linen. She thought it was only a moment since she had said those words, but it was an hour or so later when she became conscious again. "I pay Minna my good money and she is not here." She slipped into unconsciousness again. When she came out of it, she felt cold and numb. She tried to lift her arm to set the checkbooks down so she could get up. She could not move her arm. She felt herself slipping into unconsciousness again; the numbness had moved from her feet up to her breast. Darkness swept over her body, she slept. When she came out of it for the last time an hour or so later, she said only two words before she died, still clutching the checkbooks she could not let go of if she had wanted to. "Richard. . . . Richard. . . . God?" Then, her old heart stopped and she was gone. Minna found her two days later. Minna had been mad at Carlene for something she could not remember and had only just returned.

Minna cried and cried all over the little town. People wondered at all her tears. Finally Hosanna asked her, "Do you really miss Carlene Befoe so much?"

"No," Minna wailed, "I couldn't stand that ole woman! I'm crying cause I got to look for another job and there ain't nothin in this ole town to find," and off she went into tears again.

There was a short funeral service for Carlene Befoe. Carlton couldn't make it because of business commitments, he said. Richlene, Emily and Sally attended, riding in the funeral car together on the dismal, rainy day. A few people who did not come sent flowers in their place.

After Mrs. Befoe's funeral, Emily came back to the old house, looking it over to decide where her apartments would be when Carlton moved back. His return was imminent now. It was clear that they did not like each other, and she wanted to watch him when she could. She wanted Richlene to return again to Philadelphia with her.

"To stay with me for awhile," she told Luke. "But you might as well go on and make another life for yourself, Luke, because I don't think she will be coming back to this house with you and the Indians."

Luke nodded his head because this was Richlene's daughter and he thought she could keep Richlene if she really wanted to. Emily continued in a snide voice, "You seem to have done alright by yourself since . . . you and mother have been friends, so I'm sure you won't miss her."

"Miz Emily? Everything I have I have worked and paid for with my own money. I didn't take anything from Richlene. And I will miss her."

"I'm sure," came the terse reply.

After that, it was just natural for Lil Wisdom to become closer to Luke. They did not want to live in Richlene's house. They kept it clean and gardened, ready for her whenever she wanted to visit. Luke built another house near his store. Then . . . Luke and Lil Wisdom got married. They named their first child Lulene after Luke and Richlene.

chapter
4 9

One pleasant day, Hosanna was doing odd jobs around her house, singing and polishing, picking up and putting down things, just enjoying her home. She had been thinking about Homer and how happy they were now. She went and found her diamond ring and put it on. It was one of the signs that she wanted to make love, be in Homer's arms. He was working outside on the house. She was admiring the ring again when she heard a knock on her door. She answered with a smile, thinking it was Homer, playing games. It was Yinyang.

Yin had just returned from another of her trips and came to Hosanna's house to bring her a gift. She had been away two months this time. She was older, maturing, but she looked very good and still beautiful. Her clothes were of the best, as usual, and Yin knew how to use them to her best advantage. Her hair was done up expertly by herself. Her teeth were in excellent condition. Her nails and skin glowed. All that money could buy, she had.

She looked at all the improvements being made at Hosanna's house, the room being built. "What's all this, Hosanna? You married into money?"

"We are expecting a baby, Yin." Hosanna glowed with happiness.

"Well, I don't envy you what you will have to go through." Yin smiled.

"Nothing comes that's good without some pain." Hosanna smiled back. "Sit down, Yin, I'll get you some iced tea." She started from the room, looked back over her shoulder, "We got us a ice refrigerator!"

While she was gone, Yin looked around the little house at the pretty things that showed Hosanna and Homer were expecting a new baby, at the evidence of their love for each other. When Hosanna came back into the room with tea for both of them, Yin looked closely at her.

"Hosanna?"

"Yes, Yin."

"Hosanna, you've been here almost as long as I have. You washed clothes and cooked for a living. You've never seemed to have anything special, yet here you are, living a special life. You are . . . happy. You seem . . . satisfied."

"I am."

"And Sally. Sally was cheated out of her money for all those years. Yet, when I see her now, she is happy. She has her grandchildren, Russell. She's got all that money, yet she stayed here. Even opened a school for the poor, with her money! She could have gone anywhere! She is not making a dime from that school. Yet . . . she seems happy. Satisfied."

"I think she is."

"And look at Lovey. She has a rich husband practically. Her, a woman with no legs, no real education. Has a husband and . . . a future."

"Oh, she is happy. And so is he."

"Creed is trying to take Aunt Ellen away from me and marry her. Aunt Ellen is happy. And she is going to go someday. Now . . . she is old. She is not good-looking; of course, neither is Creed, but . . . they have something. They seem happy, at least satisfied."

"I think they are."

"Well . . . what happened to me? I had so much more than you all, I have so much more than you all. I am attractive. I'm not too old. Early forties. I am educated enough. But, I am not happy. I have almost never been happy since I first left my home years ago, and I can't even say I was happy then. I wanted my mother . . . and she was an alcoholic . . . she didn't really see me."

"Oh, Yinyang. Sure she did."

"What I am saying, asking, is what is wrong with me? Why am I left out of all the good things?"

"You wanted something else, maybe."

"I just wanted to be happy, satisfied. Like all of you."

"Well, Yin, I guess there is more to happiness than just wanting it. I know you worked hard at what you were doing to get some money. But I never saw you work hard at anything else. Not even your children, dear."

"I take good care of my children."

"Aunt Ellen takes good care of your children."

"Well . . . it's still me, I pay her."

"There is more to a mother than that. Your mother saw that you were taken care of, yet you missed out on her."

"Hosanna, I wanted money. But you need money. A person has to have money!"

"Yin . . . I'll tell you something. I turned my heart to God. No . . . No, I'm not going to preach to you, but I will tell you what I learned about life." Yin inclined her head to listen.

"I was alone early in life, just like you were, only earlier. I find you have to do a lot more thinking than you do living when you are trying to learn about life. I've thought long and hard in my life on the things I should love and the things I should leave alone. Real things, real people. I had to know what would make ME happy. Now . . . I have never been rich, but I have been loved, am loved. I couldn't have bought it. I have never been beautiful or handsome even, but I have been desired and am desired now. And isn't that what it's all about? I've never had any great power in this world, but I've got respect, from my family, my friends, my husband. And love, I've got love. I have never been famous, but I've got friends I can count on. What is fame after everybody knows a name? I've never even known any famous people, but I haven't missed them. I have never been a playaround girl with loves all around, but I have a good husband and I've had some good times. Never been no sex siren, but I have been loved . . . good . . . warm and real love . . . gentle, chile, sweet. And, you know, I've been on a yacht, seen the men change rooms, heard the rich, lonely ladies crying at night, alone. I've been alone, real alone, but I have never been that lonely. I never slept in any castle, but I got a good bed, and I get a good, warm, full night's sleep. I have slept in some mansions. They were full of gloom and confusion . . . and money. Never been no queen or king of a country, but I got God and He is all I need and kneel to. Never owned no grand business, but I own myself. Never was cultured, but I can read and I learned from life how best for me to live it. I can go on and on, Yin. I never been a bird, but I hear music and I love it." Hosanna took Yin's hand; Yin looked down at that hand and saw the diamond ring. "Oh, Yin, my soul has soared with life when I was at my poorest, because I had me and I respected me. I am no genius, but I got good sense. So see, I never have had everything . . . but best of all . . . I have been satisfied many times, and I am satisfied now, most of all, when I need it most."

Yin frowned, looking at Hosanna with wonder. And thinking about the ring.

Hosanna laughed, "Oh, don't get me wrong. Don't let me fool you! I have been scared, lots of times. But that made me study that little map I had made of life. A plan. I'm smiling now, but I fought, sometimes had to fight myself, to get here. I lived it, I know it. Blive that!" She smiled and held Yin's hand.

Yin tried to smile, but couldn't. She asked, "Hosanna, where did you get that ring?"

Hosanna smiled, lifted the ringed finger up. "Isn't it beautiful? It was my mother's, from my father. I found it buried in the chicken house, of all places."

Yin tried to smile back, "It is a beautiful ring. I have been looking for it for years." Hosanna turned a startled face to Yin. Yin continued, "It belonged to my mother and it was stolen from her by my father."

"Your father? Well, how did my mother and father come to have it? I'm sure my mother didn't even know your mother."

"Hosanna, that ring means a great deal to me. But . . . I see it means a great deal to you, too. I'll . . . tell you about it." Yin took a deep, deep breath, let it out and looked miserable. "My father was a Negro man." Hosanna could only look at Yin, frowning. "My father was your mother's father, too."

Hosanna opened her mouth in surprise. "Hush the fuck up!"

"It's true, Hosanna. You are my half-niece. I am your aunt."

"You mean to say you are kin to me . . . family . . . and you have never tried to help any of us? Even Lovey? Who needed help?"

"I was trying to help myself. That is why I never told a soul that I was part Negro. Now, I don't care. I have enough money and I am free. And you can keep that ring because I am free. I need a bigger family now. I need to learn about love. I haven't known it since my father Josephus died. He was good to me, you've been good to me. I was proud of you, but I couldn't afford to be your aunt until I did what I had to do. Now . . . I want a family. I want somebody to really care about what happens to me."

"I always have."

"So," Yin sighed and stood up, "Now what?"

Hosanna put her hand on Yin's arm. "Girl, life ain't something you grab, life is something you accept and make grow. I'm . . . glad you're my aunt. It makes me a little closer to my mother. I need that because I lost her so early. Everything is going to be alright, Yin. And I won't tell anyone what you've told me, I'll just hug it to myself, in my heart, right over my baby."

"You are so lucky, Hosanna, to have the man you love." Yin moved to the door. "And he be a good man."

"I know. Oh, God, do I know."

Yin held Hosanna's arm. "Carlton Befoe is moving back to Yoville. He intends to stop all this school business and he wants all his land back. He says things are going to change around here when he returns."

Hosanna patted Yin's hand, saying, "But we won't let him, will . . . we?"

"Hosanna, you don't know anything. Money can do a lot."

Hosanna smiled. "Yin, you don't know God. Money can't do everything."

Hosanna spoke to Yin as she prepared to leave. "Yin, you have two children at home, a white one and a colored one. A whole world to learn about. You have an old woman living with you who is full of wisdom learned the hard way. Creed is full of wisdom. Sally is over there with a different kind of road to her wisdom, maybe. You have them all to choose and learn from. Why don't you think about that? And you've got all of us and the future. You're gonna make you some love."

After Yin had gone away, looking thoughtful, Hosanna ran outside to find Homer. "Hooooomeerrrr! I'm calling you. I just want to see you!"

And so we arrive at the end of this little story. We move away from Yoville, which is pregnant with future stories and dreams of all those living there right now. They are still on the road, searching, living, striving for some satisfaction.

Satan loves to fly as close as he can to the heavens and he did that as he was leaving Yoville, thinking with pleasure of Carlton Befoe junior's return there and, of course, all the other things that were happening on earth and would happen on earth. This time he flew close enough to even hear the voices of angels speaking together.

One voice said, "Satan smiles over the tribulation on earth."

"In pity, Jesus weeps."

"The earth trembles, knowing that in this century, blood and destruction on its lands and waters will be worse than ever before."

"Everything is disappearing from the earth. Things the people need . . . to live."

"Satan cannot smile long, he knows his time is very short now."

"Ahhh, the End of him. Such joy will be on the earth."

"Soon now, soon."

Then, the angels flew away.

Satan face contorted into a deep, angry frown full of hate. Then he flew away with a roar, swiftly to the streets like a lion, devouring everything his power allowed him to. In his search for satisfaction.

about the author

J. CALIFORNIA COOPER is the author of the novel *Family*, and four collections of short stories: the winner of the 1989 American Book Award, *Homemade Love; Some Soul to Keep; A Piece of Mine;* and *The Matter Is Life*. She is also the author of seventeen plays and has been honored as Black Playwright of the Year (1978), received the James Baldwin Writing Award (1988), and the Literary Lion Award from the American Library Association (1988). Ms. Cooper lives in Texas.